Outsourcing Professional Body of Knowledge

Outsourcing Professional
Body of Knowledge

INTERNATIONAL ASSOCIATION OF
OUTSOURCING PROFESSIONALS

Colophon

Title:	Outsourcing Professional Body of Knowledge
Author:	Compiled by International Association of Outsourcing Professionals®
Copy Editor:	Jane Chittenden
Publisher:	Van Haren Publishing, Zaltbommel, www.vanharen.net
ISBN:	978 90 8753 613 8
Print:	First edition, first impression, June 2010
Layout, design and typesetting:	CO2 Premedia bv, Amersfoort, The Netherlands
Copyright:	© 2010 International Association of Outsourcing Professionals® (IAOP®)

For any further enquiries about Van Haren Publishing, please send an e-mail to: info@vanharen.net

Copyright and use statement

The *Outsourcing Professional Body of Knowledge (OPBOK)* describes the generally accepted set of knowledge and practices applicable to the successful design, implementation, and management of outsourcing contracts. It provides:

- a framework for understanding what outsourcing is and how it fits within contemporary business operations
- the knowledge and practice areas generally accepted as critical to outsourcing success
- a glossary of terms commonly used within the field.

This publication is designed to provide accurate and authoritative information about the subject matter covered. It is provided with the understanding that the publisher is not engaged in rendering legal or accounting service. If legal or accounting assistance is required, the services of a competent professional in those fields should be sought.

The International Association of Outsourcing Professionals (IAOP) is a global membership-based organization shaping the future of outsourcing as a management practice, as a profession, and as an industry. Its members are line and staff, executives and managers, with the vision and expertise it takes to design, implement, and manage tomorrow's global corporate ecosystem.

This new breed of outsourcing professional enhances the success of the companies they work with and advances their own careers by taking advantage of a wide array of association services including knowledge transfer, networking, research, training, and certification.

Preface and purpose of this guide

The Outsourcing Professional Body of Knowledge (OPBOK) represents a cohesive and comprehensive outline of the commonly accepted practices and skills required to ensure outsourcing success.

This guide does not attempt to capture the entire breadth of knowledge – which exists only within the field's practitioners and evolves constantly – but to present a guide to the most common and generally accepted principles and practices within an organizational framework that facilitates its sharing and learning.

On the latter purpose, this guide is the foundation for the International Association of Outsourcing Professionals' (IAOP) professional certification, the *Certified Outsourcing Professional® (COP)*.

Contributors

A major revision of the Outsourcing Professional Standards (OPS) and Outsourcing Professional Body of Knowledge (OPBOK) cannot be accomplished without the contributions of the field's practitioners – the outsourcing professionals. In 2008 and 2009 there were more than 100 pieces of material contributed to Firmbuilder.com® and considered during the preparation of this revision. Many of IAOP's Corporate Members demonstrated their commitment to the profession by providing material and case studies. We want to acknowledge these professionals for sharing their experiences and ideas.

We also want to acknowledge the Outsourcing Standards Board for its leadership on the Outsourcing Professional Standards (OPS) that form the base for OPBOK.

Finally, 2007 marked the year when the COP Master Class went global. Since then it has been delivered many dozens of times all around the world. We want to acknowledge the faculties of these classes, who provided feedback from their teaching.

Encouragement:

A professional organization such as IAOP will grow and prosper when the professionals, such as you, contribute to the knowledge and experience database. IAOP's Knowledge Center (Firmbuilder.com®) is a fountain of this knowledge and we depend on it to improve and enhance this OPBOK. We encourage you to provide articles and presentations for inclusion and expand our collective knowledge.

Contents

Index of figures:

What has changed in Rev. 9

The following table highlights the major revision sections. In addition to these changes, minor edits were applied to slides and OPBOK to make them more consistent in terminology etc. Also, each section has embedded revised standards (as per previously published Rev. 9.01).

Templates have been reviewed and revised. New templates have also been added for the new sections identified below (e.g. knowledge management)

Module	OPBOK	Master Class Slides
1	1. Additional definitions for offshore outsourcing (near shore) 2. Emerging trends in outsourcing	3. Slightly changed the order. CEO speech is before discussion 4. Provided new definitions – including an "alternate" definition for outsourcing (covering risk) 5. Inserted G100 profile for diversity of processes
2	Additional feasibility assessment section added to cover legal and labor issues	Minor edits
3	1. Significantly enhanced section on change management and associated communication 2. New template added for change management assessment 3. Moved communication plan material from other modules to be consistent with standards and MC slides	1. Added new section change management and enhanced one slide previously there 2. Moved communication plan and action to this section from later modules (consistent with the standards) 3. Added slide on legal impact on decision making
4	Moved communication plan to module 3	Moved communication plan from this module to Module 3
5	1. Added clarity on where baseline is not defined 2. Added section on appropriately selecting the process and use of documents	1. Added further clarity on use of RFI/RFP/RFQ
6	1. Addition and clarification of due diligence framework 2. A more detailed discussion on various geographies around the world (more than just India/China)	1. Added due diligence framework 2. Added G100 information on global locations of providers 3. Added new slides discussing India, China and Eastern Europe in more depth (we can encourage other locales to create a slide for their location, if desired e.g. Malaysia) 4. Added a slide from Duke on offshore destination
7	1. Further discussion on evaluating value proposition – including definition using Value Health Check Survey categories 2. Further discussion on provider's pricing methodology 3. Discussion on volume based pricing methodology (ARC, RRC)	1. More clarity on evaluating value proposition 2. Included classification of value from Value Health Check Survey 3. Further discussion on how provider creates pricing 4. Clarified two slides (previously, they were incomplete)
8	1. Contract renegotiation section added	1. Added a number of slides from Kirkland & Ellis class presentation 2. Clarity in the renegotiation and termination slides
9	1. Employee transition section expanded 2. Knowledge management added	1. Additional slides in the employee transition 2. New material for Knowledge Management

Module	OPBOK	Master Class Slides
10	1. Knowledge management as part of governance added 2. Exiting – transitioning to a third party 3. Introduction to Value Health Check Survey	1. Value Health Check Survey slides added 2. Regional addenda slides added
Appendix A	1. Some definitions edited. 2. New definitions added	
B	See Table below for changes	
C	Reviewed	
D	Reviewed	
E	Reviewed	
F	Reviewed	
G	Updated to 2009	
H	New Appendix – Governance article to supplement governance material (it is also used in the Governance workshop)	

Original	New	Template - Revised Version	Disposition
1.1	1.1	Defining Outsourcing	No Change
1.2	Deleted	Examples of Current Business Relationships	Deleted
1.3	1.2	External Business Drivers	Edited
1.4	1.3	Internal Business Drivers	Edited
1.5	1.4	Organizational Evaluation Factors (Shared Services and Outsourcing)	Edited
1.6	1.5	Anticipated Outsourcing Benefits	Edited
1.7	1.6	Gauging Organizational Outsourcing Maturity	No Change
1.8	1.7	Common Business Process Framework	No Change
1.9	1.8	Outsourcing and Offshoring Considerations	Edited
1.10	1.90	Outsourcing Professional Roles	Edited
1.11	1.1	Ethics and Business Practice Assessment	No Change
2.1	2.1	Outsourcing End-to-End Process	No Change
2.2	2.2	The Outsourcing Business Plan	No Change
2.1	2.3	Organization Capability Assessment	No Change
3.1	3.1	Integrating Outsourcing into Business Strategy Top-Down Strategic Planning	No Change
3.2	3.2	Integrating Outsourcing into Business Strategy Bottom-Up Strategic Planning	Edited
3.3	3.3	Outsourcing Decision Matrix	Edited
4.2	3.4	Stakeholder Analysis	Edited
4.3	3.5	Stakeholder Communication Plan (Change to Strategy)	Edited
4.4	3.6	Communication Plan Framework	No Change
3.4	3.7	Outsourcing Risk Assessment and Analysis	Edited
3.5	3.8	Offshore Outsourcing: Country Specific Risk Assessment	No Change
3.6	3.9	Impact of Business Regulations and Statutes	Edited
3.7	3.10	Scoping an Outsourcing Opportunity	Edited
3.8	3.11	Prioritizing Outsourcing Opportunities	No Change
9.5	3.12	Public Affairs Risk Analysis	Edited
4.1	4.1	Creating and Leading Outsourcing Teams	No Change
5.1	5.1	Checklist for Objectives and Boundary Conditions	Edited
5.2	5.2	Checklist for Developing Outsourcing Requirements	Edited
5.3	5.3	Critical Success Factors (CSFs) and Key Performance Indicators (KPIs) for Outsourcing	Edited
5.4	5.4	RFP (Request for Proposal) Document Development	No Change
5.5	5.5	Collaborative Business Case Development	No Change
6.1	6.1	Identifying Potential Outsourcing Service Providers	No Change

Original	New	Template - Revised Version	Disposition
6.2	6.2	Evaluating Potential Outsourcing Service Providers	No Change
6.3	6.3	Scoring and Selecting Outsourcing Service Providers	Edited
7.1	7.1	Cost Elements for Creating Baseline Costs	No Change
7.2	7.2	Financial Analysis of an Outsourcing Decision	No Change
7.3	7.3	Selecting the Optimum Pricing Model	Edited
new	7.4	Value Proposition	New
8.1	8.1	Outsourcing Contract Structure	Edited
8.2	8.2	Common Outsourcing Contract Terms	No Change
8.3	8.3	Description of Interests for Outsourcing Contract Negotiations	Edited
8.4	8.4	Negotiation Checklist	No Change
9.1	9.1	Outsourcing Transition Plan	Edited
9.2	9.2	Human Resources Planning	No Change
new	9.3	Knowledge Management Readiness Assessment	New
new	9.4	Knowledge Management Strategies	New
10.1	10.1	Outsourcing Governance Plan	No Change
10.2	10.2	Project Management Office (PMO)	Edited
10.3	10.3	Assessing Results versus Expectations - Critical Success Factors (CSFs) and Key Performance Indicators (KPIs) for Outsourcing	Edited
10.4	10.4	Financial Review of an Outsourcing Decision	No Change
10.5	10.5	Outsourcing Governance Assessing Current Providers	No Change
10.6	10.6	Outsourcing Process Maturity	No Change

1 Defining and communicating outsourcing as a management practice

1.1. Standards

1.0 Defining and Communicating Outsourcing as a Management Practice

1.1 Ability to define outsourcing in terms easily understood by individuals at all levels of the organization and by outside stakeholders, including shareholders and the public at large. This includes:

1.1.1 Identify business models and change agenda that will end up driving a decision for a change in the business model (e.g. focusing on core functions)

1.1.2 A working definition of outsourcing that is consistent with generally accepted concepts as commonly used by professionals within the field

1.1.3 Establish definition of common outsourcing terms such as BPO, ITO, forms of outsourcing (transactional, transitional and transformational) and provide differentiation between outsourcing and offshoring, out-tasking

1.1.4 A framework for comparing and contrasting outsourcing and other forms of outside business relationships, such as suppliers, contractors, temporary and supplemental staffing, strategic alliances, and joint ventures. Characteristics to be considered include: costs, benefits, risks, advantages, etc.

1.1.5 Identify and understand various recent developments that may/will impact outsourcing and define terms such as Cloud Computing, Bundled Sourcing, Rural Sourcing, Consortium Sourcing

1.1.6 Define and understand the concepts of "outsourcing portfolio management" and its impact on sourcing strategies

1.1.7 A working knowledge of all commonly used professional terms as defined, for example, in the Outsourcing Professional Body of Knowledge (OPBOK).

1.2 Ability to identify market potential, availability of services and service providers and case studies for various outsourcing opportunities, including: benchmarking, utilizing market knowledge in helping to define outsourcing strategy and direction for the organization

1.2.1 Identify market size and economic impact of outsourcing on business

1.2.2 Ability to identify viability of offshore destinations and specifically to be able to discuss strengths and weaknesses of leading offshore destinations

1.3 Ability to define the business drivers, timeframes, and commonly anticipated benefits of outsourcing in terms easily understood at all levels of the organization and by outside stakeholders, including the public at large. This includes:

1.3.1 External business drivers, such as, competition, globalization, technology, regulation and deregulation, economic, political and others.

1.3.2 Internal business drivers such as process improvement, competition for resources, competition for capital, core versus non-core considerations, mission criticality, etc.

1.3.3 Common benefits, including: cost savings (direct, indirect, cost avoidance), improved focus, more variable cost structure, access to skills not available to the organization internally, reduced capital requirements, improved management focus, innovation, speed to market, etc.

1.3.4 Timeframes for realizing these benefits based on market conditions and the organization's business plans and capabilities.

1.4 Ability to identify and develop organizational solutions to address the business drivers and provide clear differentiation between outsourcing and creating an inter/intra organizational solution (such as shared services)

1.4.1 Clearly identify similarities and differences between shared services and outsourcing

1.4.2 Provide management guidance on the benefits / shortcomings of outsourcing and/or inter-intra organizational solution

1.5 Ability to identify the common challenges that impede organizational success with outsourcing, including:

1.5.1 Setting realistic expectations; choosing the opportunities for outsourcing with the highest probability of delivering the intended results; choosing the most qualified providers; crafting a balanced relationship that offers sustainable benefit to customer and provider alike; properly managing outsourcing's organizational impacts; managing the ongoing relationship, including its disengagement.

1.5.2	Identifying internal barriers to outsourcing such as fear of loss of control; activities and processes being seen as too critical to be outsourced; perceived loss of flexibility; negative customer, employee, community reactions, dependence on vendor due to loss of skilled resources
1.5.3	Identify behavioral and organizational issues that may occur during the transition to an outsourced operation, including those that can result from the transfer of existing employees into the service provider(s) organization(s) and its impact on the retained employee base.
1.5.4	Identify regulatory restrictions on outsourcing – including offshoring
1.6	**Ability to define the role that a Certified Outsourcing Professional® plays in achieving intended organizational outcomes through outsourcing. This includes:**
1.6.1	Strategic roles, such as input into corporate strategic planning and the formulation of outsourcing policy and strategies
1.6.2	Management roles, such as team management, leadership, and managing outsourcing suppliers (selection through governance)
1.6.3	Topic expert roles, such as financial and process analysis, contracting, pricing, and negotiating.
1.6.4	Ability to interpret and apply The Code of Ethics and Business Practices for Outsourcing Professionals (Appendix E)
1.6.5	Ability to benefit from and contribute to the industry-wide body of knowledge through participation in the work of applicable professional associations.
1.7	**Ability to map the structure and operational components of an organization to a common business process framework using a standard model such as that defined in the Outsourcing Professional Body of Knowledge (OPBOK), including:**
1.7.1	Providing an organizational process map model and developing a custom model for a specific organization
1.7.2	Mapping at the activity, function, and business process levels and identifying dependencies
1.7.3	Mapping of an organization's value-chain and its support services
1.7.4	Developing and applying a framework for comparing and contrasting the use of outsourcing across functions and companies, including:
	1.7.4.1 Classifying current and emerging forms of outsourcing, including departmental-level outsourcing, functional process outsourcing, business process outsourcing, knowledge process outsourcing, etc.
	1.7.4.2 Comparing and contrasting the measurable benefits organizations are realizing through each form of outsourcing within each structural area of the business.
1.8	**Ability to understand and create a framework for offshoring and differentiate between offshoring and offshore outsourcing including relevant dependencies created**
1.9	**Ability to establish a framework and criteria for selection of offshore destination and appropriateness for an organization, including:**
	1.9.1 Offshore destination selection criteria and application
	1.9.2 Appropriateness of location for various forms of offshoring (BPO, ITO, LPO, KPO, etc)
	1.9.3 Models for offshoring (captive centers, build-operate-transfer, full-time, part-time, home-based, etc.)
1.10	**Ability to define the unique considerations associated with offshoring, near-shoring (including rural-sourcing), etc., including:**
1.10.1	The strategic and operational benefits offered by various offshore locations
1.10.2	Financial, regulatory, political, cultural risks, etc.
	1.10.2.1 The risks of operating in an alien political and legal environment
	1.10.2.2 The effect of cultural, work-practice, time zone differences
	1.10.2.3 The impact of tax (for example, VAT), currency, and regulatory compliance differences

Table 1.1: Standards for defining and communicating outsourcing

1.2.   What is Outsourcing?

Outsourcing is a long-term, results-oriented business relationship with a specialized services provider. The services contracted for (including manufacturing services) may encompass a single activity, a set of activities, or an entire end-to-end business process. In most cases, and especially for larger organizations, what's being outsourced was previously performed by the customer organization for itself and is being transferred to the provider. In other cases, however, these may be activities the customer organization never performed for itself.

The use of the term, 'long-term' does not necessarily imply a contract of a fixed length. Although many outsourcing contracts are 5, 10, or even 15 years in duration, others can be cancelled on 30-days notice. What long-term means is that it is the customer's intention to essentially 'divest' itself of the capacity to perform the work itself, choosing instead (some might say choosing *strategically*) to acquire the services in the future from the marketplace of available providers.

The term 'results-oriented' carries specific meaning, as well. It suggests that the service provider is assuming responsibility for the people, processes, and technologies employed along with responsibility for ensuring that those resources deliver the results for which the customer has contracted. Responsibility for the results, not just for the resources, is what differentiates outsourcing from more narrow and more traditional supplier, supplemental staffing, and task-level contracting.

1.2.1   Continuum of Business Relationships

Outsourcing occupies a unique position along the continuum of outside relationships common to the operations of most businesses. These relationships range from the traditional procurement of specific resources to highly collaborative relationships, such as strategic alliances and joint ventures.

The axes of this continuum can be best thought of as 'ownership' and 'risk.'

Ownership refers to the level of ownership of the people, processes, and technologies used to do the work that is assumed by the service provider.
Risk refers to level of risk assumed by the provider for achieving the customer's intended outcomes – conformance to requirements, operational outcomes, or business outcomes.

At the low end of the continuum are traditional supplier relationships. A traditional supplier only can assume the risks associated with ensuring that what the company supplies conforms to the agreed-to requirements. It cannot assume any risk associated with whether the customer achieves its operational outcomes through their use, let alone its sought after business outcomes, since it has not assumed responsibility for the people, processes, *and* technologies employed.

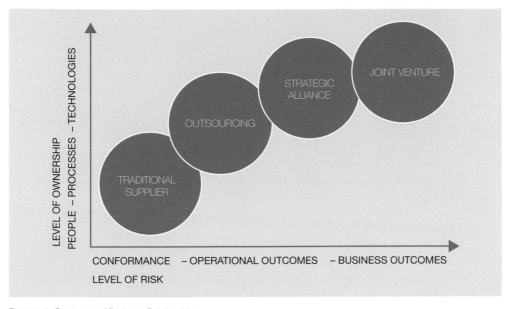

Figure 1.1: Continuum of Business Relationships

Outsourcing exists further along this continuum where the provider owns most, if not all, of the people, processes, and technologies needed to deliver the results the customer seeks. The provider now also assumes more of the risk associated with meeting the operational outcomes – service levels, throughputs, quality measures, and the like. Further along the continuum, the organizations take on shared investments and shared risks through a strategic alliances or joint ventures.

Most outsourcing relationships sit in the middle of this continuum. The provider owns most of the people, processes, and technologies needed to do the work and takes on many of the risks associated with achieving the customer's operational outcomes. In other cases, however, the business relationship may, at its core, be an outsourcing relationship – that is a long-term contract for services – but have elements that reflect aspects of relationships on either side of the continuum.

Where a particular relationship should exist on this continuum depends on various factors including long term and short term expected benefits. For certain offshore related outsourcing activities there may be additional factors such as product and brand positioning in the marketplace, economic and political advantages/disadvantages from the relationship.

1.2.2   Definitions
Although different marketing terms have been used to describe outsourcing and forms of outsourcing; there are certain industry commonly used terms (also see the appendix).

Term	Definition / Explanation
BPO	Business Process Outsourcing (BPO) puts together two powerful business tools - business process management and outsourcing. Business process management uses technology to break down barriers between traditional functional silos, such as those found in finance, order processing, and call centers. Outsourcing uses skills and resources of specialized outside service providers to perform many of these critical, yet non-core activities. BPO means examining the processes that make up the business and its functional units, and then working with specialized service providers to both reengineer and outsource them at the same time.
	Recently, the term Knowledge Process Outsourcing (KPO) is becoming prevalent to describe BPO services where there is a greater content of utilizing deeper level knowledge (domain, topic, data mining) as a part of the process.
ITO	Information Technology Outsourcing – when a company outsources its technology management and processing functions to a service provider. This includes managing data center activities, networks as well as business applications management. Many times, business applications management is further divided into applications development or applications maintenance and enhancement. APO, at times refers to Applications Process Outsourcing
Forms of outsourcing	Businesses outsource for different business reasons. These terms are applied in a 'shorthand' to explain the principal reason behind outsourcing:
	Tactical outsourcing is when a business outsources to achieve a single objective (generally cost savings) and the transaction stands on its own merit.
	Transitional outsourcing is when a business outsources in order to migrate from the current business process environment to a new one and expects the outsourcer to support the existing business process until it is no longer required. This is often used in the Information Technology area when replacing an existing application environment with a new one.
	Transformational outsourcing is to take advantage of innovation and new business models. Transformational outsourcing is approached as a way to fundamentally reposition the organization in its markets. The term Business Transformational Outsourcing is also used to combine this idea with that of Business Process Outsourcing.
Offshore / Offshoring	Performing or sourcing any part of an organization's activities at or from a location outside the company's home country. Companies create captive centers offshore, where the employees work for them, or outsource offshore, where the employees work for the outsourcing provider.
	Although the term Offshoring implies crossing the ocean, it simply means providing services from a country other than where the services are performed presently.
Nearshore	When the sourcing destination is chosen based on proximity to the country where the work is performed, it is referred to as Nearshore. For example, outsourcing work to Canada or Costa Rica from US or Ireland from England. The major benefits of choosing a Nearshore destination are to limit time zone difference and leverage potential closer cultural and economic relationships
Outtasking	Occasionally, the term outtasking is applied in the context of manufacturing process when a business engages a third party manufacturer to perform a manufacturing task (such as anodizing a formed part). Outtasking implies that the business is responsible for the entire process except for a task which is done by a third party provider.

Table 1.2 Definitions of outsourcing

1.3. Why Organizations Outsource

Outsourcing professionals work in a world that can best be described as hyper-competitive. Globalization is inextricably linking the world's major economies. Today's standard of excellence is not just best-in-class; it's best-in-world. In this global economy every company must compete against customer choices coming from everywhere and anywhere. Barriers to the marketplace are dropping quickly, with new competitors just a mouse-click away from any customer.

1.3.1   Core Competencies

It is against this backdrop of hyper-competition and increasing pressure for performance that the classical view of organizations as vertically-integrated and self-sufficient has changed. It's an approach that dates back to the industrial revolution that may be no longer possible, practical, or even desirable today. The accelerating pace of change dramatically compresses investment cycles, making the competitive advantage from an organization's internal investments last for shorter and shorter periods of time. At the same time, all the operational activities across an organization are becoming increasingly specialized and knowledge-driven. Rapid advancement in every field makes it a practical impossibility for any organization to develop and sustain best-in-world expertise in every facet of its operation.

As a result, organizations are moving away – even being forced away – from this classical structure. Increasingly organizations are finding that the better approach is to focus their internal resources on the activities that provide them a unique competitive advantage, their *core competencies*, while engaging the external market of service providers through *outsourcing* for more and more of their critical, yet non-core activities

Outsourcing, then, is nothing more and nothing less than a management tool. It is used to move an organization away from the traditional vertically integrated, self-sufficient structure; one that is increasingly ineffective in today's hyper-competitive, performance-driven environment. Through outsourcing, the organization moves toward a business structure where it's able to make more focused investments in the areas that provide its unique competitive advantage. Along the way, the organization creates interdependent relationships with specialized service providers for many of its critical activities that must be performed extremely well, but where the organization gains little competitive advantage by doing the work itself. Along the way, outsourcing creates new business opportunities for companies to become providers of outsourcing services and for advisory firms to work with both parties in the design, execution, and management of these business relationships.

1.3.2   Outsourcing's Drivers

Outsourcing decisions are driven by a combination of three sets of drivers – external drivers, internal drivers, and the availability of sourcing alternatives.

Generally, speaking external drivers that increase outsourcing are: shortening product or service lifecycles, and changes in the external business environment that impact the customers and their expectations, competitors (who, where, etc.), macro- and industry-level financials, technology, government actions (such as regulation, deregulation, and laws), and mergers, acquisitions, divestitures and other structural changes in the industry.

Common internal drivers and historical norms that lead organizations towards, or away, from greater levels of outsourcing can include: historical sourcing decisions (the more organizations currently outsource the greater they tend to in the future); organization-level characteristics, such as, industry, size, rate of growth; the use of benchmarking, reengineering and other improvement programs; the decision-making structure of the organization (centralized, decentralized); how visible a particular function is; the desire for management control; and employee practices that may restrict or encourage change.

Finally, of course, sourcing decisions can only be made when there are, indeed, outside options to be considered, that can demonstrate the ability to deliver high-quality, low-cost solutions.

1.3.3   Selecting outsourcing as a business model

Once the business has decided to focus on their core functions and explore the alternatives for outsourcing, a model is developed where the drivers (and hence benefits from outsourcing) are balanced against the risks associated with it (specific risks associated with the outsourcing and how to avoid/mitigate them are discussed in a later module). Businesses tend to balance the risks and rewards and when a point is reached where the balance shifts towards outsourcing, a decision is made to consider outsourcing. In fact, one can argue that *a business would consider outsourcing when it believes that performing a function in-house contains greater risks than having a service provider do it.* This may be used as an "alternative" definition for outsourcing.

1.3.4   Outsourcing's Benefits

The basic reason cited for outsourcing is most often to reduce costs. However the organization chooses to spend those savings, whether they are passed along to its customers, reinvested into other areas of its operations, or returned to its owners and shareholders, the need for every organization to continually drive down its costs is constant. About 50 percent of executives state that reducing costs is the top reason for outsourcing. In most cases, the cost savings are in the 10 to 20 percent range, but can be much higher depending on how large the gap is between the company's current cost of operations and the money it will be paying the outside provider.

Although cost savings is an important reason for outsourcing, it is actually only the primary reason for about half of the outsourcing projects companies undertake. This means that the top reason for outsourcing for the other half of the projects is, in fact, something other than cost savings.

The second most frequently cited reason for outsourcing is the ability to focus more company resources – its people, its physical and intellectual resources, and its capital – on the core parts of operations – the activities that provide its unique competitive advantage; thereby improving the company's ability to leverage its most valuable capabilities.

The third most frequently cited reason is to achieve a more variable cost structure. Through outsourcing, instead of having relatively fixed investments in its internal operations, the company shifts to a more on-demand business model. This reduces the effective cost of operations by enabling the company to adjust expenses in response to changes in the marketplace.

Access to skills not available to the organization internally is the next most frequently cited value from outsourcing. After all, few organizations, regardless of their size, can hire all of the talent they need. Because service providers are more specialized and are serving many customers, they have a much deeper talent pool upon which to draw. Measurable improvements in quality can result as well. Areas of the business that do not produce unique competitive advantage are often the last to be funded and invested in, making continuous improvements in quality difficult to achieve.

Another tangible benefit of outsourcing is that not only is the need for new capital significantly reduced – since the provider often brings in the needed resources – but current assets may be sold to the provider, freeing capital dollars already invested. This cash can then be reinvested in other parts of the business or used to improve the company's overall balance sheet and reduce its future cost of capital.

Most recently, companies have begun to find that bringing in outside specialists spurs much needed innovation in their operations. Some have equated outsourcing to having a dedicated R&D department; as the provider innovates new solutions they can be immediately put into practice in the company's own operations. As James Brian Quinn has put it, "No one company acting alone can out-innovate all its competitors, potential competitors, suppliers, and external knowledge sources."

A final, and often-overlooked benefit, is the ability through outsourcing to free an executive's time to focus outwardly on strategy and customers as opposed to inwardly on current operational issues. For many executives, dealing with the day-to-day details of operational activities robs them of time that would be better spent on customers, shareholders, investors, and suppliers.

As business understands the drivers and embarks on the strategy to consider outsourcing, it embarks on collecting the relevant information to help them validate their assumptions about outsourcing market in general. The sources of information for data collection include:

- Industry organization such as IAOP (through its website and Outsourcing World Summit)
- Industry reference organizations such as Gartner, Forrester Research who publish industry and market information
- Industry publications and reference books (see the end of the module for references)
- Engaging advisors who can bring industry knowledge and experience
- Industry trade groups where other businesses in the same/similar industries have had experience in outsourcing

The objectives for such a study include:

- Understanding market potential for the service. This helps identify whether the particular service is in its infancy or is reaching a mature stage. This is important to understand the risk profile associated with the particular process outsourcing
- Establish the trends in the marketplace associated with the particular process outsourcing. This will determine whether there are potential changes in the marketplace that may affect the efficacy of outsourcing decision.
- Learn from previous experiences the potential as well as pitfalls associated with the process outsourcing
- Create a preliminary list of service providers who later on may be contacted for further information

Once the preliminary study is completed, the organization can review its business drivers and priorities and look at the market data to understand alternatives and case histories to frame a more detailed outsourcing strategy.

For service providers, understanding market requirements and potential is important in identifying business opportunities and tailoring their solutions to the demands.

1.4. Outsourcing versus Shared Services

Shared services are common activities that are used by more than one division or unit within the company. When these services are combined into a central operation they are often referred to as shared services centers.

In order to address the business drivers, businesses consider creating a shared services center to consolidate common processes from different business units. Some consider this to be an alternative to outsourcing those processes. Figure 1.2 shows how the two forms of organizational structure are both similar and different in their concepts. In both forms, a service center is established that provides services to the business units under a services agreement. It is the ownership of the center that is different between a corporate shared services center and a service provider's processing center under an outsourced agreement. Since the shared services center is a part of the same company, there are inherent limitations on how far it can create synergy, different management environments and productivity levels. Typically, it would be difficult to create a market-focused organization within a corporation, which would be the case when it is managed by a service provider. Investments, employee issues, and infrastructure constraints all become hurdles faced by shared services centers pushing the envelope for higher performance.

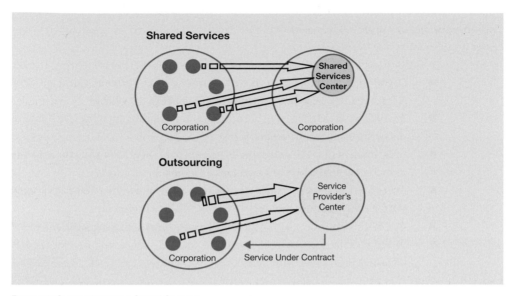

Figure 1.2: Outsourcing versus Shared Services

The following table shows some of the common benefits and shortcomings of both forms of organizational structure:

	Benefits / Advantages to Business	**Shortcomings / Barriers**
Shared Services	■ Can be implemented with lower disruption to organization and processing ■ Savings accrue directly to business (without paying profit to a provider) ■ Familiarity with processes and organization ■ Retention of skills and knowledge within corporation ■ Reversing the decision is easier ■ Easier to manage sharp changes in volume	■ Organizational resistance becomes harder to overcome ■ Greater chances of retaining historical divisions and function separation and not take a "Greenfield" approach ■ Corporate infrastructure restraints remain the same (e.g. compensation scheme, systems environment) ■ Little built-in incentive to continue to improve operation and productivity ■ Continuance of the same management team prevents "new" ideas and market perspectives
Outsourcing	■ Avoids management focus on non-core activity ■ Eliminates need for capital and other investments ■ Creates a higher potential for greater productivity in the process ■ Becomes a more responsive organization due to the nature of "market facing" organization culture ■ Creates ability to share volume and best practices with other businesses managed by the same provider	■ Creates an organizational disruption that needs to be managed effectively through change management ■ Potential loss of skills and knowledge to outside; making it difficult to reverse the decision ■ Requires greater energy in establishing the agreement and providing on going governance ■ Selection of the service provider and transition of work becomes critical and poses greater danger of disruption ■ Need to deal with "societal" impact of the decision (within and outside company)

Table 1.3: Benefits and shortcomings of shared services and outsourcing

The following factors are generally considered when deciding between creating a shared services center or outsourcing the functions:

- Organizational maturity to create a shared services center and deal with the change management and political/functional boundary issues
- Availability of investment in creating a center and then applying it to improve the performance of the center
- Commitment of multi-year capital and expense investment while the center is brought to a level where savings can be accrued
- Availability of the subject matter expertise in the process as well as a systems platform for creating a productive operational environment
- Availability and adequacy of staff for the center in the chosen location
- Willingness to organize staffing around volume changes and provide the HR infrastructure to deal with multi-types of employees (contractors, employees)

1.5.   Creating an overall business model

As an organization looks at various alternatives for business strategy and outsourcing, it is important to create a business specific model that encapsulates the full range of concepts and options, as Figure 1.3 shows.

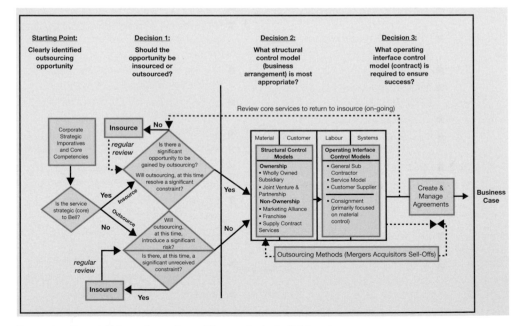

Source: Jean-Francois Poisson, Former General Manager, Contracts, Bell Canada

Figure 1.3: Decision model

1.5.1   What organizations outsource

Outsourcing began decades ago in the manufacturing parts of businesses and has gradually spread across the entire operations of most companies in developed countries all around the world.

1.5.2   Mapping activities

Figures 1.3 and 1.4 show a high-level mapping of the activities present in most organizations. In both cases, a common set of support activities (corporate services, information, communication, document management, and financial management, etc.) surrounds a value chain for the development, delivery, and support of the products and services the organization delivers.

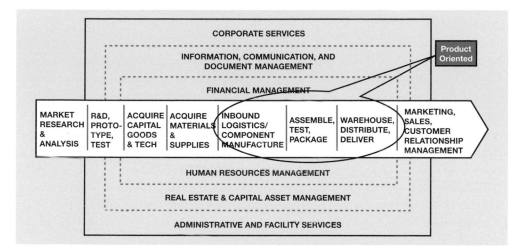

Figure 1.4: Mapping activities: product company

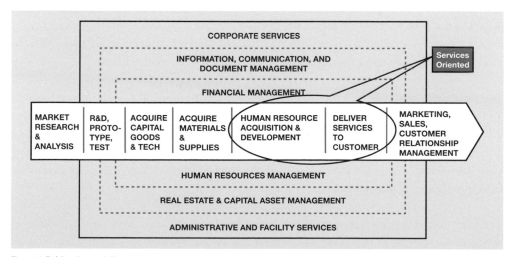

Figure 1.5: Mapping activities: services company

A more detailed listing of each activity is presented in the Appendix.

Outsourcing takes place across all of these areas of the business, based upon a careful strategic and tactical evaluation of the risks and rewards.

1.5.3   Selecting activities

Experience has shown that many of the best candidate areas for outsourcing are likely to be those where there is a robust marketplace of providers, and solid proof points of success from the experiences of other organizations. While these more mature segments of the market offer proven results, emerging areas offering opportunities for organizations to gain an early and unique advantage should be considered, as well.

In either case, one of the first steps in evaluating any outsourcing opportunity is to first match that opportunity with what other organizations are already doing and then against the maturity of the marketplace of service providers. Mapping and scoring the opportunities an organization is considering, in terms of where the marketplace is in its maturity curve, can be a very effective first step in the process of selecting the best candidates.

Generally, the most mature outsourcing markets – those in which the largest percentage of organizations outsource and where the marketplace of providers is the most robust – are in the physical parts of a business's operations. Activities such as facility services and maintenance, cafeterias and mailrooms, manufacturing, warehousing, shipping, and information technology (IT) infrastructure are all examples of this.

Next comes what might be called specialist areas of the business. There are highly specialized professionals from across a wide range of disciplines – from advertising to travel to information technology – who work within the typical company. These individuals and their departments often have a greater affinity to their specialty than to the particular company they work for. Highly sophisticated service providers exist across all of these specialized areas.

The next most common area for outsourcing is in the transactional parts of the business – activities such as telemarketing, customer order processing and inquiries, employee benefits administration, receivables and payables. These all represent repeatable, process and technology-centric activities. Outsourcing in these areas often provides the added opportunity to simultaneously reengineer the business process, implement new technologies, and streamline the supply chains that support them.

The final areas that organizations typically look at are the high-touch, high-sensitivity areas of the business – activities that play a more direct role in the organization's relationship with its customers and that are more central to the planning and development of future products and services. Service delivery, field sales, and research and development are all examples of high-touch, high-sensitivity areas.

1.5.4   Portfolio management approach for outsourcing

As businesses decide their strategies for outsourcing, there will be a need to establish a management process where the processes are grouped and analyzed as a portfolio. This enables the management to make a decision on the entire portfolio or a partial portfolio and also determine the priority of outsourcing implementation, based on portfolio characteristics and benefits.

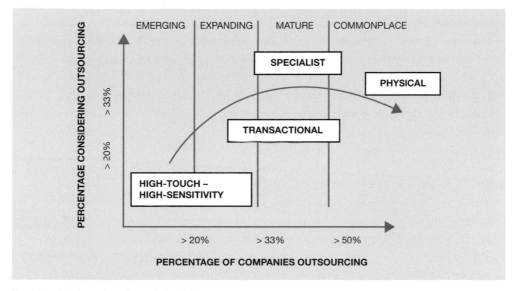

Figure 1.6: Gauging outsourcing market maturity

1.5.5   Business process outsourcing

In many cases, the scope of an activity under consideration for outsourcing exists entirely within the boundaries of an individual department or function. Increasingly, however, organizations are looking at their operations as end-to-end business processes. This leads to looking at activities under consideration for outsourcing in the same way.

The benefits of this business process approach to outsourcing can be significant. The organization gains a clearer understanding of how the various pieces of its operation connect to, reinforce, or take away from its ability to deliver value to the customer. The key performance indicators for the work can be defined in terms that are meaningful from a customer perspective, not simply from the perspective of an internally focused performance standard. Finally, all of the underlying technologies and supply chains are clearly identified and can be evaluated for inclusion in the scope of services to be outsourced.

A business process approach to outsourcing begins with the development of a process diagram – a tool that is well documented in the many texts on business process analysis and reengineering. It is often an iterative process typically beginning with a "white board" exercise that captures the activities that make up the process and their relationships. From that, a common set of diagrams, using a consistent symbolic language as well as supporting textual descriptions, is created. These textual descriptions follow a consistent template that describes the purpose, triggers, timings, durations, and resource requirements for each process, sub-process, activity, and task. All required resources are identified, including skills, technology infrastructure and applications, and the physical environment. Data flows are captured in the same template-driven manner, including the sources, destinations, characteristics, and inputs and outputs for each activity. Key performance indicators are documented as well. These establish the base for determining how well the process is operating overall in relationship to the customer value it is intended to create.

This process analysis and mapping forms the basis for all subsequent planning and decision making, including defining the scope of the work to be outsourced, determining current costs and performance, quantifying the measures of success and specifying how it is managed.

1.6.   Outsourcing versus offshoring

Taking parts of a company's operation offshore, or offshoring as it is commonly called, is certainly not a new idea. The label MADE IN CHINA has appeared on products for decades. As Western companies took their process expertise overseas, and as the global transportation infrastructure developed to make shipping of raw materials, sub-assemblies, and finished products practical and cost effective, offshore manufacturing became commonplace.

What is new is that the global digital infrastructure built in the 1990s is now making it just as possible to perform information-based activities anywhere in the world and to instantaneously deliver the results anywhere else in the world. This development has essentially made much more of the work of the modern organization "placeless." Designs can be drawn, programs written, bills generated, and customer calls answered just as easily halfway around the world as they can be across the street. The resulting offshoring of knowledge-based work is quickly becoming just as cost-effective and commonplace as it has proven to be for manufacturing in the past.

Cost savings are clearly the most compelling driver for offshoring at this moment. The largest portion of these cost savings typically come from the wage differential between employees in highly developed Western countries and those in the emerging economies, such as Africa, Asia, Eastern Europe, and Latin America.

Another important benefit to off-shoring is the creation of an operating structure that can "follow the sun." Global companies are operating somewhere in the world every hour of the day. Customer calls need to be made and received. Invoices need to be generated and payments processed. Software problems need to be worked on in real-time, regardless of the time zone of the user who first encountered it. Restructuring the business's operation into a global web helps do this.

Another benefit can be quality. Highly educated and motivated employees can perform tasks that would simply be unjustifiably expensive at Western wage rates.

Competition is another important way that offshoring leads to lower costs and better service. When locations around the world are included in the mix, each with its own unique advantage, the bar is raised even higher for everyone, and improvements through competition flourish around the globe. Offshoring can also create a presence and knowledge in the region that yields other very important advantages – advantages that accrue back to the company's home country, customers, employees, and investors alike.

A summary of the terms used to describe various geographic-based forms of outsourcing is provided below.

Onshore: Home country outsourcing – obtaining services from an external source in the home country.

Near-Shore Outsourcing: Refers to contracting a company in a nearby country, often one that shares a border (but not always). Canada and Mexico, for example, are near-shore countries for United States-based organizations.

Offshore Outsourcing: Refers to contracting with a company that is geographically distant, like India, Ireland, China, Philippines, Israel and Rumania from the United States or your home country.

Best-Shore Outsourcing: A recently coined term that describes which "shore" will offer better communications, lower costs, higher productivity and the most value, considering the risks versus the benefits.

1.6.1   The offshoring decision
Just as outsourcing is not appropriate for everyone for all processes, offshoring is not equally appropriate either. There are critical business factors that must be considered before deciding to offshore work. These factors include:

- Maturity of the business to manage a remote location (regardless of distance)
- Maturity of the business to manage a location in a different country/culture
- Stability of the process, including documentation, performance measures and reporting requirements
- Ability to provide knowledge transfer to processing people remotely
- Regulatory and legal constraints surrounding the process (such as certification requirements)
- Dependence and availability of technology infrastructure
- Market availability of skills – at offshore locations
- Management views and concerns with the societal impact of offshoring (including dealing with communication with stakeholders)

Many of these factors require an outsourcing professional to review the process details and market availability of providers first, according to other sections in this OPBOK.

1.6.2 Examples of offshoring

Offshoring began initially with lower end activity processing, such as airline tickets, keypunching, transcription services, data entry and programming conversion tasks (especially during Y2K programming changes). Since then, offshoring has matured and now there are many examples of higher level processes being managed offshore. The following are just some of the examples.

ITO

- Applications development and enhancement
- Monitoring data networks
- Data center operations management

BPO

- Claims processing
- Check image processing
- Procurement processing (requisition to checks)
- HR-benefit administration
- Legal – litigation support
- Data mining

KPO

- Capital market analysis
- Legal – copyright management
- Vendor analysis
- Medical payment assessment

1.6.5   Key differences between onshore and offshore outsourcing

The following are some of the key differences between onshore and offshore outsourcing to keep in mind:

- Provider cost/pricing structure
- Tax implications
- Regulatory implications
- Political concerns
- Data protection and security
- The sourcing process itself
- Management and governance process is more complex and time consuming
- Legal and arbitration adjudication
- Intellectual property protection

1.6.6   Models of offshoring

Although offshoring models do not differ significantly from onshore models of outsourcing, there are a couple of significant variations that should be noted and understood.

Since there is a significant impact of the governance requirements on offshoring, some businesses have taken a stand that they will only establish a captive operation offshore. However, some of them have felt that they do not possess the requisite knowledge and/or local experience to be able to establish the captive operation on their own. As a result, a new form of outsourcing model has emerged in recent times. This model is that of build-operate-transfer (BOT). In this model, the business outsources the task of establishing a center to a local company – from building the infrastructure to initial staffing and operating the center for a finite period – and then takes over responsibility of the center from the outsourcer. Other variations have emerged. There are some significant benefits with this model:

- Depending on a local provider to bring their expertise in setting up operation and thereby lowering the risk of start-up issues
- Reduction in the time it takes to set up the center
- Lower balance sheet impact of initial capital cost, since the start up capital cost can be amortized differently and then applying it during the purchase of an operational center.
- Gaining knowledge and experience by observing the initial operational period and learning the local requirements.
- Creating local market awareness through an established name and thereby reducing staffing challenges and then transferring the "goodwill" of an operational center through an established name.

1.7.   Overcoming outsourcing's challenges

Any change as significant as outsourcing has risk. Not all organizations execute outsourcing well. Not all providers deliver well for every customer. Even when both companies execute well, other internal and external factors can keep the relationship from delivering its intended benefits. As a result, various surveys regularly report a surprisingly high rate of outsourcing failures.

Outsourcing is hard work, and the role of outsourcing professionals is to use their acquired skill and knowledge to help direct the organization's efforts in ways that produce better, more consistent results. Particular areas of focus are: setting realistic expectations; choosing the right opportunities for outsourcing; choosing the right providers; crafting a balanced relationship that offers sustainable benefit to customer and provider, alike; properly managing outsourcing's organizational impacts; and managing the ongoing relationship.

Another barrier generally expressed by businesses is a fear that they will lose the knowledge and skills once the process (or technology) is outsourced. This is true if there are not appropriate governance processes put in place to document and retain the skills and knowledge through the life of the agreement. A good contract will also ensure that the service provider is responsible for significantly lessening the buyer's dependence on that knowledge or skill.

1.7.1   Barriers to outsourcing

There are also a number of barriers inside the organization that must be addressed for outsourcing to be successful. Managers fear a loss of control. They often believe that although an activity may not be core, it may still be too critical to be outsourced. They are concerned about losing flexibility by getting locked into a long-term contract with a service provider. They are concerned about how their customers may react. They are concerned about employee, and especially union, reactions. They are concerned, particularly when it comes to offshore outsourcing, about community and political backlash over lost jobs.

Although each of these concerns is based on often strongly held opinions, more often than not they reflect more a fear of the unknown than an objective assessment of the facts.

Loss of control

It can be argued just as effectively that, if done well, organizations do not lose but gain control through outsourcing. A contractual relationship with a top service provider tied to measurable outcomes often gives executives greater control than they had over their previous typically less formal and less well-defined internal management system.

Too critical to be outsourced

Can organizations outsource critical activities and still be successful? They can and do every day. The GM executive who outsourced payroll, for example, would go out of his way to make sure that other executives understood that the outsourcing decision was not made because payroll was not critical. "If we don't make payroll, the union walks. If the union walks, we don't make cars. If we don't make cars, we don't make money," he would say. GM outsourced payroll precisely because it concluded it was too critical not to outsource it to a specialist who could do it better and more efficiently.

Loss of flexibility

Instead of reducing flexibility, outsourcing can actually increase it. Through outsourcing, the company gains access to the provider's larger resource pool. Those resources can now be tapped by the customer "on demand."

Negative customer reaction

Although outsourcing may be a sensitive issue for some customers, improved service quickly puts many of these concerns to rest. The fact that a third party is involved does not need to be visible at all, if the company chooses. In other cases, the provider's brand may actually enhance their customer's.

Employee resistance

Barriers also exist because of concerns over outsourcing's impact on employees and even its impact on the status and power of the middle- and upper-level managers who have direct authority over the function. This issue is particularly sensitive when the outsourcing involves off-shoring. Even there, as we shall see later, organizations have tremendous latitude in preparing and assisting their people and managers through these changes.

Poor or lack of effective outsourcing process, performance metrics and project management

In a recent market survey on outsourcing by Forrester Research, above 50 percent of the respondents reported additional outsourcing challenges due to: (1) poor project management skills; (2) lack of an effective outsourcing process; and (3) inadequate or poor metrics and communications vehicles for measuring and monitoring performance. Poorly designed and implemented communication plans during the outsourcing process can also act as a barrier to completing the agreement.

All of these challenges can be overcome by establishing a comprehensive outsourcing governance policy, process and controls, adequate training and certification for project management and meaningful management re-enforcement.

1.7.2   Balancing customer and provider views, needs, wants and concerns

As part of the outsourcing decision considerations, customers want and/or need to have a number of factors satisfied:

- quality equal to or better than the current service
- reduced costs and reduced capital expenditures
- availability, reliability, dependability, credibility, bench strength, financial accountability and service
- redundancy, contingency and disaster recovery (no single point of failure)
- wants measurable results with realistic and enforceable metrics
- wants governance and escalation with single (limited) point of provider contact (to build relationships and resolve issues quickly)
- dependability, credibility and certification (ISO 9000, SEI's CMMI, PMP, others, etc.)
- global contract for volume discounts (think global, act local)
- pay as you grow
- easier transition from old to new technology
- disengagement options

Customers have also raised a number of issues and concerns:

- security and privacy of data
- business continuity assurance
- provider maturity and stability
- quality and timeliness of work, including service levels
- presence (representation) in home country
- communications and culture – distance, time difference,
- management time to coordinate, language, etc.
- protection from and avoidance of high tech 'scams' (e.g. Citibank call center – India)
- loss of control
- compromise of intellectual property potential
- high provider employee turnover rates (as in India)
- providers

Outsourcing providers have specific needs, wants and concerns:

- substantial revenue stream potential
- growing global market
- long-term customer relationship
- competitive environment
- bid process expensive
- technical complexity
- pricing sensitivity – making provisions for change
- cost estimating difficulty (over multi-year contracts)
- increased pressure to be certified (e.g. ISO 9000, SEI's CMMI, PMI's PMP, ITIL, other)
- account control for cross-selling and up-selling
- attracting and retaining skilled employees
- understanding the expectations of the customer
- customer industry, application, function and/or process knowledge
- economies of scale

1.8.   The outsourcing professional

Outsourcing professionals now exist in organizations around the world and, most importantly, are increasingly taking the lead on topics like outsourcing process design, project team management, strategy and policy setting, outsourcing implementation, and governance. At the same time, these outsourcing professionals are seeking to pool their efforts through development of a common robust outsourcing body of knowledge, networking and learning from each other, and through the establishment of professional skills, standards, and certification.

Outsourcing is here to stay. It is inextricably linked to the globalization of business. As this globalization continues to connect the world's economies, few if any companies will be able to meet the challenges they will face by relying solely on their own internal resources. As a result, companies will increasingly turn to partners, often through outsourcing, to help them better leverage what they are best at, gain greater flexibility and reach, and drive down their overall business costs and risks.

But this increased reliance on outsourcing brings with it its own challenges. Many studies point to less than desirable and certainly less than consistent outsourcing results. The reason is that in today's world, companies need more than simple cost savings and contractually-based service levels from outsourcing. What they need is a way to build a dynamic network of global partners able to adapt to and even anticipate ever-changing business realities.

As the use of outsourcing goes up, companies also need to lower the total cost of outsourcing. Customers and providers alike are beginning to struggle with the burden of managing increasingly complex outsourcing relationships across multiple organizations with multifaceted interfaces. Most importantly, for outsourcing to continue to grow, the success rate has to go up even faster than the growth rate. If it does not, then the sheer weight of the number of 'failed' contracts may ultimately make outsourcing seem too expensive, at any price.

It is against this backdrop that companies are increasingly turning to outsourcing professionals to take charge of their emerging global corporate ecosystems. Outsourcing professionals are fast becoming the experts with the strategic vision it takes to determine the right sourcing approach and the execution skills it takes to put the right relationships in place and make them work. They are developing a unique combination of skills: the best of traditional general management along with the knowledge and experience to design, build, and operate highly complex, cross-organizational, cross-border, and cross-cultural business systems.

Today's outsourcing professional requires that he/she possesses capabilities and skills that are different from what they are generally trained for or accustomed to before outsourcing. These are:

- **Skills** – as the Certified Outsourcing Professional (COP) program demonstrates, there are critical skills required of outsourcing professionals. In many cases, the outsourcing professional must be able to change from being a 'doer' to being a 'relationship manager.' This requires more of a holistic view of the business while at the same time maintaining alignment with third parties.
- **Methodologies and tools** – successful outsourcing management requires a process orientation and hence the emphasis on methodologies and tools – including templates.
- **Management systems** – measurements and process orientation form the basis of a strong outsourcing relationship, one that is based on facts. These systems are linked to the methodologies and tools.

1.8.1 Who is an outsourcing professional?

Outsourcing professionals are now operating across the business and at many levels. IAOP's global survey of customer-side outsourcing professionals found that 44 percent work within functional areas like IT, real estate, shared services operations, and manufacturing, while 31 percent work in corporate-wide groups such as strategic planning, procurement, and sourcing, and 25 percent work as line executives with direct operational responsibility for significantly outsourced operations.

Titles vary dramatically, as shown in Figure 1.7. Within functional areas like IT, these outsourcing professionals carry titles such as global IT outsourcing coordinator; director, IT synergies; and vice president, technology vendor management. Those with company-wide responsibilities have titles such as director, outsourcing center of competency; director of strategic sourcing; global head of outsourcing management; general manager, outsourcing; and strategic relations manager.

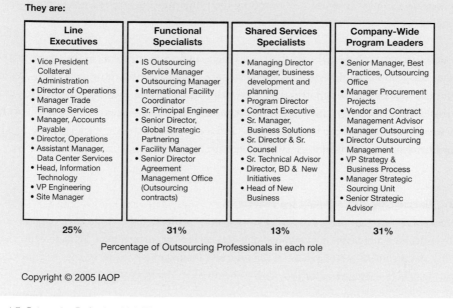

They are:

Line Executives	Functional Specialists	Shared Services Specialists	Company-Wide Program Leaders
• Vice President Collateral Administration • Director of Operations • Manager Trade Finance Services • Manager, Accounts Payable • Director, Operations • Assistant Manager, Data Center Services • Head, Information Technology • VP Engineering • Site Manager	• IS Outsourcing Service Manager • Outsourcing Manager • International Facility Coordinator • Sr. Principal Engineer • Senior Director, Global Strategic Partnering • Facility Manager • Senior Director Agreement Management Office (Outsourcing contracts)	• Managing Director • Manager, business development and planning • Program Director • Contract Executive • Sr. Manager, Business Solutions • Sr. Director & Sr. Counsel • Sr. Technical Advisor • Director, BD & New Initiatives • Head of New Business	• Senior Manager, Best Practices, Outsourcing Office • Manager Procurement Projects • Vendor and Contract Management Advisor • Manager Outsourcing • Director Outsourcing Management • VP Strategy & Business Process • Manager Strategic Sourcing Unit • Senior Strategic Advisor
25%	**31%**	**13%**	**31%**

Percentage of Outsourcing Professionals in each role

Copyright © 2005 IAOP

Figure 1.7: Outsourcing Professional Job Titles

In turn, these outsourcing professionals are creating another layer of outsourcing professionals below them. They are building their own support teams with, on average, four people reporting to them with titles such as project manager, outsourcing consultant, and alliance management specialist.

The survey also found that their expertise is increasingly in outsourcing itself, not necessarily in a particular operational area. In fact, almost 80 percent of outsourcing professionals surveyed are involved in the outsourcing of more than one activity.

Finally, the impact of these outsourcing professionals on the business is significant. The average outsourcing professional is now involved in just over $60 million per year of outsourcing spending, with some leading programs of hundreds of millions and even billions of dollars of annual spending.

1.8.2   Outsourcing professionals: roles and responsibilities

The best way to characterize the role being taken by outsourcing professionals within their companies is as designer, facilitator and implementer.

Almost 60 percent of outsourcing professionals have the lead role when it comes to designing and managing their organization's end-to-end outsourcing process. Their focus here is on establishing the steps the organization goes through in its efforts to identify and evaluate opportunities and then to move the best of those opportunities through that process effectively. Outsourcing professionals also play an active role in setting their organization's overall outsourcing strategy and policy.

But, outsourcing professionals are both designers and implementers. Many, more than 40 percent, also lead the implementation effort, manage and help set up the project teams, perform preliminary assessments of opportunities, and work on the governance of the ultimate outsourcing relationship. They also play active roles in the request for proposal process and provider selection. Even when it comes to the actual 'go, no-go' decision, which is more typically in the hands of senior management and the line executives, outsourcing professionals are heavily involved.

1.8.3   Outsourcing professionals: top challenges

Governance is the top challenge facing outsourcing professionals. And, governance is not a single issue; it encompasses a wide range of topics including performance management, change and risk management, development of the requisite management skills, quality assurance, and providing effective incentives for providers to better align the interests of all parties.

The second biggest challenge, which is closely related to the first, is properly selecting and qualifying providers to begin with. How do you choose? With an ever growing number of providers, constantly changing mixes of capabilities and services, and new insights gained regularly in terms of what does and does not work, selecting the right provider to assure the desired results is not easy.

Another area that is high on the list of challenges for outsourcing professionals is gaining internal executive buy-in. Although the overall case for outsourcing may be compelling, getting all of the affected executives on board on a specific initiative, particularly given the organizational politics that come into play, is never easy. This leads naturally to the fourth most frequently mentioned challenge – value assessment. Booking cost savings is one thing, but getting a true definition of value, value for money and return on investment that encompasses all of the expected impacts of an outsourcing decision still eludes many.

1.8.4   Outsourcing professionals defining the future of business

Just as other areas of business have matured to become recognized professions with a well understood role in contributing to organizational success enabled by the skills and professionalism of its practitioners, the same is now happening with outsourcing.

Outsourcing professionals are emerging across the business, operating within specific functions and in company-wide capacities. They are increasingly helping to shape the organization's policies and practices, but they are also helping to lead the effort to make outsourcing work. They are increasing the recognized, go-to resource for ensuring better outcomes. At the same time, outsourcing professionals face many challenges themselves and the effort to develop and codify the field's body of knowledge is really just underway.

Key to ensuring high-quality outsourcing outcomes is constantly improving the capabilities of the business and project leaders responsible for defining, implementing, and managing these highly complex multi-company relationships.

The purpose of the International Association of Outsourcing Professionals' (IAOP) *Certified Outsourcing Professional (COP) Program* is to support this goal by:

- establishing a common, globally-recognized set of standards for the experience and knowledge outsourcing professionals should possess
- providing a defined process by which outsourcing professionals can demonstrate that they possess these requisite capabilities
- creating a highly-coveted professional designation that distinguishes the outsourcing professionals who obtain it as the leading practitioners in their field

The primary certification covers the non-domain specific experience and knowledge common to outsourcing as a management practice irrespective of the individual's role as a customer, provider, or advisor. Following introduction of the primary certification, programs specific to domains, such as information technology, finance and accounting, manufacturing, logistics, etc., and to specific roles as customer, provider, and advisor will be explored. Levels of certification, such as those of interest to individuals seeking a fundamental, advanced, and master certification will be explored as well.

The *Certified Outsourcing Professional (COP) Program* is made up of the following elements.

The Outsourcing Professional Body of Knowledge (OPBOK)

The *Outsourcing Professional Body of Knowledge (OPBOK)* describes the generally accepted set of knowledge and practices applicable to the successful design, implementation, and management of outsourcing contracts. It provides:

- a framework for understanding what outsourcing is and how it fits within contemporary business operations

■ the knowledge and practice areas generally accepted as critical to outsourcing success

■ a glossary of terms commonly used within the field.

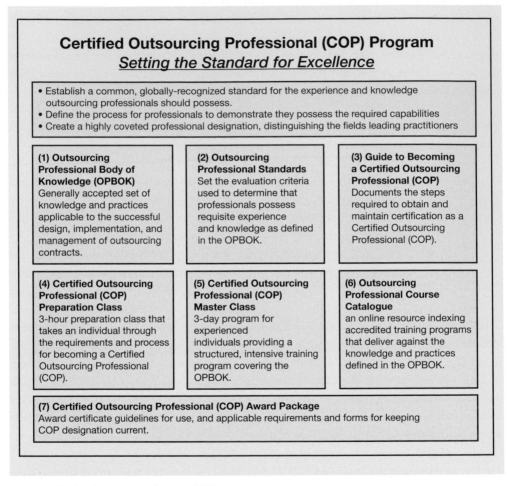

Certified Outsourcing Professional (COP) Program
Setting the Standard for Excellence

- Establish a common, globally-recognized standard for the experience and knowledge outsourcing professionals should possess.
- Define the process for professionals to demonstrate they possess the required capabilities
- Create a highly coveted professional designation, distinguishing the fields leading practitioners

(1) Outsourcing Professional Body of Knowledge (OPBOK)
Generally accepted set of knowledge and practices applicable to the successful design, implementation, and management of outsourcing contracts.

(2) Outsourcing Professional Standards
Set the evaluation criteria used to determine that professionals possess requisite experience and knowledge as defined in the OPBOK.

(3) Guide to Becoming a Certified Outsourcing Professional (COP)
Documents the steps required to obtain and maintain certification as a Certified Outsourcing Professional (COP).

(4) Certified Outsourcing Professional (COP) Preparation Class
3-hour preparation class that takes an individual through the requirements and process for becoming a Certified Outsourcing Professional (COP).

(5) Certified Outsourcing Professional (COP) Master Class
3-day program for experienced individuals providing a structured, intensive training program covering the OPBOK.

(6) Outsourcing Professional Course Catalogue
an online resource indexing accredited training programs that deliver against the knowledge and practices defined in the OPBOK.

(7) Certified Outsourcing Professional (COP) Award Package
Award certificate guidelines for use, and applicable requirements and forms for keeping COP designation current.

Figure 1.8: Certified Outsourcing Professional (COP)

Outsourcing Professional Standards

Outsourcing Professional Standards define the level of experience and knowledge outsourcing professionals need to possess to ensure consistent, high-quality results for the organizations that rely upon them to design, implement, and manage their outsourcing contracts. The *Outsourcing Professional Standards* essentially set the evaluation criteria used to determine whether or not an outsourcing professional has sufficient experience with and understanding of the *Outsourcing Professional Body of Knowledge (OPBOK)* to generally ensure high quality outsourcing outcomes.

Guide to Becoming a Certified Outsourcing Professional (COP)

The *Guide to Becoming a Certified Outsourcing Professional (COP)* documents the steps that an individual needs to take to become and maintain certification as a *Certified Outsourcing Professional (COP)*. It provides recommendations on the experiences and training needed to meet the certification requirements, all applicable forms, steps to follow, typical timelines, and requirements for meeting annual re-certification requirements. It should be noted that the certification process requires that the professional can demonstrate and validate through a reference their direct experience in meeting requirements. Although shared services and captive offshore center topics are included in this OPBOK and the Master Class for discussion, any experience involving them does not count towards the points necessary to get the certification.

Certified Outsourcing Professional (COP) Preparation Class

The *Certified Outsourcing Professional (COP) Preparation Class* is a 3-hour program that introduces the structure and content of the *Outsourcing Professional Body of Knowledge (OPBOK)*, provides an in-depth review of the *Outsourcing Professional Standards,* and takes the participant through the steps required to obtain and maintain *Certified Outsourcing Professional (COP)* certification based on the *Guide to Becoming a Certified Outsourcing Professional (COP)*.

Certified Outsourcing Professional (COP) Master Class

The *Certified Outsourcing Professional (COP) Master Class* is a 3-day program that provides individuals already experienced and working in the field of outsourcing with a structured, intensive training program based upon the *Outsourcing Professional Body of Knowledge (OPBOK)*. Individuals with solid general management skills, practical, in-the-field, outsourcing experience, and who successfully complete this program are generally fully prepared to meet the *Certified Outsourcing Professional (COP)* requirements.

Advanced Certified Outsourcing Professional Classes

From time to time, IAOP will offer 2-4 hour long classes (or webinars) that may be taken by certified professionals and thus meet the requirements for continuing education. Each of these classes have certain pre-defined points assigned and must be taken in full to receive the credits.

Outsourcing Professional Course Catalogue

The *Outsourcing Professional Course Catalogue* is an online and print resource available to IAOP members. It indexes accredited training programs, whether available from IAOP or other sources, that deliver against the knowledge and practices defined in the *Outsourcing Professionals Body of Knowledge (OPBOK)*. The catalogue also includes *IAOP's Accreditation Application* used to requesting review and inclusion of non-IAOP training programs in this catalogue.

Certified Outsourcing Professional (COP) Award Package

The *Certified Outsourcing Professional (COP) Award Package* is presented to individuals upon meeting all of the requirements for certification. It includes an award certificate, guidelines on use of the certification designation, and applicable requirements and forms for keeping the certification current and in force.

A closely related component to the *Certified Outsourcing Professional (COP) Program* is the *Code of Ethics and Business Practice Standards for Outsourcing Professionals.* By adopting and adhering to these standards, Certified Outsourcing Professionals differentiate themselves as preferred customers, providers, and advisors with whom to work. For reference the current copy of these standards are included in the Appendix.

1.8.5   Outsourcing and social responsibility

Today, Corporate Social Responsibility (CSR) is a priority item on the agenda of every business organization. At the same time, global outsourcing continues to grow unabated, and – not surprisingly – research shows leading providers have embraced CSR. Buyers and providers both expect short term and strategic value through CSR, especially in global outsourcing. In addition to customer requirements, outsourcers are reacting to societal needs, government regulations and employee expectations. They also see the opportunity to reduce energy costs while creating a smaller carbon footprint. In many cases global IT outsourcers are finding that CSR related services provide a new source of revenue. CSR has become an unavoidable issue in global outsourcing.

One of the ways IAOP advocates the management practice of outsourcing is to show how companies and professionals can embrace it in a socially responsible way, creating a positive outcome for all involved. To identify and promote discussion of socially responsible policies and practices among our IAOP membership, a Corporate Social Responsibility Sub-Committee has been created. Led by IAOP Chairman Michael F. Corbett, the Corporate Social Responsibility (CSR) sub-committee of the Advocacy & Outreach committee is chartered with identifying and promoting discussion among IAOP members on how outsourcing can be used as a powerful tool for advancing critical social, economic, and environmental issues on a global basis.

Additionally, it examines corporate socially responsible policies and practices for outsourcing, including identifying and showcasing policies that our membership have adopted, creating a framework for companies to model new CSR policies, and developing a network of resources for members.

IAOP has been interested in the topic of social responsibility as it pertains to outsourcing, and last year we identified CSR as one of the major trends to expect in 2010 and beyond. IAOP is addressing each of these areas through training programs and standards development such as:

- The Certified Outsourcing Professional® (COP) program
- IAOP chapter informational meetings and seminars
- The annual Outsourcing World Summit® – Enhancing outsourcing's image by prioritizing CSR as a main track for The 2010 Outsourcing World Summit®
- Outsourcing Hall of Fame induction for industry leaders who contribute to business and society
- The Code of Ethics and Business Practices Standards for outsourcing professionals

Examples of CSR practices embraced by our members and the outsourcing community in general are:

- expanding career opportunities and training for employees
- increasing investments in new technologies and in new ways of working
- promoting ethical standards in various facets of business operations
- supporting social and economic improvements at the community level
- improving labor and workforce practices
- addressing environmental, green, and sustainability issues

The *Survey of Corporate Social Responsibility in Outsourcing* is an initiative of the committee with findings presented at The 2010 Outsourcing World Summit. Visit the committee web page at http://www.iaop.org/content/23/126/1698/ for more information about this and other initiatives of the CSR sub-committee.

1.8.6   Some recent trends in sourcing

There are some recent trends in sourcing that are related to outsourcing and in some cases are variant models to traditional outsourcing. These developments are being followed by IAOP and outsourcing professionals need to understand them and apply them where appropriate.

Rural sourcing: this is a term created to designate rural locations where an outsourcing center is established to take advantage of lower cost of living and potential access to an underused labor pool. As the global economy continues to be difficult, there are certain rural locations that have become quite competitive and can even provide a sound alternative to offshoring from the economic point of view.

Consortium sourcing: this is a trend where multiple companies come together to form a consortium to create enough volume to attract larger, more qualified outsourcing service providers. This is a trend that is more appropriate for mid-tier and smaller companies. Although this is a new term, consortium buying has been around for many decades. As we begin to see technological innovation such as "cloud computing" "web-based process and technology tools", consortium sourcing will become more appropriate and popular.

Bundled sourcing: when a business decides to bundle multiple processes and activities and outsources to a single provider, it is identified as "bundled outsourcing". The biggest benefit to the business comes from giving service providers greater flexibility to alter the end-to-end processes, apply process efficiency and introduce appropriate technology. Procurement to Payment (Req to Check) is an example of such bundled outsourcing.

Crowd sourcing: although this has the term "sourcing", it is not yet clear as to how to categorize it as an outsourcing model. In its current form, it looks like a "web-enabled" one-on-one sourcing. As professionals, we will need to observe it and see if it ends up leading to a model where a combination of crowd sourcing and consortium service provision emanates as a model of delivery.

1.9. List of key terms

Offshoring (Near-Shoring, Rural-Shoring, etc.)
Outsourcing
Outsourcing Framework (Common Business Process Framework)
Risks in Outsourcing
Rural Sourcing
Service Provider
Shared Services Center
Sourcing
Strategic Outsourcing
Tactical Outsourcing
Transitional Outsourcing
Transformational Outsourcing

1.10. List of templates

1.1 Defining Outsourcing

1.2 External Business Drivers

1.3 Internal Business Drivers

1.4 Organizational Evaluation Factors (Shared Services and Outsourcing)

1.5 Anticipated Outsourcing Benefits

1.6 Gauging Organizational Outsourcing Maturity

1.7 Common Business Process Framework

1.8 Outsourcing and Offshoring Considerations

1.11. Additional references

Although each of the modules provides some significant references, the Knowledge Center (Firmbuilder.com®) on the IAOP website is the comprehensive source of material for all aspects of outsourcing. The articles (papers, presentations, research reports, news items) are fully categorized so as to facilitate easy research and navigation. The categorization includes:

- Standard and sub-standard as applicable
- Industry segment (e.g. financial – banking, government, retail services)
- Process specialization segment (e.g. HR, IT, real estate)
- Geography – if pertinent (e.g. US, China, South America)
- Focus of interest – customers, providers or advisors
- Type – framework, tools/templates, metrics/results, research or experiences (lessons learned),
- Revenue size where the topic may be applicable (if pertinent)

David Sibbet, "75 years of management ideas and practice 1922–1997," Harvard Business Review, Sep/Oct 1997, Supplement Vol. 75, Issue 5, p1, 10p, 1 diagram,

Peter F. Drucker, "Sell the Mailroom," The Wall Street Journal, July 25, 1989, p. A16.

C. Prahalad & G. Hamel, "The Core Competence of the Corporation," Harvard Business Review, March/April 1990, p. 79–91.

James Brian Quinn and Frederick G. Hilmer, "Strategic Outsourcing," Sloan Management Review, Summer 1994, p. 43–55.

Michael F. Corbett, "How America's Leading Firms Use Outsourcing," Michael F. Corbett & Associates, Ltd., April 1999.

Michael F. Corbett, "An Inside Look at Outsourcing," Fortune, June 9, 2003, p. S2.

James Brian Quinn, "Outsourcing Innovation: The New Engine of Growth," Sloan Management Review, Summer, 2000, pp. 13–27.

Gregg Keiser, "Gartner Says Half of Outsourcing Projects Fail," http://www.crn.com, March 26, 2003

"IT Outsourcing: Mindset Switch Needed to Improve Satisfaction with Supplier Relationships," PA Consulting Group, http://www.paconsutling.com, March 3, 2003

Atul Vashistha, Avinash Vashistha, "The Offshore Nation," TATA McGraw Hill, 2005

Michael Hammer, "The Process Enterprise: An Executive Perspective," Hammer and Company, 2001, retrieved from http://www.hammerandco.com December 12, 2003.

Michael F. Corbett, "ROI Outsourcing," Fortune, December 10, 2001, p. S8

Michael F. Corbett, "Outsourcing for Business Transformation," Fortune, June 7, 1999, p. S10.

Michael F. Corbett, "Harnessing the Power of Outsourcing's Next Wave," The 2003 Outsourcing World Summit Presentation, February 24, 2003, Palm Desert, CA, content based on previous research.

Khozem Merchant, "GE Champions India's World Class Services," Financial Times, June 3, 2003

Steven Greenhouse, "IM. Explores Shift of White-Collar Jobs Overseas," New York Times, July 22, 2003, retrieved from http://www.nytimes.com July 22, 2003.

Manjeet Kripalani and Pete Engardio, "The Rise of India," BusinessWeek, December 8, 2003, p. 66–78.

Nelson D. Schwartz, "Down and Out in White-Collar America," Fortune, June 23, 2003, p. 79–86.

John Ribeiro, "India Moves up the Outsourcing Ladder," InfoWorld, August 29 2003, retrieved from http://www. Infoworld.com on December 9, 2003.

Grant Gross, "IT Workforce Demand Lowest in Four Years," IDG News Service, May 5, 2003, retrieved December 9, 2003 from http://www.itworld.com.

David Kirkpatrick, "The Net Makes It All Easier—Including Exporting US Jobs," Fortune, May 26, 2003, p. 146.

Lisa Takeuchi Cullen, "Who's Hiring . . . And Where," Time, November 24, 2003

Jean-Francois Poisson, COP "Outsourcing Business Case", Presentation at Outsourcing World Summit Presentation, 2007

Danny Ertel, COP "Outsourcing processes, tools and skills – the right stuff," Presentation at Outsourcing World Summit"

Rick Julian and Phil Franz, "Managing outsourcing risks to ensure improved performance", Presentation at Outsourcing World Summit, 2006

Jagdish Dalal, COP "The Role of Outsourcing Professional", Presentation at Outsourcing World Summit, 2010

Wipro, " The Power of Partnering in Accomplishing your Green IT Agenda", July 2007 (A survey)

Jeremy Hockenstein, Digital Divide Data, "Socially Responsible Outsourcing from the Ground Up", Outsourcing World Summit Presentation, 2009

Robert Williams, State Street Corporation, "Socially Responsible Outsourcing: Doing Good While Doing Well", Outsourcing World Summit Presentation, 2009

Francis Meganathan; Managing Director, Cuscapi Outsourcing Sdn Bhd, Mark Yaun; Managing Director, Sonic Teleservices, "Surviving the Economic Crisis through Sound Outsourcing Principals" Asia Outsourcing Summit Presentation, 2009

Bobby Varanasi, COP, Head – Marketing & Branding, Outsourcing Malaysia and CEO, Matryzel Consulting, "Value Scale: Development of Collaboration Partnership to Create Value with Commoditized Services in Asia-Pacific" Asia Outsourcing Summit Presentation, 2009

Russell M. Bostick, EVP of Technology and Operations, Conseco, "Reimagining the Global Business Paradigm Through Outsourcing – "New Choices in the New Normal", Outsourcing World Summit Presentation, 2010

Michael F. Corbett, Chairman, IAOP, "State of Outsourcing Profession (survey results)", Outsourcing World Summit Presentation, 2010

Dr. Ganesh Natarajan, COP, Chairman, CII National Committee on IT, ITeS & eCommerce & Global CEO, Zensar Technologies Ltd. "Next Generation Socially Responsible Outsourcing", Outsourcing World Summit Presentation, 2010

Monty P. Hamilton, CEO, Rural Sourcing, Inc., " From Vicious Spiral to Virtuous Cycle: How Outsourcing Could be the Answer to Rural America's Brain Drain", Outsourcing World Summit Presentation, 2010

2 Developing and managing an organization's end-to-end process for outsourcing

Outsourcing has quickly become an essential part of the modern business. Organizations of all kinds use outsourcing every day to improve the products and services they provide to customers. They use outsourcing to free capital and brainpower for investment in research and development, leading to new products and new services. In fact, more than 90 percent of companies say that outsourcing is an important part of their overall business strategy.

Outsourcing is also critical to the growth and success of the United States and other Western economies. Harvard Business Review lists it as one of the most important new management ideas and practices of this century and noted scholar and business visionary, James Brian Quinn of Dartmouth College, has called outsourcing "one of the greatest organizational and industry structure shifts of the century."

Taking outsourcing from opportunity identification through to implementation and ongoing management requires both structure and leadership: structure in terms of a consistent and repeatable management process that is understood and followed by all, and leadership in terms of executive sponsors, project team leaders, and effective project team members.

2.1   Standards

2.0	Developing and Managing an Organization's End-to-End Process for Outsourcing
2.1	Ability to develop an organization's sourcing model – single sourcing versus multi-sourcing
2.1.1.	Define single sourcing (competitively selected or sole-source awarded) model benefits and shortcomings
2.1.2.	Define multi-sourcing model (either by process, geography, division) and describe model benefits and shortcomings
2.1.3.	Provide cogent arguments for selection of a model
2.2	Ability to develop an organization's end-to-end process for evaluating, implementing, and managing outsourcing relationships
2.2.1	Select and define the most appropriate process stages for the organization's approach to outsourcing, such as the 'idea' stage, the 'assessment and planning' stage, the 'implementation' stage, the 'transition' stage, and the 'management' stage.
2.2.2	Define the key business questions that are asked and answered in each stage.
2.2.3	Define the organizational decision-makers for each stage
2.2.1	Define the process for setting the go, no-go decision criteria for each stage and for determining if those criteria have been met
2.2.5	Define timeframes for each stage consistent with the organization's goals and objectives
2.2.6	Evaluate an organization's specific process against generally accepted process criteria, such as the Lifecycle Stages and Key Components Checklist in the Outsourcing Professional Body of Knowledge (OPBOK) Appendix C
2.3	Ability to manage an organization's end-to-end outsourcing planning, design, implementation, and management process
2.3.1	Track individual outsourcing initiatives as they move through the defined stages of the organization's process using the Outsourcing Business Plan
2.3.2	Create a 'forward-leaning' management approach that helps ensure that outsourcing opportunities move through the process in an effective and efficient manner, including ensuring appropriate levels of executive support.

2.3.3.	Set and manage to realistic timeframes for each stage of the process
2.2.4	Integrate outsourcing processes and outcomes into the day-to-day business operations and environment
2.4	**Ability to assess and enhance over time an organization's outsourcing process maturity**

2.2   Sourcing alternatives

Businesses have used multiple approaches when creating their strategy for outsourcing. Some have used a single provider strategy when outsourcing a robust set of processes while others have used best-of-breed sourcing. There have been industry examples of both types of sourcing.

2.2.1   Best-of-breed sourcing

Going back in history, when Kodak started the IT outsourcing trend in 1990, they used the best-of-breed approach (and since then it has been used by large corporations such as DuPont, JP Morgan, and Procter & Gamble). In this approach, activities within the same function (or process) are divided among multiple providers based on their capabilities and commitment. Some businesses have used best-of-breed solutions based on the geography of where the work is outsourced from. This is done so as to use the local strength of different providers.

More recently, this best-of-breed approach has been referred to as 'multi-sourcing.'

The most obvious benefit from this type of sourcing is that the business can select providers based on their best capability (either by process or geography) and be assured of a higher level of service. It also allows the business to have more than one provider compete against each other throughout the agreement period and thereby be assured of the highest level of attention from the provider.

There are two principal drawbacks from this approach to sourcing:

- the investment required to manage multiple service providers – from sourcing through governance
- the difficulty in cross-managing services when the two providers are dependent on each other to meet the contracted service levels.

One way to address this is by establishing a common set of standards (such as ITIL for information technology) which all providers are required to adhere to, thereby reducing the level of coordination required by the customer. Another approach is to use a prime sub-contractor model where the best-of-breed suppliers are selected, but the management role is taken on by a lead provider (the prime contractor).

2.2.2   Single sourcing

Again, when Xerox outsourced its information technology function, the entire function was awarded to a single provider following a competitive sourcing process. In this approach, the single provider takes responsibility for the entire process and all included functions.

This type of sourcing is easier to implement and manage through governance but creates an opportunity for potentially inferior levels of service in areas where the provider does not have the best capability. It also creates an advantage for the provider to trade off one service against the other.

Factors that would govern the decision making process include:

- Uniqueness of the process and maturity of the process involved
- Size of the activity/process being outsourced
- Complexity of the organization (geography, divisions) being serviced
- Business capacity to manage multiple sourcing process

2.3   The process of outsourcing: stages and components

The process of outsourcing begins with strategy, moves through assessment and implementation, and then continues into the management of the relationship. It forms a closed loop as the management of the current relationship sets the stage for what is strategically possible in the future. A model for this process is shown in Figure 2.1. The overall process has been broken into five stages. The end of each stage is thought of as a gate that the project must successfully pass through before it enters the next stage.

The first stage answers the essential question: Is outsourcing this business process or function appropriate for this organization at this time? What are the specific requirements? If deemed appropriate, the second stage is an in-depth assessment of the opportunity. That is, the development of the business case and analysis of the provider marketplace to confirm that the anticipated benefits are, indeed, real. It also includes the development of the plan for the remaining stages.

Once the opportunity is found to be real, then the next stage answers the question: Can we reach agreement on a deal with one or more of the qualified providers? If so, then the subsequent stages of the process cover its implementation and ongoing management. Each stage has a clearly defined and straightforward question it seeks to answer. And that answer is the starting point for the next stage.

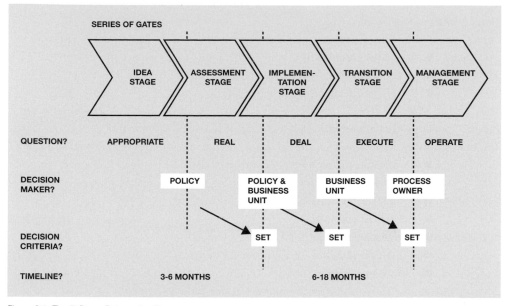

Figure 2.1: The 5-Stage Outsourcing Process

In total, a comprehensive outsourcing management process will address the following stages.

Identify outsourcing opportunity

- Develop concept.
- Perform high level strategic review of operations.
- Identify corporate direction.
- Develop "high insight" reports on outsourcing competitive intelligence.
- Perform business comparative or situation analysis.
- Identify outsourcing potential.
- Get executive concurrence and sponsorship.
- Assign steering committee.

Perform preliminary opportunity assessment

- Identify current processes.
- Understand user needs.
- Identify internal baseline costs and organization.
- Develop process requirements.
- Perform risk assessment analysis.
- Explore supplier alternatives.
- Develop preliminary outsourcing business case.
- Present to business prime.

Develop and evaluate business case

- Finalize business case.
- Verify customer approval.
- Verify board approval (where needed).

Establish outsourcing relationship

- Implement request for proposals process.
- Develop outsourcing contract.
- Finalize human resources plan.
- Finalize deal structure.
- Negotiate contract.
- Ratify contract.
- Execute contract.

Implement the solution

- Communicate project, team, and leadership.
- Develop detailed transition plan.
- Pilot development, test, review
- Finalize communication plan.
- Implement new organization structure.
- Transition activities.
- Monitor transition and implementation.

Manage ongoing relationship

- Perform daily management activities.
- Monitor performance.
- Implement relationship management processes.
- Complete outsourcing business plan.
- Change management process.
- Assess strategic review.
- Reconfirm business case.
- Review outsourcing performance assessment model.

Resistance to a change of the scope and impact of outsourcing from within and across the organization can be significant. Overcoming this resistance requires that not only the stages and gates are clearly defined, but that a forward-leaning management approach is adopted. To do this, the decision-makers at each gate and the decision criteria used must be clear to all involved.

Another key element of this staged but forward-leaning approach to making and executing outsourcing decisions is that as each decision gate is passed, the criteria for the next gate are established. When the policy decision is made that an opportunity is appropriate, the policy-level decision makers also establish the specific criteria to be used for the assessment decision. The parameters for this next decision gate are established in terms of anticipated benefits and acceptable risks. It might be phrased along the lines of "This opportunity is real if upon detail assessment we find that…" The reason it is important to establish the exit criteria for the next gate as part of passing through the previous one is to short-circuit the natural tendency of those coming onto the project at a later time to revisit the "wisdom" of the decisions that preceded them. For example, the goal of the individuals involved in the deal stage is not to reassess the appropriateness or the viability of the opportunity, it is to do their very best to complete a deal that fits the criteria established during the assessment stage.

Finally, it is important to set reasonable timeframes for the project. Although certain organizational changes can be planned and implemented in a matter of weeks or months, significant outsourcing projects will require between three and six months for scoping and assessing the opportunity, and then six to twelve months for putting the relationship together with a provider and transitioning to the new operating environment. It certainly can happen faster, but only if the level of executive attention and organizational resources applied are up to the task. Setting reasonable timeframes for each stage, whatever they are, is an important part of maintaining momentum while not forcing the work to be done in such a compressed manner that shortcuts get taken, leading to poor decisions and even poorer execution.

The gates at the end of each stage of the outsourcing process essentially represent go/no go decision points. Figure 2.2 lists select examples of deliverables and go/no go decisions at each stage.

Stage	Idea	Assessment (& Planning)	Implementation	Transition	Management
Deliverables	• Develop Concept • Perform High Level Review of Operations • Identify corporate direction • Perform Situation Analysis & Identify Outsourcing Opportunity • Get executive sponsor • Assign Steering Committee	• Analyze current processes & functions • Define proposed processes & functions • Define user needs • Perform risk analysis • Develop business case (with plan)	• Issue RFP • Finalize deal structure and terms • Develop and negotiate contract • Develop human resource and asset transfer plan • Communications Plan • Governance plan	• Detailed transition plan (with pilot) • Implement new organization structure • Transfer people, assets, functions and/or processes • Develop training plan	• Perform daily management activities • Monitor performance • Implement relationship management process • Institute change management process
Key Question and Go/No Go Criteria	**Appropriate?** • Alignment with business strategy? • Core competency? • High level cost/benefit acceptable? • Acceptable risk? • Competitive advantage? • Legal, ethical, etc.?	**Real?** • Acceptable business case? • Acceptable risk?	**Deal?** • Approved contract?	**Execute?** • Approved pilot? • Approve transition plan? • Assess transition and fix issues as necessary	**Operate?** • Governance and metrics being met? • Renew, expand, disengage?

Figure 2.2: Selected Deliverables and Go/No Go Criteria by Outsourcing Stage

Note that each go/no go decision is supported by a series of deliverables. These deliverables are contained in the Outsourcing Business Plan, discussed in the next section.

2.4   The Outsourcing Business Plan

For many, preparing the business plan for outsourcing seems to be a daunting task; what information should be made available, in what detail, and when? The Outsourcing Business Plan (OBP) provides a framework for organizing and providing the right information at the right time in a way that is consistent and useable at the various levels of the organization.

The Outsourcing Business Plan (OBP) for any opportunity is begun during the idea stage and continuously updated, expanded, and refined as the individual initiative moves through the organization's outsourcing process. It then becomes the central tool in establishing an interdependent management system with the organization's service providers.

Key sections of the Outsourcing Business Plan are:

Executive Summary

- Strategy
- Risks and risk mitigation
- Operation
- Human Resources
- Financial
- Communications

Detail sections for each as follows:

Strategy
- Overall strategy
- Business requirements
- Strategic choice
- Strategic objectives
- Structural model
- Contractual model
- Provider selection and/or recommendations
- Risk and risk mitigation

Risks and risk mitigation

- Risks by phase (strategy through governance)

- Risk appetite "boundary conditions"
- Risk avoidance and mitigation options

Operation

- Division of functions, roles and responsibilities
- Transaction activities
- Division of assets and systems
- Management of day to day operations
- Management of the overall relationship
- Management of outsourcing contract performance

Human resources

- Division of human resources
- Diagnostic of the client human resources needs
- Diagnostic of the provider human resources needs

Financial

- Financial baseline
- Incremental impact of transaction on the provider
- Provider's valuation
- Management of the financial process
- Financial studies

Communication

- Client Organization Communication Plan
- Provider Organization Communication Plan
- Customer Communication Plan
- Regulatory, Government and Community Communication Plan
- Union Communication Plan

2.5   Organizational capability assessment

As a part of developing strategy for the sourcing process and before initiating the outsourcing, it is important that the business assesses its capability to manage the outsourcing – from sourcing through governance. Organizational assessment is just as important as assessing the maturity and stability of the process. The following factors are important to consider when assessing the organizational ability to manage outsourcing:

■ Outsourcing competency: understanding the end-to-end outsourcing process, tools and techniques (ideally, having "Certified Outsourcing Professionals" on staff to help in this area) and be able to use it effectively

■ Strategic coalition: ability to create a strategy and creating alignment around the strategy from the top of the organization to the management level that would be directly affected by outsourcing

■ Customer impact: knowledge of customer impact on various processes and the sensitivity the customers will have for outsourcing of process that affects them

■ Sourcing capability: being able to have sourcing knowledge and ability to source and select the service provider without totally depending on outside consulting help

■ Process expertise: knowledge and understanding of the processes, metrics and drivers

■ Governance style: ability to manage the service provider without being involved in their day-to-day management. This is generally described as being able to manage "what" versus "how"

■ Relationship management: ability to create and sustain the relationship with an outside organization in such a way that the governance process is effective

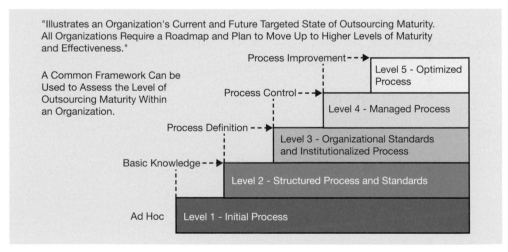

Figure 2.3: Assessing Outsourcing Process Maturity

2.6 Other feasibility assessments

Once the outsourcing organizational and process maturity is evaluated, there must be some additional factors that must be considered and decisions made before initiating the outsourcing process. Although these become a part of risk assessment, they are identified here to emphasize their importance in the decision making:

■ Implication of legal regulations and restrictions on outsourcing for the business. As some countries and states within the country establish conditions for outsourcing, its impact must be evaluated in the light of the total business scenario and not just the outsourcing options. For example, if outsourcing restricts the company from entering into any other business deals, it may affect other business plans (and revenue potential)

■ Similarly, labor requirements – including notification, consultation – must also be considered and the feasibility established that the outsourcing decision will not adversely affect the smooth operation of the business.

2.7 List of key terms

Organizational Assessment
Sourcing Options
Sole Source
Competitively Sourced
Single-Source Selection
Best-of-Breed Selection
Outsourcing Business Plan (OBP)
Outsourcing Process
Outsourcing Process Maturity

2.8 List of templates

2.1 Outsourcing End-to-End Process

2.2 The Outsourcing Business Plan

2.3 Organization Capability Assessment

2.9 Additional references

Brad Rubin, "Managing a Multi-Vendor Environment for Success," presentation at 2007 Outsourcing World Summit

Shailendra Kumar, GMAC Financial Services, Rachna Kumar, Alliant International University of San Diego, "Contrasting Captive versus Outsource Strategies for Global Talent Sourcing: Experiences from a Case Study." Outsourcing World Summit Presentation, 2009

Chresten Bruun, Senior Director, Lego Systems A/S, "Outsourcing and Offshoring: The Lego Story", European Outsourcing Summit Presentation, 2009

Stephen D. Hunsberger, Director, NewsCorp, Dow Jones, "A Toolkit for BPO Success (When the Sh*t Hits the Fan)", Outsourcing World Summit Presentation, 2010

Graham S. Pascoe, COP, Partner, PricewaterhouseCoopers "The Outsourcing Journey: Using Rich Pictures to Provide Insight", Outsourcing World Summit Presentation, 2010

3 Integrating outsourcing into an organization's business strategy and operations

3.1 Standards

3.0	Integrating Outsourcing into an Organization's Business Strategy and Operations
3.1	Ability to work within the framework of commonly accepted strategic and operational planning and assessment, tools and techniques to identify opportunities for leveraging outsourcing to enhance business outcomes, including such considerations as:
3.1.1	Mapping an organization's desired competitive advantages, whether functional, cost, or focus, to where they can best be obtained – through internal operations, outsourced operations, or blended operations.
3.1.2	Collaborating with outsourcing service providers to identify potential new opportunities for competitive advantage.
3.1.3	Defining the organizational model for post-outsourcing and its impact on the business (including a need for change management)
3.2.	Ability to develop and gain organizational agreement to a sourcing decision matrix that includes addressing critical make versus buy considerations, such as:
3.2.1.	Identification of specific criteria and weighting factors to be used by the organization for sourcing decisions, such as operational performance relative to the marketplace (benchmarking) and relative importance as a competitive differentiator
3.2.2	A consistent and repeatable process for applying the methodology across the organization's operations
3.3.	Ability to develop and communicate a program for change management, including:
3.3.1.	Understanding the impact of change management *before* outsourcing, (this will be covered under transition management)
3.3.2.	Create communication framework and identify stakeholders
3.3.3.	Development and deployment of a communication plan
3.4.	Ability to define in detail the scope of activities to be included in, and not included in, an outsourcing opportunity, including:
3.4.1.	Describing the operation in terms of the discrete activities that comprise it
3.4.2.	Identification of the inputs, outputs, and resources used in each activity
3.4.3.	Grouping of processes, activities into logical work breakdown structures suitable for an outsourcing project that can be integrated as part of steady state business operations
3.5.	Ability to define a process for prioritizing outsourcing opportunities, including assessing key factors to be considered in the evaluation and prioritization process, such as:
3.5.1.	The benefit of the opportunity in financial terms
3.5.2.	The readiness and stability of current and potential suppliers
3.5.3.	Other potential benefits, such as freed resources, increased flexibility, quality improvements, capital cost avoidance, reduced time to market, etc
3.5.4.	Ease of execution factors such as ease of migration to the new environment, stakeholder issues, employee considerations, etc.
3.5.5.	Constraints and obstacles to be overcome (e.g. resistance to change, 'not invented here' syndrome, etc.)
3.6.	Ability to develop a comprehensive risk analysis matrix that includes:
3.6.1.	Strategic risks, such as loss of control over future business decisions, loss of domain knowledge, the stability of the provider, etc.
3.6.2.	Operational risks, such as its impact on the organization's people, integrating the provider's processes into the business's, risks from poor performance, security, data protection and privacy, business disruption etc.
3.6.3.	Result risks, such as how likely the organization is to achieve its intended results, governance, and the ability of the organization to work collaboratively with the provider
3.6.4.	Transactional risks, such as termination clauses, dispute resolution, liability, indemnity, warranties, asset transfers, and intellectual property ownership

3.6.5.	Financial risks, such as underlying cost and currency fluctuations, and other risks that can have a financial impact on the organization
3.6.6.	Unique risks, such as those associated with offshoring and with outsourcing at the customer interface, where the providers' employees work directly with the organization's customers
3.6.7.	Identification of the probability, impact, and mitigation of these risks, including business continuity, contingency, security and disaster recovery plans
3.7.	**Ability to identify and assess the implications of applicable business regulations and statutes, including: the Sarbanes-Oxley Act, HIPAA, Privacy Act and other country specific laws**
3.7.1	Regulations and statutes that apply to most businesses, such as the Sarbanes-Oxley Act
3.7.2	Regulations and statues that apply to selected industries, such as, the Health Insurance Portability and Accountability Act (HIPAA)
3.7.3	Regulations and statutes unique to individual countries, including specifically the EU regulations (since they are similar to most non-EU country laws and customs).
3.8.	**Ability to identify and assess the requirements of various operational standards and certifications such as CMM, eSCM, Six-Sigma (black belt), TPA, NASD, ABA compliance requirements**
3.9.	**Ability to effectively gain consensus and agreement to and lead scope and prioritization evaluations across the organization**

3.2   A strategic approach to outsourcing

For outsourcing to be truly effective, it needs to be integrated into an organization's overall business strategy.

There are many ways of doing this, but most fall into one of two overall approaches:

■ a top-down approach where outsourcing is an integral part of the development of the organization's overall business strategy.

■ a bottom-up approach where the business systematically reviews each aspect of its operation to identify those areas where specific benefits might be achieved through outsourcing.

Both approaches work and can be used simultaneously.

3.2.1   Top-down approach

Strategy is essential to the success of any organization. It answers the critical questions about what is happening in the environment and marketplaces the organization serves, how it makes a unique and competitively-viable difference in serving the needs of the customers in those markets, and how it allocates and invests its resources toward the achievement of those ends.

Top-down approaches to integrating outsourcing into a business's strategy focus on identifying where the organization's competitive advantages will come from – whether that source is internal or external or both – and then ensuring that its investments and execution plans are aligned with that strategy (see Figure 3.1). Outsourcing decisions then become an integral part of the organization's investment decisions, all geared toward maximizing its competitive advantages.

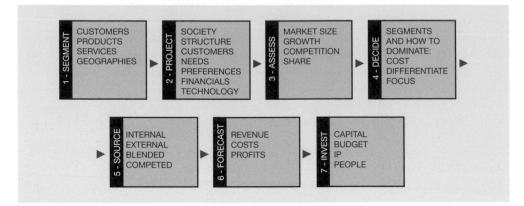

Figure 3.1: Top-Down Approach to Integrating Outsourcing into Strategic Planning

Step #1: Segment the marketplace

Segmentation is typically done by identifying the combinations of customers served by the company and its products and services. These segments may then be further broken down by geographies or other delineations. This segmentation may result in as little as two or in dozens of segments.

Step #2: Project changes in each segment

Changes in the environment are typically examined in terms of society, business, and their overall structures; changes in the customers themselves, including their needs, preferences, and financial situations; and changes in technology, regulations, the economy and the competitive environment. Techniques like scenario planning are often used to describe more than one possible future along with the unique characteristics and probabilities of each.

Step #3: Assess size and growth

Next the size and growth of each segment is assessed. Just as importantly, each segment is looked at in terms of current competitors, likely future competitors, and how each may fair in terms of market share.

Step #4: Segment selection and how to dominate

The fourth step is to decide, based on the opportunities available to the organization, which segments to pursue and what it will take to dominate in those selected. These required competitive advantages should be stated in specific, measurable terms. At the end of step four, the organization has created a list of market segments it desires to serve and what it believes is needed to compete and win in those segments.

Step #5: Sourcing

The fifth step, sourcing, is the mapping of the required competitive advantages across the operational activities of the business to determine where and how each will be created.

Certain competitive advantages will only be available through the organization's internal operations, while others can be acquired through outsourcing and other forms of external relationships. All other activities – those that need to be done and done well but offer little or no competitive advantage – are non-strategic and are sourced at the operational level on a competition-driven basis.

Step #6: Forecast business outcomes

For commercial organizations, this forecast is in terms of revenue, costs, profit, and other key financial indicators. For noncommercial enterprises, these outcomes may be forecasted in different terms, such as budget targets and the number of constituents served. It's the process of taking the strategic plan and turning it into a set of forecasted outcomes.

Step #7: Invest in execution

This means allocating all the forms of investments available to the organization: its capital, its operating funds, its people, and its intellectual properties. The alignment between the organization's strategic plan and its execution plan transforms strategy into action.

Figure 3.2 illustrates another common business planning framework that answers six questions:

- Where are we today? (e.g. Situation Assessment and Reference Base)
- Why change? (e.g. Opportunities and Threats)
- What could we do? (e.g. Analyze Alternative Scenarios based on Vision and Goals)
- What should we do? (e.g. Focus areas based on direction, objectives and constraints)
- How do we get there? (e.g. Strategic imperatives [must do's] to achieve vision and objectives and initiatives [one of which is may be outsourcing]
- Did we get there? (e.g. Assessing the results of the plan deliverables)

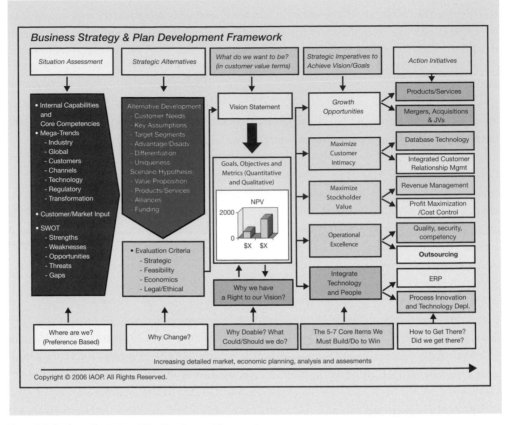

Figure 3.2: Business Strategy and Plan Development Framework

Whatever approach is used, a top-down process helps makes outsourcing an integral part of the organization's strategic planning process. It also requires that the strategic plans of the organization and of its key outsourcing service providers be interconnected. The result is a weaving together of this network of business relationships at the strategic levels of business.

3.2.2 Bottom-up approach

The bottom-up approach focuses instead on identifying on a continuous basis activities that do not contribute a unique competitive advantage of the organization, and then competing these activities against the marketplace of service providers.

Doing this requires establishing a criterion for asking and answering whether an activity does, or does not provide a unique competitive advantage. The following 3-Question Test can form the basis for this:

1. If started from scratch today, would the business build the capability internally?

What would the organization do if it was being formed today? Would it invest in creating the capability internally or would its first inclination be to look for sources available in the external marketplace? Similarly, are new competitors entering the company's market building this capability for themselves, thereby validating its unique contribution or suggesting that adequate external sources are not available, or are they acquiring the capability from the outside and then focusing their internal investments elsewhere?

2. Is the business so good at the activity that others would hire it to do it for them?

The external marketplace of service providers for virtually any business activity is increasingly robust. Could your company compete in that marketplace for that activity? If not, then the marketplace should at least be tested as opposed to continuing to perform the activity internally, as simply a matter of course.

3. Is this an activity of the business where its future leaders will come from?

The third question asks how valued the skills needed to perform the activity are to the organization. Are they the skills that are so highly prized that they are reflected in the knowledge- and experience-set of the company's top leaders? Activities that are based on highly valued skills naturally receive the lion's share of internal funding for their development and support. The people in those areas are likely to be able to see a career path leading to the company's corner office. The organization is likely to be attracting the best and brightest in those fields.

If the answer is yes to all three of these questions, then continued internal sourcing is likely to produce the best results. If not, then further evaluation as an opportunity for outsourcing is more appropriate. These three questions, although simple in nature, provide an easy-to-apply 'litmus test' to appropriate sourcing

3.3   Outsourcing Decision Matrix

An Outsourcing Decision Matrix that addresses the fundamental 'make versus buy' decision is required. Using characteristics such as 'performance relative to the market' and 'importance as a differentiator' in combination produces a four-quadrant view and a more granular decision model.

Where the organization's performance relative to the market is weak and the activity offers little opportunity for differentiation, then outsourcing makes the most sense. When the opposite is true, continued internal sourcing would be recommended.

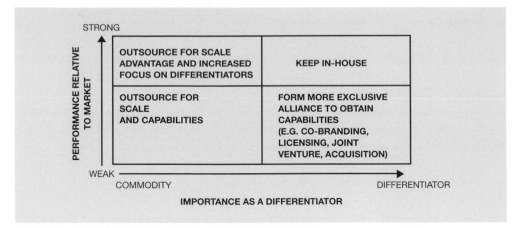

Figure 3.3: Outsourcing Decision Matrix

At the opposing corners, there will be cases where an organization's performance relative to the market is strong, yet outsourcing might still produce incremental value based on scale or the ability to redeploy the resources being used. There can also be cases where an organization is weak in an activity that could provide a marketplace differentiation. Here, more exclusive forms of relationships, such as licensing, joint ventures, or even acquisition might make the most sense.

This analysis cannot, however, be subjective if it is to be effective and to gain acceptance among the key decision makers. As a result, specific criteria, including a weighting system, needs to be developed. In this example, the relevant question for each dimension might be **performance relative to the market.**

Financial:

- Is expense/revenue ratio favorable compared to best-in-class (BIC)?
- Have ratios been moving in a positive direction over the past two years?
- What is the volume compared to the largest provider?

Process:

- Is performance in key quality measures favorable compared to BIC?
- Is cycle-time competitive?
- Is process positively/negatively affecting time to market?

Technology:

- Has technology investment kept pace with the marketplace?
- What is our bench strength with this technology?

Employees:

- Employee attrition/satisfaction compared to BIC?
- Is an adequate labor pool available geographically?

Organizational strength:

- Does change management/sponsorship exist?

Core versus non-core:

- Is there a highly valuable, unique asset involved in the activity?
- Do we have institutional capabilities/experiences that are hard for our competitors to replicate?
- Is this a unique source of leverage?

Brand:

- Is the activity done to raise brand awareness?
- Can the activity strengthen/weaken the brand?

Impact of customers:

- Does the activity involve direct interaction with customers or prospects? Is the activity important to our customers in the long run?
- Is the activity directly related to the delivery of product versus a support function?
- Would loss or disruption of this service hurt the organization? What would be the impact?

There are several sections in the OPBOK that discuss in more detail the various aspects of identifying, defining and evaluating the outsourcing opportunities. However, the following strategic, value, delivery and execution questions can help to provide an initial filter to identify the best outsourcing opportunities

Strategic questions; are we doing the right thing? Is the outsourcing investment:

- In line with our business vision?
- Consistent with our business principles, plan and direction?
- Contributing to our strategic objectives and sustainable competitive differentiation?
- Providing optimum value at an acceptable level of risk?

Value questions: are we getting the benefits?

- A clear and shared understanding and commitment to achieve the expected benefits.
- Clear accountability for achieving the benefits, which should be linked to MBOs and incentive compensation schemes.
- Relevant and meaningful critical success factors and key performance indicators.
- An effective benefits realization process and sign-off.

Delivery and execution questions: are we deploying well and effectively?

- Scalable, disciplined and consistent management, governance and delivery processes
- Appropriate and sufficient resources available with the right competencies, capabilities and attitudes for the providers.

Finally, Figure 3.4 summarizes a number of make versus buy factors that should be considered when evaluating the outsourcing opportunity.

BUY	MAKE
Cost deduction	Competitive advantage (proprietary requirements)
Speed up time-to-market	Expertise available in-house
Lack of critical skills	May be less expensive than buying
Aggressive schedule	Can be completed on time
Politically correct	Opportunity costs trade-offs
Lower risk	No suitable vendors available
Easier to maintain	Core competency
Staff/skill/resource supplementation	Strategic
Known costs	

Figure 3.4: Summary of Key 'Make versus Buy' Considerations

3.4 Change management

Once the organizational decision making process is established and initiated, organizational change management must be considered and a plan developed for addressing the change. There are three stages when the change management must be implemented:

- **Decision making stage**. At this stage, the uncertainty about the future begins to prevail in the organization and it must be addressed. The change management at this stage begins with the communication process and establishes the framework and boundary conditions for all stakeholders to comprehend. Even though the details about outsourcing are not yet known, a clear communication of objectives, steps in decision making and ultimate options that the business will consider must be provided to all stakeholders – not just to directly affected stakeholders.

- **Outsourcing implementation stage**. Throughout the sourcing process, change management plays an important role in making sure all dimensions of change are addressed. This includes dealing with facts and addressing non-facts; providing all stakeholders with potential outcome scenarios and options and addressing all expressed (and some unexpressed) fears. It is during this stage that the service provider needs to be a member of the change management team and communicate their operational plans, philosophy and expectations. This combined communication also helps establish a joint ownership of the entire process and removes a "we-they" syndrome. Again, communication is quite important in making sure that the facts about the service providers are known through proper channels.

- **Post implementation stage**. At this stage, change management provides the framework for working with the service provider. This includes not only what is required for governance but day-to-day operations. New sets of processes need to be communicated in dealing with the outsourced processes and the impact of the change defined and communicated to all stakeholders.

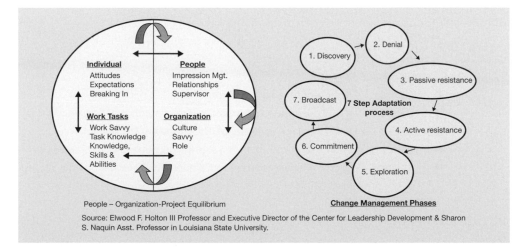

Source: Elwood F. Holton III Professor and Executive Director of the Center for Leadership Development & Sharon S. Naquin Asst. Professor in Louisiana State University.

Figure 3.5: Change Management Cycle

Change management practice deals with addressing the acceptance of change through people, organization, work process and eventually through the output from the work effort. It also addresses the management of change through the change adoption cycle. Many publications have addressed the topic of "managing fear" and change and have described how people adopt to change by going through various stages. The change management context and the cycle of change is described as "people-organization-project equilibrium" as shown in Figure 3.5.

3.4.1   Implementing a change management program

There are three phases for implementing a change management program. In phase I, a change management program is defined, an implementation team established and trained and a champion appointed who will lead the change. In phase II, the change management program is fully developed and deployed throughout the organization. In Phase III, the impact of change management is assessed through a feedback process (surveys, meetings – formal and informal) and the change management plan is further refined and revised. This revised plan is used to reinforce the change.

3.5   Stakeholder analysis

The success of an outsourcing business initiative also requires identifying, gaining and keeping the appropriate levels of support and involvement of all individuals and groups having a stake in the outcome.

A stakeholder is any individual or group of individuals with an interest (stake), something to be gained or something to be lost, in the outcome of the outsourcing initiative.

Understanding and developing communications and participation strategies for all stakeholders using the following matrix can be an effective planning and management tool

Stakeholder Involvement and Commitment Matrix

- ■   Oppose: Will attempt to block an action.
- ■   Allow: Will allow the project to proceed but may not directly support it.
- ■   Assist: Will help in some way to ensure the success of the project.
- ■   Perform: Will take responsibility for a significant portion of the project.
- ■   Sponsor: Will provide the resources and leadership necessary for the success of the project.

Communications plans should then be developed to address the unique considerations of each and every stakeholder.

3.6   Communication with stakeholders

Communication is an important dimension of change management and must not be underestimated. As a part of the sourcing process, a communication strategy must be established during the strategy phase and stakeholders as well as means of communicating with them established. There are five components to an effective communication process and they must be recognized and dealt with. Cultural diversity must also be understood and accounted for when dealing with all five components.

The intensity and impact of communication is different based on each of the phase of the outsourcing project. Figure 3.6 below shows the communication level and intensity:

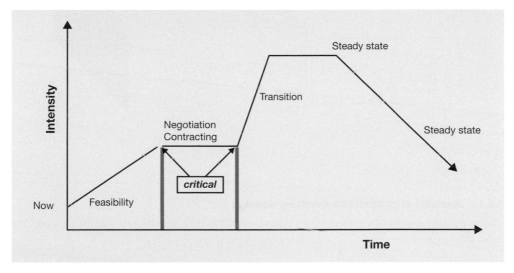

Figure 3.6: Communication Intensity

The components of communication are:

- Thinking
- Listening
- Understanding
- Observing
- Talking

Effective communication requires that all five areas are addressed.

It is also important to clearly define the stakeholders and establish a communication plan with each of them. There is a differing level of communication required when dealing with different stakeholders (such as employees need to know about their job and processes while the customers only need to understand how and if they are affected by the outsourcing decision). Figure 3.7 identifies a framework that can be used to establish the communication plan (by phase and objectives).

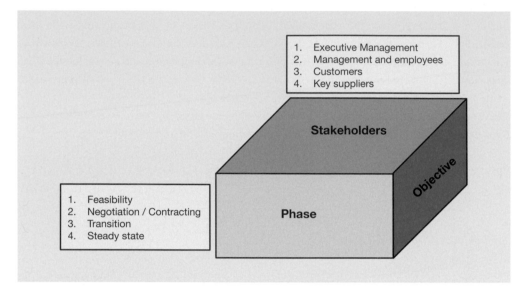

Figure 3.7: Communication Framework

3.6.1   Elements of an effective outsourcing message

There are nine points to consider when communicating with stakeholders about outsourcing. They are:

- The compelling need for change
- Cost of doing nothing
- Change techniques to be employed
- Role of outsourcing
- Outsourcing benefits and implications for the organization
- Outsourcing benefits and implications for the customers
- Outsourcing benefits and implications for employees and the community
- Timelines
- How will the business measure success?

The compelling need for change

The compelling need for change will typically involve a number of factors such as: changes in customer needs and demographics; competitive pressures; technology; financial performance and structures; regulatory changes; and other factors specific to the business itself. Outsourcing should be clearly connected to addressing one or more of these needs for change.

Cost of doing nothing

Communicating the cost of doing nothing – in terms of its likely impact on the business's performance and its ability to serve its customers, employees, and shareholders – makes the need for change much more real and compelling. Outsourcing professionals need to help all of the stakeholders make this connection in terms that are relevant and tangible.

Change techniques to be employed

Outsourcing is just one of a wide range of changes available to management and taking place within the business. All of the changes under consideration as well as their relative roles should be communicated.

Role of outsourcing

Within that framework, how is outsourcing likely to be used? What is the process that management will use in evaluating outsourcing opportunities and their potential to contribute to the organization's goals?

Outsourcing benefits and implications for the organization

What are the benefits and implications for the organization of outsourcing? Will it reduce costs? And how will those funds be reallocated? How will it affect the speed, innovation, and flexibility of the organization? How will these benefits actually be realized, and when? Employees are far more likely to embrace change when they understand how the change will create a positive outcome for the organization in total.

Outsourcing benefits and implications for the customers

How will the quality of the organization's products and services be enhanced by outsourcing? How will its resources be redeployed? Why will customers react favorably to the change? In the absence of this information, outsourcing may be viewed as simply a cost-cutting tool for improving the bottom line, reinforcing the negative portrayal of outsourcing that is prevalent in the press.

Outsourcing benefits and implications for employees and the community

How will outsourcing affect the individuals – both those in-scope and those out-of-scope? What is the organization prepared to do to work with those affected? What is it not prepared to do? These questions are of immediate concern to in-scope employees, but the answers are just as important to those who are out-of-scope and certainly realize that their area may be under consideration for outsourcing in the future.

Timelines

When will decisions be made, and once made, what is the timeline for their implementation? A framework for these management processes should be shared, thereby avoiding the speculation that will otherwise ensue.

How will the business measure success?

How will the organization know that the desired outcomes are being realized? How will that information be captured and shared with stakeholders? What corrective actions might be taken if the desired results are not achieved? Answers to these questions are central to demonstrating a well conceived management plan that justifies the changes being made to the organization.

Just as important as the message is its preparation and delivery. Four considerations here are:

- **Content**: What are the key points? What outcomes are we targeting? Who will do what by when? If you are requesting a change in behavior on the part of others, be clear about what your request is and to whom it is directed.

- **Context**: What are the factors/drivers, inside the organization and outside it, that led us to make the decisions we made? Who was involved in the decision-making? What alternatives did we consider? What criteria did we use to select the course of action we have chosen?

- **Impact:** Complete the sentence: "This is what this means to you …," the "you" being the people you are speaking with. Do not take for granted that the listeners will automatically "get" how your message affects them. This needs to be made explicit. Also, let them know who the "point person" is to contact if they have questions about this in the future.

- **Follow-up**: When will you follow up with additional information and project status updates? How will the audience/stakeholders provide input and make requests for specific information in the future?

Finally, there is a wide-range of communications techniques available for communicating. Large formal meetings are just one. Others include: smaller, less formal meetings; newsletters; e-mail; voice mail; websites and chat facilities; town-hall style meetings. Communications should first be with supervisors and managers, since they are the front-line for communications with employees.

3.7   Managing outsourcing risks

3.7.1   Understanding and identifying risks

Gauging and managing risks may be the most important factor to consider. When companies evaluate outsourcing, they are constantly balancing perceived benefits and perceived risks.

There are four major classes of risks that organizations evaluate: strategic risks, operational risks, result risks and transactional risks.

Strategic risks

Strategic risks include the loss of control over future business decisions; loss of knowledge, especially protection of intellectual properties; future changes in the service provider's business that may affect the customer's; and, particularly when offshore outsourcing is involved, risks associated with cultural differences and geo-political risks. Strategic risk can also include impact of security violation, affecting the customer's ability to conduct business (e.g. when personal information is involved).

Operational risks

Operational risks are associated with the impact of outsourcing on the organization's people, both those who may be transferring to the service provider and those remaining with the company; risks associated with integrating the provider's processes into the business's; risks from poor performance; and, particularly with offshore outsourcing, risks associated with the impact of future legislation and changes in regulatory compliance. Business continuity, contingency, back-up and disaster recovery plans must also be considered.

Business disruption is one of the major operational risks, where the services or products for the customer is affected by a failure of the service provider in delivering the services. There have been examples of a major Canadian bank, which had to suspend banking due to a systems failure at their service provider; or a major airline had to shut down operations for several hours at a major hub due to computer operations failure at their provider's location.

Managing security of operational environment – especially when involved in certain industry/ process outsourcing – can also be a major risk. Compliance with security standards can mitigate the risk but a lack of discipline may end up creating an operational risk during the performance of the contract.

As more industry/government/professional regulations are enacted, continuous compliance with them becomes a major responsibility for the provider and any violation may result in a significant risk to the business. The regulations may affect:

- Country/state/region control regulations (e.g. banking, health, data related laws)
- Public company related regulations (e.g. SEC for US publicly traded companies)
- Industry group defined rules of certification (e.g. American Bar Association, medical association, ISO, IEEE)

Another operational risk may be the lack of defined knowledge management process and the discipline required to implement it. As discussed later, a flawed knowledge management process can present a risk to both the provider and the company.

Result risks

How likely is the organization to achieve its intended results? Governance and the ability of the organization to manage collaboratively with the provider to achieve the intended benefits is the big consideration here.

Transactional risks

Termination clauses, both for cause and convenience, dispute resolution, liability, indemnity, warranties, asset transfers, intellectual property ownership, and payments are all examples of transactional risks.

Financial risks

All of these factors, as well as considerations such as changes in underlying cost levels, exchange rates, and others, translate into potential financial risks for the organization.

An assessment of these risks and how well prepared the organization is to manage them is an inseparable part of selecting the best candidates for outsourcing.

The following are additional risk considerations associated with offshore outsourcing:

- Government support
- Labor pool
- Physical infrastructure
- Educational system
- Cost advantage – direct/indirect
- Quality
- Cultural compatibility
- Time/distance advantage
- Language proficiency
- Geopolitical environment
- Process maturity/competitiveness
- Supportive people factors
- Supportive economic scenario

Figure 3.8 provides a management process schematic listing and relating the key activities for identifying, quantifying, and mitigating risks.

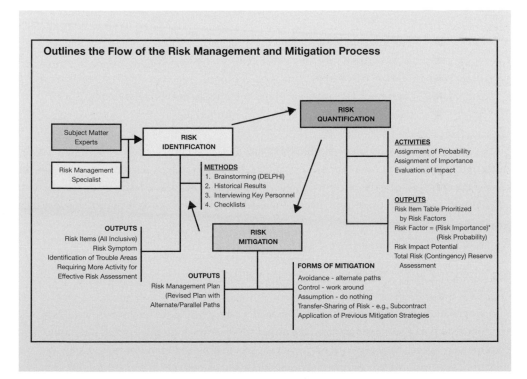

Figure 3.8: Risk Management Process

3.7.2   Creating a risk management framework

As part of forming the strategy and identifying the risks, it is important that a framework is established that identifies them and creates a plan for avoiding or mitigating them. Both service providers and the business need to work together to accomplish this. The framework building block includes:

- Identifying and defining the organization's operating model (people, processes, technology) for risk topics and exposure
- Defining the business's risk management capabilities and appetite for managing the risk
- Identifying and defining acceptable risk mitigation alternatives and approaches and a framework for managing them (such as disaster recovery versus business continuity)
- Identifying the governance principles that will monitor and, as needed, adjust the risk factors and risk management activities.

3.7.3   Portfolio management approach to outsourcing

Once the risks are identified and risk appetite established, a portfolio approach can be applied to managing the outsourcing decision. A portfolio approach may include the following options:

- Multiple providers for the same process
- Different providers for "dependent" processes
- "Tower" based implementation of process
- "Staggered" termination points for agreements (vs. co-terminous)
- Balance between off and on shore outsourcing

Some of the recent negative outsourcing experiences (e.g. fraud implication with Satyam) can be mitigated to some extent with the use of such an approach. However, the business case must be closely examined so that the outsourcing benefits are not limited as a result of the selection of one of the above options (see discussion on "bundled outsourcing" for an argument against such an approach).

3.8   Scoping outsourcing opportunities

The scope of an outsourcing initiative is best developed using a standard process-mapping technique such as a process diagram. The actual work of developing a process diagram is well documented in the many texts on business process analysis and reengineering. Generally, the most successful approach is to hold a series of modeling workshops with participation from the subject-matter experts involved in the process and facilitators to help describe and depict the process using consistent terminology and documentation.

This is often done as an iterative process that typically begins with a "white board" exercise that captures the activities and their relationships. From that, a common set of diagrams, using a consistent symbolic language as well as supporting textual descriptions, is created. These textual descriptions follow a consistent template that, for each process, sub-process, activity, and task, describe its purpose, triggers, timings, durations, and resource requirements. All the required resources are identified, including skills, technology infrastructure and applications, and physical environment. Data flows are captured in the same template-driven manner, including the sources, destinations, characteristics, and inputs and outputs for each activity. Key performance indicators are documented as well. These establish the base for determining how well the process is operating overall in relationship to the customer value it is intended to create.

This process analysis and mapping forms the basis for all subsequent planning and decision making, including defining the scope of the work to be outsourced, determining current costs and performance, quantifying measures of success, and how the activities are managed.

3.9   Prioritizing outsourcing opportunities

Once the candidate areas have been filtered and scoped in process terms, they need to be prioritized. The goal here is to ensure that the opportunities that offer the organization the greatest return at the lowest level of risk are pursued first.

Prioritization is typically based on a number of factors. These factors and the weight given each may change over time. Many organizations develop a formal scoring sheet for evaluating and ranking opportunities. Others choose a more iterative, discussion-driven approach.

In either case, gauging the size of the opportunity in financial terms is often the first factor considered. Unless the opportunity is affecting a large enough portion of the business's operations, it may simply not be worth the effort to pursue.

A second factor is often an assessment of the marketplace of suppliers. The questions to be answered are: Do providers of sufficient size, expertise and geographic presence exist for this opportunity to be pursued? Or, is there a unique advantage to be created by becoming the anchor client for a new provider in a new area?

The third factor is a preliminary assessment of the potential benefits to be realized. Questions here are: What level of savings is likely? How would the freed-up resources be redeployed? How much can the flexibility of the organization be increased, as measured by the percentage of costs or resources that can be ramped up and down quickly? How large is the gap between current internal quality levels and where the marketplace of service providers is performing? What level of capital spending can be avoided?

A fourth factor is ease of execution. How well is the process understood, defined, and measured? How easy will it be to migrate to the new environment? Who are the stakeholders, and how easy will it be to bring them into agreement on the changes proposed? How many employees will be affected and how? If disengagement is necessary, what actions and responsibilities must be instituted?

The fifth factor is risk. How significant are the strategic, operational, result, transactional and overall financial risks? How well can they be mitigated? At what cost?

3.10 Special considerations: governmental/ industry regulations and certifications

Although many of the governmental regulations do not directly affect outsourcing decision making or implementation, there are several regulations that have a direct impact on it. These include regulations surrounding controls imposed on public companies – in the US as well as in other countries. Additionally, there are regulations that affect certain industries in different countries and they have to be adequately addressed when going through the outsourcing process. It must be noted that a qualified legal support through the outsourcing process (from decision to implementation to governance) is necessary to understand the impact of these and other regulations and provide actions to meet them.

Some of the US laws affecting outsourcing are listed below (some affect only certain public companies while others affect all companies):
- Privacy Act of 1974 (5 USC. § 552a)
- Graham-Leach-Bliley Act for financial institutions
- Federal Trade Commission (FTC) Act dealing with disposal of information and records and liability associated with disclosure
- Penalty for Unauthorized Participation by Convicted Individuals (12 USCA § 1289)
- OCC regulations for banks affecting subcontracting of work including offshoring
- Health Insurance Portability and Accountability Act (HIPAA) of 1996
- Telecommunications Act of 1996 – Section 222 dealing with Customer Proprietary Network Information (CPNI)

- US Patriot's Act of 2001 dealing with approving (and identifying) people with whom business is conducted or employment offered. The most commonly used legal requirement is that the company must "certify" that the employees (or contractors) are not on the US Government's list of undesirable/dangerous people (known as "OFAC" list)
- Sarbanes-Oxley regulation requiring public companies (of a certain size) to certify internal controls; including controls over outsourced processes

Some of the European laws (although they are EU regulations, many non EU countries have adopted them) affecting outsourcing include:

- Data Protection Act (known more commonly as "Safe Harbor Provision" as well as "trans-border data flow") that regulate how information is shared and communicated between countries and companies
- Acquired Rights Directive (ARD is EU law that is adopted by various nations and in some cases, named slightly differently; for example, it is known as TUPE in the UK), which requires businesses to follow certain procedures during outsourcing and also provides for employee rights through the outsourcing action (such as pension provision)

In addition to the governmental regulations, there are certain industry regulations and certifications that are required as a part of company operation. These regulations and certifications also apply to the service provider when working on outsourced processes. For example, USfinancial institutions are required to comply to NASD regulations and one of the dimensions is the requirement of obtaining NASD certifications for employing certain practices (such as advising public on investment matters). In the insurance industry, US state governments requires licensing of businesses (and people) who provide "third party administration" (such as adjudication of a claim).

In addition to these certifications, many outsourcing providers seek additional certifications to demonstrate their capabilities and maturity in managing processes. These certifications do not have any legal standing except businesses may require their providers to obtain them as a way to reduce their risk in outsourcing. Some of the more commonly known certifications are:

- CMM (Capability Maturity Model) and its derivatives (CMMi and pCMM) deal with establishing levels of capability and maturity in Information Systems processes
- ITIL is a similar certification for managing Information Systems infrastructure
- Various ISO standards dealing with security (ISO 20007) or quality (9000.1) also provide for a framework for certification. For example, the ISO standard for computer security has been adopted by the British Standards Board (and classified as BS1779) and offer certification through independent assessors.

Lastly, there are various quality related certifications and designations/disciplines that service providers adopt to show their commitment to improving process quality. 6 Sigma (and Lean 6 Sigma) is the best known example of such implementation.

3.11   Special considerations: outsourcing at the customer interface

The relationship between an organization and its customers is among the most critical of all of its activities. Outsourcing at the customer interface, where a third party directly interacts with the organization's customers, introduces additional considerations. This is true whether that interaction is face-to-face, over the telephone, via mail, or electronically.

One way of evaluating outsourcing at the customer interface is to examine the activities involved along two dimensions: the level of judgement and the value of interaction.

Level of judgment

Interactions that last for an extended period of time are complex in nature. They may involve the exchange of a great deal of information. Many alternative paths may exist, requiring discretion on the part of the individual performing the work. The greater the level of judgment, the greater the potential risk.

Value of interaction

The second dimension is how much value the customer places on the interaction. Was the interaction customer-initiated? Is it central or peripheral to the value the customer is looking for from the overall relationship with the company? Is the interaction key to customer retention? Interactions that represent a high level of customer value also represent a higher risk.

Looking at both dimensions at the same time, highly valued interactions requiring the greatest judgment are the most sensitive of all. This does not mean that these more sensitive customer interactions should not be considered for outsourcing, but it does suggest that consideration should be given to:

- beginning with lower level risk interactions and then migrating based on experience and a track record of success to higher risk interactions
- investing even greater care into the planning, and monitoring of performance.

A key consideration in outsourcing at the customer interface is to recognize that the client organization maintains full control over what services its customers receive and the nature and character of that 'customer experience.' While in some cases the provider's brand may actually increase the customer's perception of value, generally customers are not even made aware of the fact that the service they are receiving is outsourced.

3.12   List of key terms

Change Management
Critical versus Core
Just-in-Time Sourcing
Make versus Buy
Market Driven Sourcing
Outsourcing at the Customer Interface
Process Enterprise
Regulatory Compliance
Risk
Governmental Regulations
Sourcing-as-Strategy
Stakeholders
Zero-Based Sourcing

3.13   List of templates

3.1 Integrating Outsourcing into Business Strategy Top-Down Strategic Planning
3.2 Integrating Outsourcing into Business Strategy Bottom-Up Strategic Planning
3.3 Outsourcing Decision Matrix
3.4 Stakeholder Analysis
3.5 Stakeholder Communication Plan-Messages
3.6 Stakeholder Communication Plan Framework
3.7 Outsourcing Risk Assessment and Analysis
3.8 Offshore Outsourcing: Country Specific Risk Assessment
3.9 Impact of Business Regulations and Statutes
3.10 Scoping an Outsourcing Opportunity
3.11 Prioritizing Outsourcing Opportunities
3.12 Public Affairs Risk Analysis

3.14 Additional references

Jagdish Dalal, COP, "Offshore Outsourcing: Creating a Compelling Case," The 2003 India Outsourcing Summit Presentation, October 15, 2003, Bangalore, India.

Michael F. Corbett, "Best Practices in Managing Outsourcing at the Customer Interface," Michael F. Corbett & Associates, January 2001.

Ian Rushby, "Outsourcing at BP Amoco," The 2000 Outsourcing World Summit Presentation, February 22, 2000, Lake Buena Vista, FL

PricewaterhouseCoopers, "How Outsourcing Providers Can Capture Profits and Manage Today's Increasing Risk", Presentation at The 2006 Outsourcing World Summit

The Delve Group, "Change Resistant? Why selling change within organizations is so hard and what you can do about it.", October, 2007

Phil Fersht and Derek Sappenfield, Deloitte Consulting LLP, "Preparing the New Organization Post-Outsourcing", September, 2007

T. Wilson & J. Bergman, Thomson Legal & Regulatory, "Professional Staffing Sourcing Guidelines: A Decision Matrix for Evaluating Sourcing Decisions", Outsourcing World Summit Presentation, 2008

Scott Lever, Tamara Kett, Doug Plotkin; PA Consulting, "Sourcing – why gamble, there is a better way", Outsourcing World Summit Presentation, 2008

Stephen Hunsberger, NewsCorp Dow Jones, "Where the rubber meets the road", Outsourcing World Summit Presentation, 2009

Till Lohmann, PricewaterhouseCoopers, "People And Change: Leading Across the Outsourcing Journey", Outsourcing World Summit Presentation, 2008

Jagdish Dalal, COP, JDalal Associates, LLC, "Outsourcing – game changer: Manage it or Accept it" Outsourcing World Summit Presentation, 2008

Danny Ertel, COP, Vantage Partners, "Help Me, Help you: Value creation takes two", Outsourcing World Summit Presentation, 2009

Jens Nielsen, Head of Outsourcing & Analysts Nordea Bank Danmark A/S, "Using Outsourcing to Support the Business Strategy In the Economic Downturn and Preparing For the Upturn" European Outsourcing Summit Presentation, 2009

Nitin Bhatt; Senior Vice President, ICT Practice, Asia Pacific, Frost & Sullivan, "Featured Destination – Malaysia", Asia Outsourcing Summit Presentation, 2009

Beverly Honig; CEO, Honeylight Enterprise Pty. Ltd., "The Future of Outsourcing and the Cultural Surprise", Asia Outsourcing Summit Presentation, 2009

Dr. Leslie P. Willcocks, Professor, London School of Economics and Political Science, "Outsourcing Decisions, Bundled or not Bundled", Outsourcing World Summit Presentation, 2010

David Caldwell, Director of IT Effectiveness, Compassion International, Mark Hendrickson, IT Multi-Sourcing Consultant, Compassion International, "The Seven Mistakes of First-Time Offshoring (and How to Avoid Them!)", Outsourcing World Summit Presentation, 2010

4

Creating, leading and sustaining high-performance outsourcing project teams

The successful planning, execution, and management of outsourcing requires multi-disciplinary skills applied over an extended period of time. Because of this, project teams, often made up of different individuals with different skills, are typically formed at various stages of the outsourcing process.

Understanding the role and make-up of these teams is central to outsourcing success.

4.1   Standards

4.0	Creating, Leading and Sustaining High-Performance Outsourcing Project Teams
4.1	Ability to identify specific skills required to support project teams and their roles and responsibilities at each phase of the outsourcing initiative, including:
4.1.1	*Policy Team* with responsibility for setting the organization's overall policy toward outsourcing and for determining the appropriateness of outsourcing in the specific areas under consideration.
4.1.2	*Idea Team* tasked with generating ideas for review by the policy-level team.
4.1.3	*Assessment Team* tasked with performing the detail evaluation and plan development for an outsourcing initiative.
4.1.4	*Implementation and Transition* that executes the initiative.
4.1.5	*Management Teams* responsible for the ongoing oversight of the outsourcing relationship
4.2	Ability to assemble and train effective teams for each stage of each outsourcing project.
4.3	Ability to identify and design cultural and operational assimilation requirements and drive change management process
4.4	Ability to effectively direct project teams at each stage of the outsourcing process, including winning and maintaining the support of team members given the numerous demands on their time.

4.2   Skills required for the outsourcing project team

Outsourcing project team skill make-up varies depending on the phase of the outsourcing project. Some specialized skills are required during certain phases while there are certain skills that are common for all phases and teams, as identified later.

Skills that are common to all teams include:

- Subject matter knowledge (not expertise) in the field of outsourcing process
- Fundamentals of outsourcing
- Business acumen
- Project management
- Communication
- Relationship building and management
- Team orientation

The following are some of the specialized skills that are required for the teams:

- **Policy Team:** Business knowledge, long-range planning, strategic management
- **Idea Team:** Outsourcing knowledge (ideally as a COP), strategic thinking, business planning, organizational impact management
- **Assessment Team:** Finance (accounting, reporting, planning), HR (organizational development, communication), legal (contract law, foreign law – if applicable), Subject Matter Experts
- **Implementation and Transition Team:** Finance (accounting, tax, treasury, asset management, liability and insurance understanding), HR (change management, organizational development, communication, employee relations management), legal (contract law, intellectual property law, foreign law – if applicable)
- **Management Team:** Measurements, process management

4.3   Outsourcing process teams

Policy team

This team has responsibility for setting the organization's overall policy on outsourcing and for determining the appropriateness of outsourcing in the specific areas under consideration. Since the factors that go into answering these questions are complex with long-term implications for the organization, the policy team typically involves the organization's senior executives with overall policy-making responsibility.

Idea team

Another important team is the one tasked with generating ideas for review by the policy-level team. This team is typically small, led by a well-respected, experienced person. It should have high quality technical and business people assigned to it, and typically does not report directly to the management of the operations being examined for outsourcing.

Assessment team

As an idea moves from the idea stage to the assessment stage, a larger team is typically needed. Often one or two members of the idea team may continue as members of this team to provide continuity. An executive from the policy team is often selected as the executive sponsor for the project at this point. A functional or process executive typically becomes the assessment team leader, joining functional managers; process experts; information technology experts; representative customers or end-users of the process; and purchasing, legal, finance, human resources, and, possibly, external consultants.

Implementation and transition

The assessment team typically evolves into the implementation and transition teams, adding and subtracting team members based on the needs of the particular project.

Management teams

The structure for managing outsourcing relationships typically includes layers of teams focused on the operational, tactical, and strategic aspects of the relationship. These teams are comprised of individuals from both organizations – customer and provider – representing all the needed disciplines and interests – operations, finance, end users, and others.

Operating committees, made up of individuals directly involved in the operational activities, help ensure day-to-day communications between the organization and the provider, resolve issues as they occur, and report up issues that cannot be resolved at their level. A management committee, with overall responsibility for the contract and its deliverables, ensures that both organizations understand how performance compares to expectations. They are also the focal point for approving changes in scope or deliverables and are the arbitrator for unresolved operational issues. Finally, an executive steering committee should be led by the executives with overall strategic responsibility. This team has the role of ensuring the ongoing health of the relationship and resolving any major issues that develop at lower levels.

Given all of the multi-level and inter-disciplinary teams that can be involved in the outsourcing decisions, Figure 4.1 identifies the key attributes of successful and effective teams.

Clear purpose:	The vision, mission, goal or task of the team has been defined and is now accepted by everyone. There is an action plan.
Informality:	The climate tends to be informal, comfortable, and relaxed. There are no obvious tensions or signs of boredom.
Participation:	There is much discussion and everyone is encouraged to participate.
Listening:	The members use effective listening techniques such as questioning, paraphrasing and summarizing to get ideas out.
Civilized Disagreement:	There is disagreement, but the team is comfortable with this and shows no signs of avoiding, smoothing over, or suppressing conflict.
Consensus Decisions:	For important decisions, the goal is substantial but not necessarily unanimous agreement through open discussion of everyone's ideas, avoidance of formal voting, or easy compromises.
Open communication:	Team members feel free to express their feelings on the tasks aswell as on the group's operation. There are few hidden agendas. Communication takes place outside of meetings.
Clear Roles and Work Assignments	There are clear expectations about roles played by each team member. When action is taken, clear assignments are made, accepted and carried out. Work is fairly distributed among members
Shared Leadership:	While the team has a formal leader, leadership functions shift from time to time depending upon the circumstances, the needs of the group, and the skills of the members. The formal leader models the appropriate behavior and helps establish positive norms.
External Relations:	The team spends time developing key outside relationships, mobilizing resources, and building credibility with important players in other parts of the organization
Style Diversity:	The team has a broad spectrum of team-player types including members who emphasize attention to task, goal setting, focus on process and questions about how the team is functioning
Self-Assessment:	Periodically the team steps back to examine how well it is functioning and what may be interfering with its effectiveness.

Figure 4.1: Key Attributes of Successful and Effective Teams

4.4 Outsourcing project leadership

Managing these teams, as well as the overall outsourcing project, is a complex task requiring strong leadership skills and is one of the most important roles that outsourcing professionals play.

The characteristics common to these professionals are outlined below.

Ability to embrace and champion change

Outsourcing is, first and foremost, a tool for organizational change. Outsourcing professionals leading these efforts must not only be able to embrace the changes that outsourcing entails, but be able to champion them across the organization.

Earned credibility across the organization

To be an effective change agent, the individual must have a high degree of credibility across the organization; credibility that typically has been earned through a proven track record of contribution to the organization and its success.

A desire to manage, not to do

Another critical leadership skill is the desire to manage, not to do. Engaging the marketplace in a way that is overly proscriptive detracts from creativity and the ultimate value of outsourcing. The provider must be reasonably free to control how the work gets done while the client organization focuses on defining and leveraging the results.

Ability to build trust

Consistency, fairness, objectivity, principle-based decision making, open communications, and a demonstrated desire for both organizations to succeed are important professional characteristics. If present, the relationship between the organizations will be well grounded and poised for success; if not both trust and, ultimately, results suffer.

Communications skills

Communications is required throughout the process both externally and internally. It includes all media: written, verbal, small and large groups, traditional and electronic forms. Most of all, listening intensely can minimize the lingering affect of poor decision making by best incorporating all insights.

Negotiation skills

Negotiation is not just a matter of getting the best deal, it is a matter of maximizing the value of the relationship for the client organization while, at the same time, fairly meeting most (if not all) of the needs of the provider. Negotiation takes place every day, at every level of the organization, as both parties constantly adjust to changing situations.

Strategic planning skills

A disciplined, consistent approach to evaluating each decision as to its future implications is needed, as well as an ability to communicate these considerations throughout the organization and, of course, to the service provider.

Project and team management skills

Leaders of an outsourcing team are, by the very nature of the work, operating in a team environment. Many individuals representing different disciplines and functions are involved on the customer side. Just as importantly, the provider's representatives are operating as a team. The leader must be able to effectively bring both of these groups together, keep them focused, recognize and reward each individual's contributions, and balance everyone's interests.

Marketing skills

The ability to use communications, negotiations, and many of the skills just discussed to support, gain commitment, and action from others is the essence of marketing. The leader of an outsourcing team constantly markets the value of the project within the organization, ensuring that interests are understood and met, dealing with exceptions, and overcoming resistance.

Process expertise

Finally, the project leader, the outsourcing professional, must have an understanding of the processes being evaluated for outsourcing. Expertise on the process and process analysis enables the leader to understand the issues being faced, the value of what is being accomplished, and the ways that results are achieved.

4.5   Outsourcing project team management

The principles and practices for managing outsourcing project teams are essentially the same as for other projects. There are numerous and excellent references on project management and it is not the intent of this short section to replicate them. However, the key principles and practices of successful enterprise-wide program and project management include, but are not limited to the factors outlined below.

Creating the right environment and culture:

- Establish the appropriate organizational mindset, culture and environment
- Obtain executive sponsorship, commitment and multi-level management buy-in
- Obtain customer/other stakeholder/project team commitments and ownership
- Success depends on creating a sustainable foundation (e.g. policy, process, metrics,) for managing programs and projects and integrating results and methodologies into the culture of the organization
- Define roles – get the right people involved in every program/project phase
- Establish matrix management goals, expectations and measurements for performance assessment on the project
- Market and re-enforce (e.g. training, rewards, mentors, tools, flexible processes) the value and benefits of good PM practices
- Adopt a flexible and scalable PM process (phases, templates, repository, tools) [tailor when required] to accommodate different program and project types (complexity, size, value, etc.) based on current and emerging industry best practices

Developing program/project plans (based on a flexible and scalable process)

- Define the project's scope, objectives, requirements and deliverables
- Establish well-defined phases/tasks, go/no go gates and milestones (break the job down into manageable work packages – 80 hour rule) with realistic baselines (costs, time, resources and contingencies) based on short term incremental and visible deliverables
- Establish a responsibility assignment matrix to clarify roles and responsibilities – Responsible, Inform, Consult and/or Approve
- Establish formal change management and risk management processes

Ensuring governance and excellent communications

- Establish a governance, control, reporting and escalation policy and process
- Manage expectations of all stakeholders proactively
- Identify, measure and track performance indicators, metrics, key issues and take necessary actions quickly – knock obstacles out of the way
- Establish frequent and open communications with stakeholders (both formal and informal review meetings – daily, weekly, monthly, quarterly

- Ensure accurate, timely and meaningful monitoring and progress reporting and take decisive actions

Institutionalizing a project management policy with flexible and scalable processes

- Create PM Centers of Excellence (e.g. Advocacy Center, Help Desk, Education, Training, Expert Help, Process, Project Tracking, Certification, etc.)
- Create a reward and/or recognition policy to re-enforce and sustain
- Conduct formal program/project reviews
- Develop and use consistent, flexible and scalable PM processes (e.g. Fast Track versus Full Risk Mitigation Projects and Automate processes and tools (Web based))
- Capture and apply lessons learned and focus on continuous improvement

Figure 4.2 illustrates the phases and their key components applicable to each team, stage, and overall end-to-end project management. Each organization will have to use those components that are important for their environment and may need to tailor the process. This project management lifecycle supplements the Outsourcing Process Stages, identified earlier.

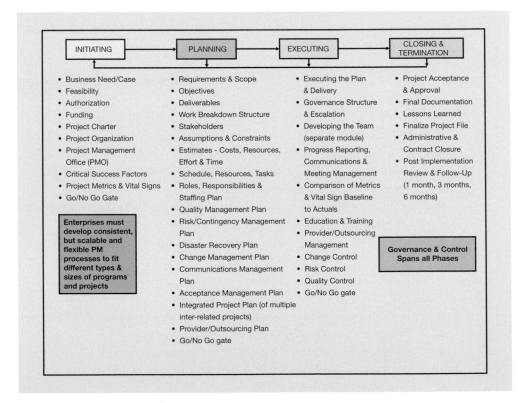

Figure 4.2: Project Phases and Key Components

4.6 List of key terms

- Governance
- Outsourcing Teams
- Project Management Skills

4.7 List of templates

4.1 Outsourcing Professional Roles

4.2 Creating and Leading Outsourcing Teams

4.8 Additional references

Roger Fisher and William Ury, Getting to Yes, (New York: Penguin Books), 1983.

Michael Useem and Joseph Harder, "Leading Laterally in Company Outsourcing," Sloan Management Review, Winter 2000, p. 25–36.

Jean-Francois Poisson, COP, "Managing Outsourcing as a Core Competency," Outsourcing World Summit Presentation, February 24, 2003, Palm Desert, California.

Sarah Parker Enlow; Vantage Partners, "Outsourcing Renegotiating - Threat or Opportunity?", Outsourcing World Summit Presentation, 2008

Sara Enlow; Principal, Vantage Partners, "Critical Skills for Outsourcing Professionals", IAOP Global Human Resources Conference, 2009

LeAnne Andersen, Senior Director, HR Operations, Best Buy Company, Traci Egly, Partner, Accenture Technology Solutions, "Inside Outsourcing: Roles, Responsibilities and Skills Needed to Manage an Outsourcing Engagement Successfully", IAOP Global Human Resources Conference, 2009

5

Developing and communicating outsourcing business requirements

Outsourcing is a very complex, long-term business relationship. Outsourcing providers are engaged for both their expertise and their ability to deliver consistent, high-quality, financially advantageous results. For this reason, building the right business relationship with the right service provider is likely to be the single most important factor in an organization's outsourcing success.

This process of first defining the customer needs, then engaging the marketplace of providers, and ultimately selecting the right provider requires a well-orchestrated interplay of internal assessment and consensus building, coupled with an effective and practical interaction with the marketplace of potential providers.

5.1   Standards

5.0	Developing and Communicating Outsourcing Business Requirements
5.1	Ability to develop a clear statement of the organizational goals and required outcomes.
5.2	Ability to establish multi-year goals and objectives as a framework for contract and establish operating guidelines for the duration
5.3	Ability to develop an accurate and complete baseline of current costs, environment, processes, and performance levels (current state) as well as a gap analysis between these and the required performance levels.
5.4.	Ability to develop *critical success factors* that define business measures of success associated with the area under consideration for outsourcing aligned with the organization's overall business objectives and key performance indicators (e.g. process improvement, financial, service levels, changed business model, customer satisfaction etc.)
5.4.1	Describe various approaches and industry experience when existing measures do not provide baseline for future agreement and are needed for a good contract
5.5	Ability to translate the organization's goals into one or more documents that effectively communicate current and future requirements and the selection criteria that organization plans on using to the marketplace. The types of documents required include, but are not limited to:
5.5.1	Prequalification letters and Request for Information (RFIs), Request for Quotation (RFQs) that state the customer's expectations of any potential provider, including such factors as, the length of time the provider has been in business, its financial health, its current suite of services, its experience in the customer's industry, and its current clients, and its pricing.
5.5.2	A Business Case Document that explains such factors as:
5.5.2.1	What the organization believes is likely to occur in its industry and business over the next few years
5.5.2.2	The challenges and opportunities these changes will create
5.2.2.3	The types of approaches to addressing and leveraging those changes that are currently under consideration.
5.5.3	Requests for Proposals (RFPs) that provide a detailed description on the part of the customer of its business requirements, scope and deliverables including:
5.5.3.1	Communicating the organization's objectives and desired results in clear, complete, and measurable terms.
5.5.3.2	How those results will be measured using metrics and service levels.
5.5.3.3	The factors that will go into evaluating the providers' proposals including the relative weight of each.
5.5.3.4	The information and format required so that the proposals can be readily compared to each other.

5.6.	Ability to use alternative collaborative approaches to defining and developing outsourcing solutions, such as the business case approach, an independent qualification process for providers that can then be brought in by project teams to design and prototype solutions.
5.7	Ability to ensure that a well defined and agreed to process and checklist for development and dissemination of the outsourcing business requirements to potential service providers is followed, such as that defined in the OPBOK Appendix.

5.2   Objectives

Before starting the outsourcing project, it is important to clearly establish the objectives to be accomplished through outsourcing. This is completed during the idea stage and is validated with the Policy Team. The objectives should include longer term (generally established as the length of the initial contract term) objectives as well as shorter term objectives (to be accomplished within the first year of outsourcing). In addition to the objectives, the idea team must identify "boundary conditions" for the outsourcing and agreement.

A framework for establishing objectives is based on the reasons for outsourcing discussed in Section 1. During the idea stage, each of the reasons for outsourcing must be definitively established so that progress against them can be measured.

- Cost savings – define cost savings expectations against current baseline costs (usually measured in percentages)
- Changing cost model – define how outsourcing pricing will be sensitive to the volume of work. This will help convert from bigger "fixed cost" basis to a bigger "variable cost" model This can be expressed as a percentage of the current baseline variable cost component changed to the future one.
- Access to skill – define how skills – either currently deficient in the workforce or not to the level of proficiency required – will be improved over the life of the agreement. This is expressed as a skill mix ratio of current staff versus the staff supplying services or percentage of projects not being able to initiate/ complete as a result of skill deficiency.
- Management focus – this is one of the most difficult objectives to be able to define in a measurable term. It can be defined as time spent by management in managing day-to-day operations or reduction in management level staffing.
- Innovation – define how processes and technology can be changed to an improved state through outsourcing. It can be established as implementation of specific innovative technology or process or as a benchmark comparison against industry standards (or best in class).

In addition to establishing the objectives, idea team should establish boundary conditions. Boundary conditions are business requirements that form the restrictions on what can or cannot be implemented as part of outsourcing. These boundary conditions will guide the implementation team as they establish RFP and contract terms. Below are some of the examples of boundary conditions:

- Strategy and planning functions for the process will not be outsourced
- No part of outsourced work can be offshored
- A single provider will not be chosen for all process outsourcing
- Current employees that transition to the service provider will not be adversely impacted on their benefits
- Outsourcing provider will be compliant with Information Technology standards and architectures established by corporate function

5.3 Defining requirements

Before engaging the marketplace, organizations need to first develop a clear understanding of their own goals and requirements. This takes collaboration between the business leaders and the actual customers of the processes under consideration for outsourcing. A series of meetings with these users, process experts, and others is needed to define the current process in detail and to gain a clear understanding of the results required. These business requirements need to be defined in a way that can be translated into contractual requirements including establishing baseline services and service levels.

To accomplish this, the organization should ensure that:

- The team developing the requirements document has representation from functional management, process experts, customers/users, procurement, finance, human resources, and legal.
- The current process is documented as a diagram, including a clear distinction and rationale for in-scope and out-of-scope activities.
- Current costs are captured for each activity, including people, supplies, equipment, overheads, and capital costs.
- Critical Success Factors and Key Performance Indicators are documented and measured for the current process's quality, customer satisfaction, timeliness, financial performance, conformance to requirements, speed, flexibility, and innovation.
- Future process requirements, based on reasonable potential scenarios, are identified and documented.

During this process, a natural byproduct that should be captured and documented is a clear understanding of the types of competencies and capabilities an outside organization will need to have in order to be successful in taking over the process .

5.4   Baselining current costs

An accurate and complete baseline of current costs and performance levels is required, as well as a gap analysis between these and best-in-class performance levels. This analysis then needs to be extended over the strategic planning horizon, considering how the very nature of the process may need to change in response to changing customer preferences, technologies, and competitors.

In addition to establishing the cost baseline, it is also important to create a baseline of the environment and current process. The environmental baseline would include:

- Physical requirements for the process (such as specialized equipment/ workstations)
- Policies and procedural requirements (such as privacy and security policies)
- Training requirements (such as initial and remedial or recurring training as well as certification)

A process baseline requires that the current process is documented to the level necessary to establish the services and service level agreement part of the contract. This baseline assures that the changes in the future are tracked and appropriate knowledge transfer takes place when and if the process is migrated back (or awarded to a different service provider).

Despite the desire to establish a baseline cost before engaging a service provider, it may not be possible under certain conditions where the historical information may not be available (or captured in the right format). In such cases, it may be necessary to create a phase within the implementation where the baseline is established and becomes a part of the measurement for the contract term. For example; under contract, both parties agree to establish a baseline (given certain boundary conditions) over a fixed period of time – generally six months. They also further agree to use that baseline beyond the six-month period for the remainder of the contract term, as if it was established at the beginning of the agreement.

5.5   Defining critical success factors

Defining desired results in clear, complete, and measurable terms is key to managing any business process, whether it is outsourced or not. Service level agreements, or SLAs, are often used to define process measures, while balanced scorecards are typically used to define business outcomes.

These scorecards essentially define what is important. They describe what both organizations are trying to accomplish and the objective means by which those results will be tracked and reported. If a scorecard for the process does not already exist, then the organization, as part of mapping the process and developing its own business requirements, creates it. Since the scorecard describes what is important, it is essentially the same whether or not the process is outsourced.

Categories are typically used to describe the highest level characteristics used to measure the process. They address such characteristics as quality, customer satisfaction, timeliness, financial performance (costs, revenue), conformance to requirements (regulations, audit requirements), speed, flexibility, and innovation.

For each category, one or more attributes are then defined. These attributes are unique to the process and to the customer's business objectives. They are the tangible and actionable elements of each category. Next, each attribute requires a metric by which it can be measured. The metric must be supported by one or more tools that will be used for collecting the data. Finally, the results of the metric for each attribute, and collectively for each category, must be rated against the desired outcomes. That is, what was the score and does it meet, fail to meet, or exceed the desired result?

You get what you measure, so it is critical to measure the right things. Figure 5.1 identifies select critical success factors (CSFs), key performance indicators (KPIs) and their performance or predictive attributes. Each organization should select those CSFs and KPIs that are most relevant to their outsourcing deals.

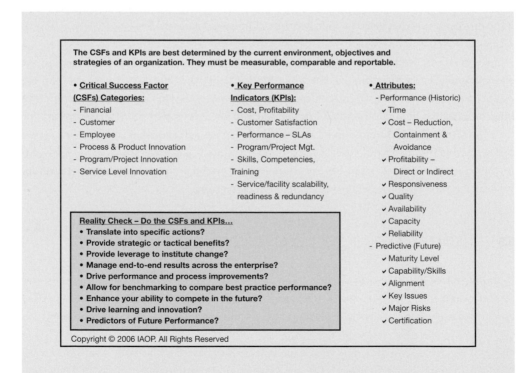

Figure 5.1: CSFs and KPIs for Outsourcing

5.6   Communicating requirements: RFIs, RFQs and RFPs

Once the organization's requirements are fully understood, an approach for communicating those requirements to the marketplace of potential outsourcing service providers needs to be established. There is a range of approaches that organizations can use to capture their requirements internally and then communicate them externally.

The more structured approach, typically following a purchasing model, can begin with a prequalification letter stating the customer's basic expectations of any potential provider. These requirements might include the length of time the provider has been in business, its financial health, its current suite of services, its experience in the customer's industry, and its current clients. Prequalification letters are typically sent to a fairly long list of potential providers with each requested to respond with the information demonstrating that the company meets the customer's stated qualifications.

Similar, and used instead of or following the prequalification letter is a request for information or RFI. Like the prequalification letter, the RFI is, implicitly, a statement of what the customer is looking for in the providers that will receive full consideration. The request for information goes further, however, in that it typically asks for a wide range of information not only about whether the organization meets specific qualifications, but its overall operations - essentially asking how it does what it does. A request for information will often ask about the size and scope of the various elements of the provider's operations, its process for transitioning into a relationship and managing it in on ongoing basis, how it allocates its resources, how it evaluates and minimizes its business risks. The request for information focuses on any and all aspects of the potential provider's operations that might have a bearing on the customer's ultimate selection decision.

The key document used by most organizations when following this more structured approach is the request for proposals, or RFP. A request for proposals is a very detailed description on the part of the customer of its business requirements. It requests a formal, binding response in a predefined format that facilitates the customer's comparison of the responses it receives. Generally, an RFP is only sent to a relatively few organizations, those that have been qualified through a prequalification letter, an RFI, or some other similar process.

Although the layout of the sections of an RFP may vary, there are a few, generally accepted, principles that apply. The first is the need to focus on objectives and results, not resources and methodologies. The purpose of the RFP is not to document what the client organization is currently doing, but to describe its business objectives and the results it is seeking.

The second principle is to define those desired results in clear, complete, and measurable terms. The RFP answers two questions: What results does the organization seek? How will the organization determine whether or not those results are being achieved? The scorecard that the organization plans to use to measure these results is the centerpiece of most effective requests for proposals.

The third principle is to describe all of the factors that will go into evaluating the providers' proposals including their relative weight. Certainly the financials of the proposal will be important, but so will a number of other factors: the organization's confidence that the approach being proposed will deliver the intended results both today and in the future; the level of risk involved and how those risks are mitigated and shared; the proposed terms and conditions of the contract, especially acceptance of any specific contract terms the organization defined in its RFP; the proposed transition plan, especially its human resources elements; and how the provider will manage the relationship over time.

The fourth principle is to specify the information and format required so that the proposals can be readily compared to each other. This means identifying the frequencies and volume drivers of the business activities that make up the process so that all proposals are based on a similar set of base workload assumptions. It also means specifying the actual information requested from organizations responding to the RFP and the format in which it is to be presented.

5.6.1 Summary of RFIs, RFQs and RFPs

As previously stated, some organizations use all three documents, while others may only use the RFP or another type of requirements document. In any event, the following section describes the use and general topics included in each respective document.

Request for Information (RFI)

The RFI is used to collect information (business, financial, product, service, other, etc.) about companies. The desired information is:

- Company profile
- Products and services – current and future research and development
- Focus and funding
- Financial stability (growing or shrinking)
- Plans and direction
- Customer base and references
- Key players in organization
- Number of locations and strategic alliances
- Service, support and training facilities and resources
- Pre-installation and post-installation
- Support, maintenance and service
- Other (list)

Request for Quote (RFQ)

The RFQ is primarily used to solicit pricing and/or cost information from providers. The desired information is:

- Requirements and deliverables (from RFP or high level before RFP)
- Contract type, terms and special conditions
- Pricing and discounts
- Change criteria and their impact on pricing
- Payment terms
- Other (list)

Request for Proposal (RFP)

The RFP is used to define the buyer's requirements, scope, objectives and deliverables in order for the provider to provide a proposal to supply the product or service for evaluation by the buyer. The desired information is:

- Background
- Objectives and scope
- General/detailed requirements
- Functions, features and performance criteria
- Standards and regulatory compliance
- Constraints – time, business, technical, other
- Governance, reporting, dispute escalation and key performance indicators
- Customer/vendor contacts
- Backup, recovery and contingency plans
- Vendor's quality assurance and risk mitigation plans
- Detailed schedule of deliverables
- Insurance
- Contract information and type
- Contract clauses – discretionary or mandatory clauses
- Recourse, remedies and warranty
- Pricing
- Change management – triggers, criteria and approvals
- Licensing and intellectual property protection
- Security and privacy
- Acceptance criteria
- Disengagement conditions, actions and responsibilities
- Other (list)

In summary:

Does the requirements document describe:

- Objectives and desired results, while allowing providers to propose specific resources and methodologies to be employed?
- Current and future volumes in sufficient detail for providers to forecast workload levels?
- The number and location of recipients of the services?
- The desired relationship between the companies, including such considerations as transfer of assets, people, exclusivity, sharing of risks and rewards, and pricing?
- How the relationship should be managed over time?
- Current problems and costs; projects currently underway, status and expectations for provider to assume and complete?
- Key contract considerations, such as, intellectual properties, length, termination options, liabilities and warranties?
- Why the organization will be a good customer for the provider?

5.7   The RFP process

In setting up and managing the requirements process, consider the following.

Does the management of the requirements process include:

- A defined process for identifying the companies to receive the document?
- Compilation of the appropriate contact information for the individuals at the companies to receive the document?
- Definition of the key activities and dates for the distribution, response, review and selection process?
- Sufficient guidance on response structure; the evaluation criteria described; what constitutes a valid response?
- A definition of the internal review process, including roles, responsibilities, and timelines?
- A weighted evaluation criteria; a standardized format for documenting reviewer notes and positions?
- Completion of all required internal reviews and approvals before any providers are contacted?
- When and by whom responders are advised; the next steps to be followed with the selected provider(s)?

5.8   Alternatives to the RFP

Although the Request For Proposals and other elements of this structured process are most common, other approaches are frequently used and should be considered. One is the use of a two- to four-page Harvard Business Case-style document, explaining the current state of the process, what the organization believes is likely to occur in its industry and business over the next few years, the challenges and opportunities these changes will create, and the types of approaches to addressing and leveraging those changes that are currently under consideration. This case study is then provided to potential providers. These providers respond to the case study through both a written management brief and an executive presentation, describing how they would approach solving the challenges the organization faces. The resulting dialogue leads to the selection of a preferred approach and a preferred provider. This, in turn, kicks off a collaborative process involving the two companies in the joint design, development, and implementation of the ultimate solution. The final design, essentially covering everything that would have been in the response to an RFP anyway and more, develops out of this process.

Another collaborative approach is to separate the qualification of potential providers from the design of the solution. This can be done by having providers go through an independent qualification process with a central group, such as purchasing, to get onto a preferred supplier list for a range of processes or business functions. Once on that list, providers can then be brought in by any of the organization's project teams to work with them in the design and prototyping of solutions for specific outsourcing opportunities. The final contract is awarded to the provider whose solution is selected by the project team through the design and prototype process. This is a well-tested supplier-management strategy in manufacturing, and it can work just as well for other business processes.

5.9   Appropriateness of documents

Use of all of the above mentioned documents – RFI, RFP, RFQ – can be an overwhelming process where a lot of resources and time can be wasted. Also, providers may not enthusiastically participate in the process if they believe that it is too long and a rigid process and, therefore, a greater chance of the outsourcing initiative being cancelled or changed. As described, each of these documents has a purpose:

- RFI – Collect market information
- RFP – Obtain detailed information directly relevant to the process being outsourced
- RFQ – Get competitive pricing information on a common baseline.

Figure 5.2 shows how these documents can be combined to create an effective and efficient process.

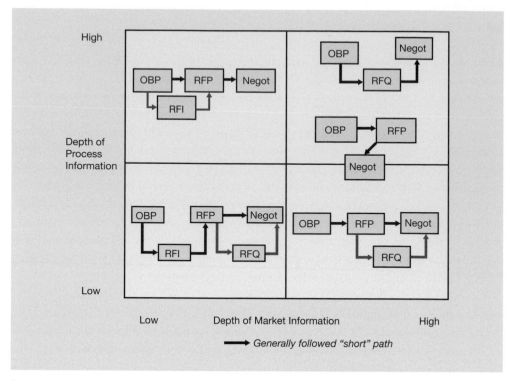

Figure 5.2: Appropriateness of Communicating Documents

5.10   List of key terms

Activity-Based Costing

Boundary Conditions

Case Study

Critical Success Factors (CSF)

Key Performance Indicators (KPI)

Objectives (Goals)

RFI (Request for Information)

RFQ (Request for Quotation)

RFP (Request for Proposal)

Scope of Services

Scorecard

Service Level Agreement (SLA)

5.11   List of templates

5.1   Checklist for Objectives and Boundary Conditions

5.2   Checklist for Developing Outsourcing Requirements

5.3   Critical Success Factors (CSF) and Key Performance Indicators (KPI) for Outsourcing

5.4   RFP (Request for Proposal) Document Development

5.5   Collaborative Business Case Development

5.12   Additional references

WNS Global, "Global Operating Model Version 2.0 Capturing stratiegic benefits in a "flat" world", Published January, 2007

Jill Smart, Accenture, "Outsourcing: A Blue Print for Attracting Talent" Outsourcing World Summit Presentation, 2009

6 Selecting outsourcing service providers

6.1   Standards

6.0	**Selecting Outsourcing Service Providers**
6.1	Ability to take the organizational model for sourcing and developing a list of criteria for the identification and selection of outsourcing service providers
6.1.1	Ability to define the process and use of tools such as RFI, RFP, RFQ and develop an understanding of the most appropriate use of the tools and sourcing methods – within the context of organizational sourcing model
6.2	Ability to use a wide range of techniques for identifying potential outsourcing service providers, such as:
6.2.1	Identifying opportunities to expand current relationships with already successful providers.
6.2.2	Using the organization's professional network to determine what other organizations are doing and who they are working with.
6.2.3	Direct research, including, reviewing articles in the press, research on the internet, and attending conferences and trade shows.
6.2.4	Working with consultants and other advisors.
6.2.5	Industry benchmark data, if available
6.2.6	Utilize professional industry associations
6.3	Ability to establish and gain organizational agreement on an objective and consistent process for reviewing, assessing, weighting, and scoring potential outsourcing services providers, including such factors as:
6.3.1	*Competencies* as reflected in the provider's people, processes, and technologies.
6.3.2	*Capabilities* in terms of its financial strength, overall infrastructure, management systems, and its complete suite of services.
6.3.3	*Relationship dynamics* as influenced by the provider's mission and strategy, flexibility, relative size, importance it places on the customer and its outsourcing relationship management systems.
6.3.4	Identify and weight vendor selection criteria and methodology for selection (scoring as well as subjective)
6.4	Ability to establish a due diligence model for validating the selection of the service provider, including a framework for due diligence and process for conducting due diligence – including customer and business references
6.5	Ability to identify and evaluate offshore locations and their appropriateness to the sourcing requirement and risk management.

6.2   Provider selection process: initialization

As identified in section 1, organizations establish their sourcing strategy (versus creating an internal services organization) and models for provider identification and selection (such as single sourcing versus competitive bidding or multi sourcing). Before initiating the provider selection process, these factors must be considered and a market scan completed so that the initial list of providers is a "qualified" list.

6.3   Provider selection process

Provider selection requires the development of a comprehensive list of factors to consider, a determination of their relative impact and importance, and a repeatable, objective process for the evaluation, analysis, scoring, and decision making.

Figure 6.1 illustrates a typical provider selection process flow. It should be tailored to each organization's environment. The areas focused on in this section of the OPBOK have been highlighted.

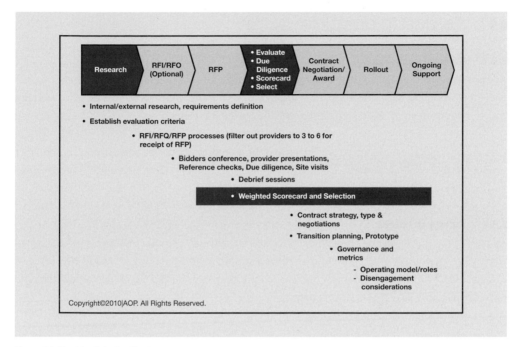

Figure 6.1: Provider Selection Process

6.4   Identifying potential providers

There are a number of ways to go about identifying potential providers. One of the best is to talk to organizations the company is already successfully working with. Another is to use the organization's professional network to find out what other companies are doing and who they are working with. This professional network includes trusted advisors, such as accounting companies, law firms, professional associations, consultants, outsourcing brokers, and other senior-level relationships, as well as, of course, the company's own operating executives' professional networks. It also includes the company's board, where board members may have direct experience with what other organizations are doing and who they are working with.

Another approach is direct research. Direct research includes such activities as reviewing articles in the press, research on the internet, and attending conferences and trade shows. Information on who is in the industry, the types of organizations they are working for, and at least a preliminary sense of the results being achieved can be easily gained in these ways. Companies will also use consultants to help them identify potential providers.

As providers are identified and engaged in preliminary conversation, their strengths and weaknesses are analyzed, and a shortlist of three to six providers is typically developed. These are the providers that will be invited to review the opportunity in detail and propose a solution.

6.5   Assessing providers

6.5.1   Bidders' conferences

After an RFP is issued, it may be appropriate for the buyer to hold a bidders' conference for all providers who have been invited to bid. The purpose of the conference is to answer any questions and clarify the desired objectives, deliverables and selection criteria.

Outside the bidder conference, providers may be asked to make individual presentations in support of their RFP responses.

6.5.2   Reference checks

As part of the due diligence process, the prospective customer should conduct reference checks with other customers of the provider as well as suppliers and partners. It would be useful to obtain a list of provider customers and make sure that you contact some customers that the provider has not suggested that you contact.

6.5.3   Site visits

If the outsourcing initiative is significant, it may be wise to visit the provider's premises and talk to some of the individuals, managers, and executives who would be performing and leading the work. It is important to make sure that the visit includes discussions with non-sales and non-marketing personnel to get a real feel for the people and facilities of the organization.

6.5.4   Due diligence process

Similar to any business engagement, due diligence is an important part of the process. The due diligence process begins before identifying the potential providers, when the due diligence framework, as well as criticality of factors, is established. The due diligence process continues through the acquisition process (RFI, RFP and contracting) and eventually it becomes a part of the ongoing governance process.

The basic tenet of due diligence is examining the process and results individually and personally rather than relying on material either provided by the customer or service provider or obtained from public sources. It is all about "checking for facts".

For customers, due diligence validates the service provider's ability to perform the work, meet the commitment and have the capability (and track record) of being able to do so for then price quoted in their response. Due diligence also examines the compatibility of the two organizations' cultures and methods of operation, so that it can provide a basis for evaluation as well as a framework for change management.

For providers, due diligence validates the information – such as volume, services and service levels – that was provided either in the RFP or in client engagements. This makes sure that their response has a stronger base for assumptions. Providers also determine the level of knowledge repository so that the knowledge management plan (acquisition and training) can be put in place and included in the transition plan.

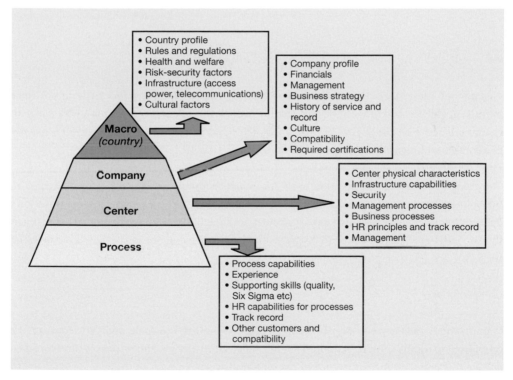

Figure 6.2: Due Diligence Framework

The due diligence framework (Figure 6.2) includes:

- ■ The service provider's business background and company stability. This includes financial, incorporation track record and validation of stated results. If validation is required through a third party audit, such as SAS-70 (type II), the efficacy of the audit is also validated.

- The infrastructure necessary to fulfill the contractual obligations. Infrastructure diligence also includes validating implementation and compliance with requirements such as security (e.g. ISO standards), physical and data protection.
- People resources (either existing or a plan for acquisition and training) necessary to deliver the services. People resource diligence would also include the providers' compliance with required requirements such as drug testing or background check as well as their process for recruiting and managing subcontracted resources.
- Tools and methodologies that assure the knowledge and expertise in the area of service
- Track record and references to prove the continuity of operation over a period of time

6.6 Scoring and selecting service providers

Throughout the process the customer is evaluating the service providers in terms of their overall capabilities and fit with the business. In making this assessment there is a wide range of characteristics to be considered. A formal list of key characteristics to be considered is usually developed and weighted to bring as much objectivity to the process as possible.

The competitiveness of the solution itself is a major factor. However, the competitiveness of the solution is only one factor to be considered. Other factors, including the organization's demonstrated competencies, its total capabilities, and the likely relationship dynamics between the two companies, have proved to be just as important, if not more important to outsourcing success.

Competencies

Organizations outsource to tap the competencies, including the scale and the scope, of the provider's operations. These competencies are reflected in the provider's people, its processes, and its technologies. A track record of ongoing investment in each of these is essential to the provider's ability to deliver over time. Customers look for organizations whose competencies are as close as possible to best-in-world. They also examine the provider's track record of innovation and its industry experience.

Capabilities

A provider's total capabilities are typically examined in terms of its financial strength, overall infrastructure, management systems, and its complete suite of services. Each of these characteristics contributes to determining the viability of a long-term successful business relationship.

Relationship dynamics

When organizations enter into outsourcing contracts, their respective cultural and value systems become very important. Other factors that will influence the relationship over time are the provider's mission and strategy, the flexibility of its business dealings, its relative size, the importance it places on the relationship with that customer, and its outsourcing relationship management systems.

Demonstrated Competencies
- People (Recruitment, Training, Experience)
- Processes (Benchmarking, Certification, Continuous Improvement)
- Technologies (Level of Investment, Leading Edge)
- Experience (Functional, Industry)
- Proven Performance; Certifications
- Track Record of Innovation

Total Capabilities
- Financial Strength & Stability
- Infrastructure and Resources (Bench Strength, Weaknesses/Points of Failure)
- Management Systems
- Complete Suite of Services (Type and Scope, Ability to Scale, Backup, Redundancy, Security)

Competitiveness of Solution
- Solution itself (Fit to Requirements, Innovative)
- Service Delivery (Quality of Processes/Tools/Resources, Performance, Management Depth and Capabilities)
- Risks and Risk Sharing
- Financial Proposal (Pricing, Volume Considerations, Structure, Switching Costs)
- Terms and Conditions (Commercial, Change, Dispute, Adjudication)
- Human Resources Requirements (Employee Transition, Career Opportunities)

Relationship Dynamics
- Culture
- Mission and Strategy
- Relationship Management (Flexibility, Partnership, Trust, Executive Presence, Governance and Reporting)
- Relative Importance (Size, as a Client)

Achievement (esp. existing relationship)
– Evaluate Performance   – Assess Value Achieved   – Continuous Improvement

Figure 6.3: Scoring and Selecting Potential Providers

Another way to develop the scoring system is look at three major groups of criteria used for evaluating and assessing a provider, depending on what is being outsourced These include provider, business and technical criteria. Each of these criteria has specific components as illustrated here.

Provider criteria and components:

- Targeted status for business (such as minority / hardship related ownership)
- Stability
- Financial viability
- Industry certification and audit (e.g. Sas-70, US banking audit frameworks such as shared assessment, AUP)
- Locations and on-site presence
- Performance track record
- Control environment and discipline
- References and reputation
- Pre- and post contract support
- Relationship/engagement model
- Growth and scalability
- Flexibility
- Training and education

Business criteria and components:

- Flexible contract terms and pricing options
- Industry, application and process/functional knowledge and depth
- Transition support
- Business continuity
- Warranties
- Disputes and resolution
- Service and support
- Governance and escalation
- Status reporting and governance
- Asset ownership
- Human resource considerations
- Security

Technical criteria and components:

- Reliability
- Availability
- Scalability
- Depth of knowledge of application, software and/or technology
- Bench strength
- Compatibility
- Support

- Back-up and recovery
- Documentation
- Certifications (ISO, PMP, CMMI, ITIL, etc)

Each organization should determine the most important factors for it and weigh them accordingly. Once the weight has been established, each criterion should be evaluated on a scale of 1 (poor) to 5 (best). The results should be evaluated by a team and each provider should be given an overall ranking.

6.7   Selecting offshore providers

Selecting offshore providers require a greater amount of due diligence encompassing not just the service provider but the locations as well. Although the framework cited above applies equally, there are some additional factors that influence the selection of offshore location and providers.

6.7.1   Factors influencing selection of offshore locations and providers

The following are some of the key factors that need to be considered when selecting an offshore location and providers in those locations.

Exogenous factors

- Government support
- Educational system
- Geopolitical environment
- Infrastructure

Catalyst factors

- Physical and time zone displacement
- Cultural compatibility
- Labor pool
- Language proficiency

Business environment

- Cost advantage – direct labor and indirect process
- Process maturity/competitiveness of suppliers
- Supportive people factors
- Security, IP protection

Although there are several legislative restrictions on what and where to outsource work (especially within the US), there are few limiting requirements that prevent any business from offshoring their work.

6.7.2   Key offshoring destinations

By all surveys and results, it is clear that India is the best known, most used and leading country for offshoring. China remains a formidable force and offers longer term options for outsourcing as the use of the English language and western business principles are more widely adopted by the Chinese providers and people.

Several of the Asian countries remain competitive but are generally limited by the availability of qualified staff. Malaysia, Philippines and Taiwan-China are more popular destinations while Korea, Vietnam, and Indonesia are still emerging with some potential for future work.

Eastern European countries are also strong candidates for consideration for offshoring – especially for European businesses. As the European Economic Community continues to expand and enroll more of the emerging nations (especially from the former USSR confederation); they will be strong economically viable destinations.

Central American countries such as Costa Rica, Dominican Republic and Panama have been strong near-shore candidates for US based companies but they suffer from not having large enough numbers of qualified personnel and a weak infrastructure (universities, telecommunication).

South American countries are emerging rapidly as destinations and Brazil, Argentina and Chile are considered strong candidates. Fluency in the English language remains one of the challenges. As these countries offer stronger, more stable political environments/economies than in the past, they will be a growing segment of offshore destinations.

The African continent is and will remain a "sleeping giant" for the foreseeable future, although there is evidence of limited offshoring done in South Africa and Nigeria.

Outsourcing professionals are encouraged to review research results from CIBRE (Duke University) on offshoring published in the Knowledge Center and presented at various Outsourcing World Summits.

6.8   List of key terms

Bidders' Conference
Reference Checks

Site Visits
Due Diligence

6.9   List of templates

6.1   Identifying Potential Outsourcing Service Providers

6.2   Evaluating Potential Outsourcing Service Providers

6.3   Scoring and Selecting Outsourcing Service Providers

6.10   Additional references

Eugene Goland, "Outsourcing Industry Trend Analysis: Results of the OOBP Vendor Selection Survey" IAOP SME Global Sourcing Chapter Webinar, July, 2006

Eric Rongley, "Managing a Talent Pool Spoilt for Choice– attracting, growing and retaining staff in China", 2006

Donald Mones; McGraw-Hill, "How not to outsource, a customer's perspective", Outsourcing World Summit Presentation, 2008

Arijit Sengupta; CEO, BeyondCore, Inc., "IAOP's OperatorEvaluator: Improving Workforce Quality and Productivity in Global Outsourcing", IAOP Global Human Resources Conference, 2009

Matthew Considine; Vice President, Athenahealth, "Building Innovation and Long-Term Value Creation Into Outsourcing Relationships", Asia Outsourcing Summit Presentation, 2009

Anurag Asthana, Manager, Global R&D Collaboration and Outsourcing, Covidien Gunjan Bagla, Managing Director, Amritt Ventures, Jeff Russell, Director of Research Operations, Duke University, Fuqua School of Business, Cliff Emmons, Director of R&D, Covidien Surgical Devices, "Outsourcing R&D and Product Development: Lessons Learned", Outsourcing World Summit Presentation, 2010

7 Developing the outsourcing financial case and pricing

At one level, developing the business case for outsourcing is simply a matter of comparing the financials of the current operation to those for the proposed outsourced operation. For most organizations, however, this is much easier said than done. Few have a complete understanding of their current costs, especially for the specific scope of activities under consideration for outsourcing. Adding to that is the need to forecast future business levels and costs, typically well beyond the usual planning timeframe. Finally, outsourcing brings with it its own costs that need to be forecasted. As a result, the financial analysis of outsourcing is complex, requiring a disciplined methodology integrating multiple sources of information.

7.1 Standards

7.0	Developing the Outsourcing Financial case and Pricing
7.1	Ability to develop a financial business model for establishing an outsourcing business case that ensures that:
7.1.1	All relevant financial implications are considered
7.1.2	Integrates with the organization's overall business case and financial analysis methodologies.
7.1.3	Provides a clear frame of reference for bid comparison
7.2	Ability to fully capture current costs, including:
7.2.1	Activity-based costing or some other methodology to capture current costs for an activity, set of activities, or end-to-end business process under consideration for outsourcing that:
7.2.1.1	Captures the direct costs of the resources consumed by the activity
7.2.1.2	All overhead costs, including but not limited to, costs for the people and equipment used in the activity, training costs, employee benefit costs, capital costs, etc.
7.2.1.3	Matches cost levels to performance levels as defined by a scorecard or service-level measurements.
7.3	Ability to forecast future costs over the outsourcing decision timeframe, considering:
7.3.1	Probable changes in the business's operations
7.3.2	In its underlying volume drivers
7.3.3.	In performance requirements
7.3.4	In potential changes in technology and other factors that can affect the way the process is performed
7.4	Ability to project costs directly attributable to assessment, planning, execution, and management of the outsourcing relationships, including:
7.4.1	Planning costs, such as staff time, travel, expenses for documenting the process, establishing the internal baseline, engaging the marketplace, and negotiating and contracting with the provider, as well as the use of consultants, lawyers, and outside experts.
7.4.2	Transition costs, such as internal and external expenses for switching to the provider's process, one-time investments in new systems and technologies, and costs overlapping the old and the new operations during an initial period of time.
7.4.3	Additional potential transition costs, such as:
7.4.3.1	Termination fees for any products and services currently used
7.4.3.2	Fees for transferring licensed materials and existing services contracts to the provider
7.4.3.3	Relocation costs for moving people and equipment
7.4.3.4	Any tax liabilities that may be created through the sale of existing equipment to the provider

7.4.3.5	Any one-time stay bonuses, incentives, or severance packages for current employees and managers.
7.4.4	Oversight costs including all upfront and ongoing costs associated with managing the outsourcing contract, both internal and external associated with training, outside services, or tools.
7.5	**Ability to project financial benefits of outsourcing over the decision-making timeframe, including:**
7.5.1	A direct comparison of these projected total costs before and after outsourcing.
7.5.2	Application of cash flow, net present value, return on investment, or internal rate of return techniques to account for the time value of money
7.5.3	Translation of less tangible (non-financial or indirect cost savings) benefits, such as increased flexibility, innovation, speed to market, risk sharing and others into tangible elements of an overall business case
7.6	**Ability to evaluate and select the optimum pricing model (contract type) for an outsourcing business agreement, including such options as: JM: Should include volume, pilot and tenure pricing options.**
7.6.1	Cost plus where the provider is paid for actual costs plus a predetermined fixed amount or percentage for profit margin.
7.6.2	Unit pricing where the customer pays based on the amount of service, number of service units, used.
7.6.3	Fixed price where the provider's fee is the same regardless of the volume of services provided.
7.6.4	Incentive-based pricing where payments are connected to achievement of specified service levels or other specific aspect of delivery or performance.
7.6.5	Gain-sharing where the provider receives a portion of any additional benefits, typically savings, it can generate for its customer.
7.6.6	Achievement bonuses which are typically one-time payments for achieving certain milestones.
7.6.7	Risk/reward sharing where both the customer and the provider have money at risk, and each stand to gain a percentage of the additional value created by their collaborative efforts.
7.6.8	Volume management principles such as ARC and RRC and its application to pricing models.
7.7	**Ability to define specific price-levels within the chosen pricing models that are reasonable and consistent with current and probable future market conditions.**
7.7.1	Ability to identify the framework for provider margin management with reference to price-levels

7.2 Capturing current costs

Some form of activity-based costing is the optimum approach for capturing current costs for an activity, set of activities, or end-to-end business process under consideration for outsourcing. Although this is the optimum, and described in more detail below, most organizations evaluate the financial impact of outsourcing at an overall budget level, not at the activity-cost level.

To get to activity costs, the costs of the resources consumed by the activity need to be understood. Existing accounting and financial data that reports labor costs, supplies, equipment utilization and overheads are typical the starting point used. The people involved in performing the activity are then a key source for taking that information, which is usually structured at the department- or function-level, and restating it at the activity level. Once this is done, it is then possible to aggregate the costs of each activity and establish the baseline cost for the entire set of activities or business process being examined.

All overhead costs, even those not normally included in the department's budget, need to be traced to the activities they support. Costs that might otherwise be missed if this is not done include occupancy costs for the people and equipment used in the activity, training costs, employee benefit costs, and capital costs. Finally, the activities and their costs need to be matched to the current process's outcomes as defined by the scorecard. This connection between how the activities are performed, their costs, and the results achieved needs to be clear.

The organization's understanding of its current process and costs are only complete when:

- The activities that make up the process are fully documented
- The costs of the resources used in each activity are known
- All relevant overheads have been traced to the activities they support
- The current performance of the process is reflected in a scorecard, and
- The volume drivers of the process and the effect of volume on costs are fully understood.

In addition to understanding current costs, reasonable projections for those costs over the financial analysis timeframe are required. This timeframe may be as short as a year or two, but it may be as long as ten years. Since the data from normal budgeting systems typically does not extend beyond a year or two, assumptions need to be made. These assumptions should consider probable changes in the business's operations, in its underlying volume drivers, in performance requirements, as well as potential changes in technology and other factors that can affect the way the process is performed and its associated costs. Additionally, not all current costs will be covered by the provider's proposal and are therefore retained.

Finally, there are investments required for the outsourcing project itself and for the ongoing management of the business relationship. Examples are outlined below.

Planning costs

These include staff time, travel, and other expenses for documenting the process, establishing the internal baseline, engaging the marketplace, and negotiating and contracting with the provider. If consultants, lawyers, or other outside experts are used, then these costs need to be included as well.

Transition costs

Transition costs include staff time, travel, and other expenses, both internal and external, for switching to the provider's process. Moving to the new environment may require one-time investments in new systems and technologies. These investments may be within the business process or in other processes that connect to it. They may also be in support areas, such as security, quality control, and scorecard data gathering. They may also include costs associated with overlapping the old and the new operations during an initial period of time.

There are a number of other transition costs to consider. These include termination fees for any products and services to be discontinued; fees for transferring licensed materials and existing services contracts to the provider; relocation costs for moving people and equipment; any tax liabilities that may be created through the sale of existing equipment to the provider; and any one-time stay bonuses, incentives, or severance packages for current employees and managers.

Additionally, transition costs should also include the productivity loss or additional expenses involved in maintaining the service levels while the service provider gets over its "learning curve". This may include items such as:

- Additional staff (temporary, back-filled)
- Additional training costs for the replacement staff or costs associated with "training the trainers"

Environmental costs for supporting extra staffing for the period (such as additional workstations, physical space)

Governance costs

The new relationship has to be managed, and there are upfront and ongoing costs associated with this. Some of these costs will, again, be internal, and others may be associated with training, outside services, or tools. Generally, these costs are not included in the baseline when the work is being managed internally and may even represent a cost that may be incurred in departments other than the one being affected through outsourcing. For example; many businesses use internal audit department or finance staff or even outside auditors to provide some aspects of governance. These costs may or may not be directly allocated to the organization benefiting from outsourcing and therefore, if it is not accounted for properly, the net benefits will not reflect the corporate-wide impact of outsourcing.

Termination costs

There are costs associated with terminating an outsourcing agreement – whether the termination is a result of completion of the full term of the agreement or a mid-contract termination as a result of cause or a matter of convenience. These costs are typically similar to the transition costs and include some of the same elements. If the termination of one agreement leads to awarding the same work to another service provider, there is additional (twice the amount) transition costs that must be identified and accounted for. These termination costs should be included in the baseline so that a full "end of life" benefit picture can be developed for the management.

Termination costs should also include engagement of subject matter experts from the provider to facilitate migration of work. Often, this type of engagement is specifically identified in the contract and the pricing is pre-defined.

Oversight costs

The new relationship has to be managed, and there are upfront and ongoing costs associated with this. Some of these costs will, again, be internal, and others may be associated with training, outside services, or tools.

7.2.1   Challenges in creating current costs and establishing the baseline

It is often believed that establishing current costs should be easy, if the budget for the process/activity is known. It could not be further from the reality. There are some significant issues and challenges when creating a baseline that is reflective of the cost of performing the operation. Some of the challenges are:

- Not all cost information may be easily available (and therefore, not included in the "budget"). This is common where capital cost and common corporate management costs are not directly allocated to the function.
- The allocated cost basis may not be consistent with the selection of the process being outsourced. This occurs when the allocated costs (such as space and utilities or HR function) are based on elements not reflecting the process intensity or have direct correlation to the process.
- Volume sensitivity may not be known and may not have historical trend to validate costs per volume and establish a relationship curve. Since future pricing will be based on the projection of volume, providers need to understand the price-volume sensitivity and if it is not known, it may be difficult to establish the relationship between the two factors.
- The currency basis and cost of money for the activities may not be recognized as a separate cost element. This becomes an issue when either the process is outsourced offshore or where the cost of money is significantly different for the customer from that of the provider (typically, financial institutions).
- The secondary impact of costs for outsourced processes may not have valid assumptions (e.g. empty space may not result in savings if the space cannot be returned/reduced)

7.2.2   Activity Based Costing:

One of the most rigid methods for developing the baseline cost is the use of Activity Based Costing (ABC). As described in Wikipedia:

"Activity-based costing (ABC) is a costing model that identifies activities in an organization and assigns the cost of each activity resource to all products and services according to the actual consumption by each: it assigns more indirect costs (overhead) into direct costs.

In this way an organization can precisely estimate the cost of its individual products and services for the purposes of identifying and eliminating those which are unprofitable and lowering the prices of those which are overpriced.

In a business organization, the ABC methodology assigns an organization's resource costs through activities to the products and services provided to its customers. It is generally used as a tool for understanding product and customer cost and profitability. As such, ABC has predominantly been used to support strategic decisions such as pricing, outsourcing and identification and measurement of process improvement initiatives."

7.3   Pricing and price levels

Pricing for outsourcing is developed by establishing baseline costs, future delivery costs and how the impact of benefit is shared. Figure 7.1 simplistically portrays how such a pricing scheme works.

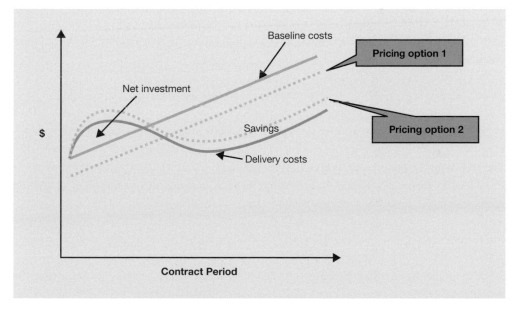

Figure 7.1: How Pricing Works

Pricing specifies how the fees for the services provided are calculated and, of course, when and how they are paid. Just as importantly, however, the pricing structure for an outsourcing contract defines how the financial risks and rewards are allocated between the parties. As a result, there are a number of ways of structuring the pricing of an outsourcing contract and each has a potentially powerful affect on the ongoing decision making of both parties.

The following are the most common, along with generally recognized pros and cons of each.

Cost plus

The provider is paid for actual costs plus a predetermined fixed amount or percentage.

This approach enables the customer to fix the profit level for the provider and gives it direct visibility into the underlying cost factors. However, it offers little incentive for the provider to improve the way the service is performed or to reduce actual costs.

Unit pricing

The customer pays based on the amount of service, number of service units, used. The rate may be the same regardless of the number of service units used, or an additional or reduced resource charge may apply for utilization above or below agreed-to levels.

Here, the service provider may be motivated to find ways to increase the customer's utilization of its services, while looking to reduce its internal per unit costs. This can be in direct conflict with the customer's desire to drive down its utilization rate and to share in the benefits of future efficiencies.

Fixed price

With a fixed price, the provider's fee is the same regardless of the volume of services provided.

The advantage for the organization is easy budgeting. The problem can be that the provider is motivated to ensure it achieves a consistent profit level, causing it to seek ways of restricting scope, volume, or costs when service demands peak.

Incentive-based

With incentive-based pricing, the organization uses payment incentives to encourage the provider to deliver services in a particular way, particularly at certain levels of performance. Penalties are, of course, the flip side of this.

The challenge is to ensure that the incentives and penalties directly correlate to the business value the organization is realizing. Higher levels of service may not actually translate into greater value for the customer, making the higher payment unjustified. On the other hand, the organization does not really want a poorer service for which it is paying less; it wants the right level of service at a fair price.

Gain-sharing

Here, the provider receives a portion of any additional benefits, typically savings, it can generate for its customer. These savings might come from driving down the costs of raw materials, implementing new technologies, or making suggestions for improvement in the organization's operations. Gain-sharing splits typically range from 50-50 to 75-25, in favor of the customer.

Achievement bonuses

These are typically one-time payments for achieving certain milestones. These milestones may be tied to earlier-than-expected completion dates, higher-than-committed service levels, or better-than-expected throughput. When multiple providers delivering the same service are involved, achievement bonuses based upon comparative rankings can be used as well, where top-performing providers receive bonus payments.

Risk/reward sharing

This implies that both the organization and the provider have money at risk, and each stand to gain a percentage of the additional value created by their collaborative efforts. For example, if the provider and the organization are able to drive down certain costs or drive up revenues, then they share them. Similarly, if costs run higher or revenues run lower than expected, they each share the downside as well.

Which pricing model works best in any given situation is a matter of matching the goals of the organization with those of the provider, and selecting the approach which best aligns their interests over the planning period.

There are a number of ways for setting the price level for outsourcing services. They include:

- Benchmarking current operations
- Projecting an 'optimum' price
- Decomposing activities
- Researching reported financials
- Gaining insights from others
- Using consultants/analysts
- Using marketplace dynamics (multiple bidders)

7.3.1   Volume based pricing principles

When a contract is established (either as a fixed price or incentive-based price), transaction volume provides the baseline around which the pricing is based. Since the volume typically varies over a period of time, most agreements establish a methodology using "banding" where the price and volume have a reasonable synchronization. In this method, both parties agree on the baseline volume and associated price. Then they establish a higher and a lower band of volume change (e.g. plus or minus 10%) where there is a pre-defined price. They also establish an outer set of bands where the pricing can be negotiated at the time that volume is reached. Finally, there may be an extreme upper and lower limit for volume at which all assumptions about pricing no longer are valid and therefore would result in an organized contract termination (or total renegotiation). The two bands beyond the baseline volume are generally known in the industry as ARC (Additional Resource Charges) or RRC (Reduced Resource Charges) – or "Arc" and "Rook".

7.4   Understanding how a provider develops pricing

It is important to understand how a typical service provider develops the basis for their cost before negotiating the deal or creating the pricing structure, so that a similar analysis can be performed by the outsourcing organization. This will help in assuring that the cost elements in the baseline are consistent and, therefore, the internally developed baseline is reflective of the true cost of operation and not just the budget for the department. Template 7.1 provides a detailed list of the cost elements included in developing a baseline as well as pricing.

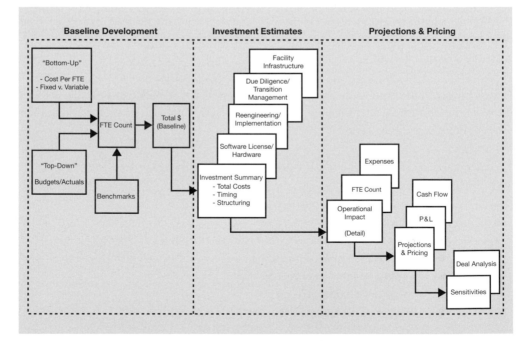

Figure 7.2: Provider Pricing Development

7.4.1   Economics of pricing

Figure 7.3 shows how economics of pricing works, based on some industry norm information. As you can see that unless the provider has a clear option of creating labor (by using a cheaper location) or efficiency (with process improvement and/or technology insertion), an overall economic model cannot work. Since this is a fairly good representation, customers can use a similar chart in validating providers' proposals as a part of the due diligence process.

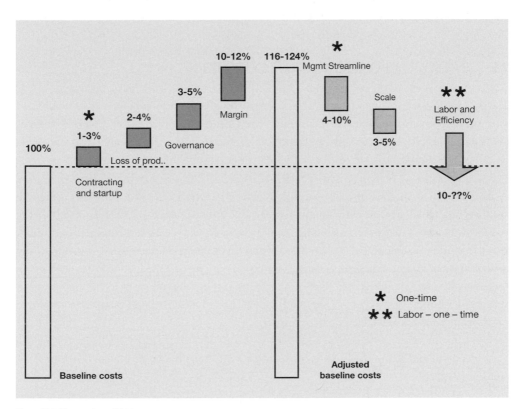

Figure 7.3: Economics of Pricing

7.5   Management presentation of baseline and benefits

One of the important tasks that the outsourcing team has to prepare is the financial analysis for presentation to the policy committee and other senior management. These presentations take various forms and are tailored specifically as to how each business looks at investment and expenses. The following are some of the standard reporting formats:

- Baseline costs versus outsourced costs – shown over the length of the agreement either as a Percent of Baseline Savings or calculated as Return on Investment using net present value (NPV)

- Net EBITDA impact of outsourcing savings (particularly useful if there is a sale of assets involved in the transactions)
- Changes in capital consumed over the length of the agreement (current state versus outsourced)

Sometimes, it is also important as part of management presentation to show the potential savings and how the selected outsourcer is planning to achieve the savings (as presented in their RFP response and ascertained through due diligence).

7.6   Projecting outsourcing's benefits

The base business case comes from a direct comparison of these projected total costs before and after outsourcing. Net present value, return on investment, or internal rate of return techniques are typically employed to account for the time value and to reduce the business case to a single cash figure that can be used to readily compare various options.

A final aspect of forecasting outsourcing's benefits is to translate what might be generally seen as 'intangible' benefits into 'tangible' aspects of the business case. With so much of the potential benefit of outsourcing coming from areas such as increased flexibility, innovation, speed to market, risk sharing and other areas of business value, a methodology for systematically identifying and quantifying these benefits is commonly employed. One approach for quantifying these benefits is to determine their likely economic impact in terms of one or more dimensions of shareholder value – such as costs, assets, and revenue, and to then develop a reasonable economic calculation for the projected level of that impact.

To understand and assure the benefits from outsourcing, benefits can be broken down in three specific categories:

- Direct savings:
  - Operational expense savings
  - Reduction in capital expenses (current and planned)
- Opportunity for revenue generation. This can be achieved as a result of higher customer satisfaction, customer retention, upsale or increased offered services.
- Reduction of recorded liability on the books as a result of reduced risks or accrual for lower performance (such as higher warranty costs)

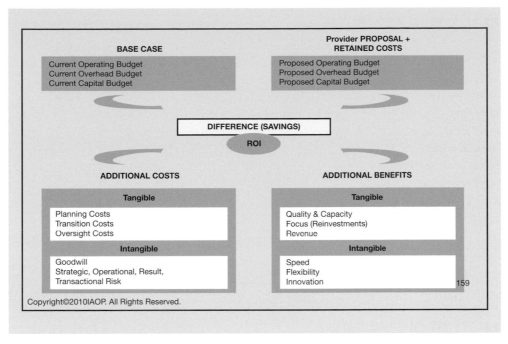

Figure 7.4: Financial Analysis of an Outsourcing Decision

7.6.1   Outsourcing value proposition

There are many ways a company may define and prioritize the value proposition that is most appropriate for their outsourcing engagement. However, the value proposition can be categorized in the following five categories. The first three of these value categories have direct correlation to the business while the last two have inverse correlation (in other words, elimination or reduction is considered a value):

1. Financial
2. Capabilities
3. Service quality
4. Risk and compliance
5. Governance
6. Other

Identifying and prioritizing these value propositions help create and communicate the objectives for outsourcing and establish a common ground rule for all competing for business. It also helps communicate internally the purpose and results of outsourcing.

Thye IAOP Value Health Check Survey uses these five categories to assess the outsourcing value and relationship health.

7.7 List of key terms

Achievement Bonuses
ARC
Cost Plus
EBITDA
Fixed Price
Gain-Sharing
Incentive-Based Pricing
Net Present Value (NPV)
Risk/Reward Sharing
ROI (Return on Investment)
RRC
Unit Pricing
Value Proposition

7.8 List of templates

7.1 Cost Elements for Creating Baseline Costs

7.2 Financial Analysis of an Outsourcing Decision

7.3 Selecting the Optimum Pricing Model

7.4 Value Proposition

7.9 Additional references

Equaterra, "Pricing alternatives and methodologies", IAOP Chapter Meeting, 2006

Guillermo Estebanez (Bank of America), "The currency forecasting tools – the art and science," IAOP San Francisco Chapter Meeting, May 2007

S. Reynolds, WNS North America "Activity Based Compensation", Outsourcing World Summit Presentation, 2008

Joe Hogan, COP, Managing Director, Alsbridge, Inc." How to Make Client Relationships Stand the Test of Time" Outsourcing World Summit Presentation, 2010

8 Contracting and negotiating for outsourcing

Contracting and negotiating focus on establishing the working framework for the outsourcing business relationship. Because every company and every outsourcing deal is different, it is the understanding and ability to apply the most appropriate pricing model and then structure the contract and its unique commercial terms for each situation that leads to successful outsourcing outcomes.

8.1   Standards

8.0	Negotiating, and Contracting for Outsourcing
8.1	Ability to define the most appropriate structure for an outsourcing contract(s), including the use of separate term, scope of services, and pricing sections including:
8.1.1	Define contractual framework for multi-process outsourcing to a single provider
8.1.2	Define multi-provider management contract to assure coordinated delivery of service
8.2	Ability to ensure that each section of the contract addresses the critical management considerations inherent in the outsourcing business relationship, such as:
8.2.1	A terms section that defines the intent of the relationship and how it will be managed, the contract terms that govern the overall agreement, the initial transition from the customer's operation to the provider's including such considerations as:
8.2.1.1	Contract termination and disengagement triggers
8.2.1.2	Contract reward and penalty considerations
8.2.1.3	Business continuity, security and intellectual property break-up and recovery
8.2.2	One or more sections on the scope of services that describe the type, scope, and nature of all the services to be provided, where and when those services will be made available, and the standards of performance, as defined by the critical success factors and service-level measures.
8.2.3	One or more pricing sections that reflect the pricing model, price points, and payment terms.
8.2.4	One or more sections that reflect employee treatment (selection, retention, pay equalization) by the service provider
8.3	Ability to ensure that all applicable legal considerations, for all jurisdictions involved, are reflected in the contract, such as those documented in the OPBOK Appendix.
8.4	Ability to negotiate an outsourcing agreement that takes into consideration the interests of all parties.
8.4.1	Ability to apply generally accepted negotiating principles to the development of an outsourcing relationship that are consistent with contemporary practices and learning.
8.4.2	Ability to develop an effective process and checklist for guiding an organization's approach to negotiating an outsourcing business relationship.
8.5	Ability to model termination events, options and alternatives and how contract terms affect the model selected
8.5.1	Contract provision for transition back or transition to another third party
8.5.2	Managing the process of "renegotiation" as a pre-requisite to normal termination

8.2   Contracting

The outsourcing contract captures:

- The intent of the relationship
- How it will be managed
- The scope of services to be performed
- The responsibilities of the parties
- How the results will be measured
- As discussed in Chapter 7, how the provider will be compensated.

Structurally, most outsourcing contracts have three distinct sections: a contract terms section, a scope of services section, and a pricing section. This also enables a modular design of the agreement where the contract terms section defines the 'master framework' of the business relationship while the services and pricing sections are treated as 'service towers' for each major service to be provided. This structure makes it easier to write agreements that include different types of services – each defined and paid for differently. It also allows for each major service area to be managed separately – added, changed, and deleted without directly affecting the other services or the overall relationship.

The terms section defines the intent of the relationship and how it will be managed. It contains the contract terms that govern the overall agreement. Common practice is to be specific in describing the intent of the relationship, its goals and objectives, and how it will be managed, while avoiding terms suggesting a common understanding but not well enough defined to carry any specific meaning. For example, describing the relationship as a strategic alliance may capture the spirit of the parties; but what does that really mean? If the relationship is truly a strategic alliance, the terms section should talk about the shared strategic planning process to be followed, the type of information to be exchanged, and the resources being committed by the parties to this shared effort.

Another important part of the terms section of the contract covers the initial transition from the customer's operation to the provider's. The transition section describes the plan for converting the customer's current operation to the provider's, including responsibilities, cost allocations, timelines, and operational certification. What equipment and facilities will be transferred to the service provider, including their valuation, responsibilities for warranties, liability for repair to bring the equipment to proper working order, taxes, and any environmental issues? Similar considerations apply if the equipment or facilities are leased and the organization wishes to either assign the lease to the provider or exercise a purchase option and then resell it to the provider. If there are lease transfer charges, whose responsibility are they? What are the organization's obligations, such as providing access to information, resources, and personnel?

If customer equipment or facilities are to be made available for use by the provider but not transferred, the terms section should specify the terms of their use, including who bears the costs of changes, repairs, and future upgrades. Other considerations might include access to customer facilities and required customer approvals for changes to equipment and facilities.

Third party services, equipment, and facilities may also be involved and need to be transferred. These third party agreements may be assigned to the provider, terminated, or continue and be managed by the organization. Responsibilities and cost should be stated, as well as the parties' rights to change and replace these third-party agreements.

To the extent that this transition will involve the transfer of personnel from the organization to the service provider, the terms section should specify the particulars around the offers of employment, including salaries, benefits, and any guarantees of employment for a specified period of time. It should also specify how the transfers are to be managed, including the organization's and provider's respective roles and responsibilities, allocation of costs, and any indemnities and allocation of risks from employee lawsuits that might arise. Another personnel consideration is training. The terms section should specify who is responsible for training the personnel on new skills or processes needed to support the new operation, how that training is to be provided, and who bears the costs. The agreement should specify the parties' responsibilities and cost allocation in relation to projects underway at the time of the transfer.

The terms section should also specify how the relationship will be managed, including project managers at the organization and provider companies, oversight and senior management committees, and operational teams. Roles and responsibilities should be clearly defined, as well as frequency and types of meetings, and how any related costs will be allocated. If formal management techniques are to be used, such as jointly developed annual business plans and formal risk assessment programs, these should be specified. The process, authorities, and responsibilities for negotiating and agreeing to additions or changes to the agreement should be described, as well.

All other relevant business and legal terms should be defined and the responsibilities of the parties clarified. A common list of terms is provided in the Appendix.

One or more scope of services sections are used to describe the type, scope, and nature of all the services to be provided, as well as where and when those services will be made available. Hand-in-hand with a description of the services is the standards of performance, as defined by the scorecard.

Services are typically described in as much detail as possible, including a description of the service and of the responsibilities and duties associated with it. The intent is to make this section specific enough that an independent third party could determine what each party's obligations are from reading it. This is key to preventing later problems that can result from different interpretations as to what services were or were not included within the scope of services.

The key performance indicators (KPIs) typically reflect, at a minimum, measures of volume, availability, timeliness, milestones, quality, safety, regulatory compliance, and customer satisfaction. Additionally this section describes how the information will be collected; who owns the measurement system; how the costs are borne; and how the integrity of the data will be ensured.

8.2.1   Additional considerations for contracts involving offshore services

Offshore contracts require additional consideration due to its nature. Generally, it is highly recommended that for offshore outsourcing contracts, local attorneys are engaged who are familiar with local customs and regulations. Some of the key points of consideration for offshore contracts include:

- Form of agreement (legal entities and their relationship)
- Intellectual Property laws and their adoptability
- Local government regulations (contractual, tax)
- Enforceability of contractual terms and potential decisions
- Escalation options and viability of common forms of negotiation (e.g. arbitration)
- Continued adjustment to contract terms due to changes in laws, regulations, restrictions

8.3   Forms of contract for multi-process; multi-provider services

Although there are no standard rules for an outsourcing contract, most contracts are developed in a standard fashion and, as explained in the previous section, contain standard sections. However, there are several variances on this contract format when there are multiple processes or service providers involved.

8.3.1   Multi-process contract form

In a multi-process outsourcing to a single provider scenario, a slightly different framework is used in order to simplify contracting and negotiating process. In such a scenario, a master services agreement is created that contain terms that would be universally applicable to all processes and a separate services agreement is created that contain process specific terms. There will be only one master services agreement while there will be as many services agreements as processes involved in outsourcing. Figure 8.1 below shows such a structure.

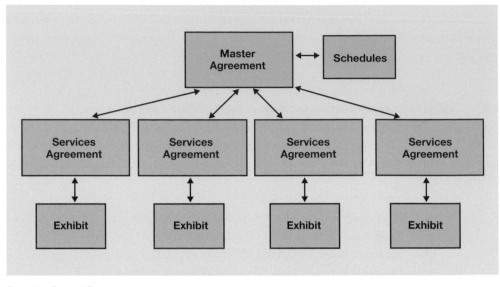

Figure 8.1: Contract Form

8.3.2   Multi-provider contract form

When there are multiple service providers involved in providing outsourcing services and where there is a dependency on each other for meeting services and service level agreements, certain additional terms need to be considered:

- A clearly defined dependency between the providers
- A dependent service level agreement (sometime it is called Operations Level Agreement) where a service provider commits to a level of service to the other service provider (as opposed to the buyer of service)
- The consequences of not meeting such dependent service levels and resultant contract violation condition for the secondary service provider (e.g. if service provider A does not meet the SLA and as a result, service provider B does not and therefore is subject to contract penalty to the customer)

A joint governance and reporting model (and terms) ensures that that the net impact of services and service level agreement is visible to the customer.

8.4   Negotiating

Negotiating is a management discipline in its own right, and there is a wealth of information available on the topic.

The following checklist offers some generally accepted principles for preparing to negotiate an outsourcing relationship:

- Have the negotiating team members and roles been defined?
- Have the organization's key interests been defined?
- Are individuals with all relevant discipline knowledge included, such as legal, human resources, procurement, functional management?
- Are individuals with sufficient decision-making authority on the negotiating team for both parties?
- Are multiple providers to be negotiated with at the same time, and if so, have dates for "best and final" offers been established?
- Have sources of objective information for evaluating proposed terms been identified?
- Have all relevant issues been reviewed and negotiated internally before negotiation with the provider?
- Has the best alternative to a negotiated agreement for each of these items been determined? (What is the fallback position?)
- Has sufficient time been allocated for planning, preparation, and negotiation?
- Have the interests of the provider been considered?
- Have areas of potential value to either or both organizations, beyond the specific services being contracted for, been identified?
- Have a meeting schedule and road map for the negotiations been agreed to by both organizations?
- Has a comprehensive list of items to be negotiated been developed and agreed to?

Introducing all relevant considerations as early in the discussions as possible, and making sure they are fully understood by both parties before negotiating any individual term, focuses attention on the outcomes sought – not the positions of the parties.

Once the contract negotiation is complete, the customer and the provider will be in a long-term business relationship where both must succeed. Therefore, the final terms must be reasonable for both parties in light of the responsibilities and risks involved. Negotiations do not end when the contract is signed; the customer and provider will be negotiating throughout the life of their relationship.

8.5 Common areas of negotiation

The following areas are common negotiation points surrounding outsourcing contracts. This list is provided from a business perspective and not a legal perspective. (A list of common legal terms is included in the glossary in the Appendix.)

- Scope, requirements, deliverables and schedule – create a mutual understanding of "in scope"; define a process for "out-of-scope" requests.

- Financial and legal arrangements – payments, discounts, rewards and penalties, pricing formulas and changes; insurance, taxes, foreign exchange, indemnities, liability limitations, escrow, ownership, and consequential damages

- Acceptance criteria – quantitative and qualitative criteria

- Metrics and service criteria – volume, capacity, speed, performance, quality, documentation, training, mean time to repair, schedule, budget, program/project, etc. Consider metrics in three different areas:
  - Outcome and performance based metrics (e.g. volume, speed, scalability, etc.)
  - Metrics for quality assurance (e.g. consistency, accuracy, satisfaction, etc.)
  - Key indicator project or operational metrics (e.g. schedule, reliability index, help desk problem resolution time, etc.)

- Governance, disputes, recourse, remedies, escalation and issues resolution

- Support services – training, documentation, maintenance, service

- Updates, new releases, upgrades

- Performance warrantees and service levels – SLAs (ranges with incentives, penalties) – including compliance with technical/security standards, staff acquisition (e.g. background check). Also included are maintaining various certifications (ISO) or clean audit reports (SAS-70, Sarbanes-Oxley) as well as compliance with local and international laws

- Status reporting periods, formats and contents – What? When? To whom? How often?

- Disengagement options – conditions, responsibilities, transition plan – define roles and responsibilities of both parties

- Ownership of equipment, software, data, etc.

- Change management triggers, process and approvals

- Confidentiality, non-disclosure and security (physical, logical)

- Intellectual property and content protection

- Termination triggers, disengagement process and provisions

- Contingency, back-up and disaster recovery plans and resources

- Detailed service descriptions with adequate metrics for each activity

8.5.1 Termination consideration

Termination for an agreement can occur for four different reasons:

1. Normal – termination at the end of the effective period of the agreement (original or extended per contract)
2. For cause – when either party has violated a contractual term that can trigger disengagement from the contract, it is considered termination for cause. There may be additional contractual remedies provided before or during such a termination. Not all violation of contractual terms can be damaging or willful. For example, change of ownership of either party can trigger a violation of contract term (generally dealing with the assignment of the contract).

   It is generally recommended that both parties agree upon various termination events and provide for the disposition according to its application. This prevents lengthy or rancorous negotiations when such events occur.
3. For convenience – when either party has a right to disengage without a cause, it is considered termination for convenience. This right, which should be used sparingly, is usually a difficult negotiating term
4. For "jeopardy" – when a contract has to be voided due to a change that is out of control of either party and is not considered either a cause or convenience. Again, a rare situation but can be applied if a legislative prohibition would make the contract unenforceable (e.g. a country prohibited from doing business with a company located in another country)

No matter what the reason is for termination, it is important that the customer decides what the normal course of action will be after the termination. The options generally considered are:

■   Bring back the work in-house
■   Engage another service provider to provide essentially the same service
■   Abandon the service (although not very common, this can occur if a customer decides to exit the business supported by the outsourced process)

Depending on the choice of the action, this will help identify the options and additional services required from the service provider upon termination. For example, if the work is brought in-house, the customer may require that certain "key employees" of the service provider remain engaged in providing service (either through "subordination" or through transferring to the customer). These types of terms are referred to as "puts" and "calls" – meaning rights of the customer to either acquire (calls) or demand service provider to provide (puts) agreed upon service or assets.

Another service that needs to be identified and agreed upon is the support for transition of work back to customer (see Chapter 7 for additional discussion on costs associated with such transition).

The key to getting the right exit provisions is asking key questions from each of the party's perspectives as an integral part of creating the agreement and negotiating it at the onset.

Regardless of the form of termination, agreement must be reached and documented as to the disposition (return, retain, clean up or destroy) of:

■   People resources
■   Physical assets
■   Technology environment (including use of tools)
■   Process documentations (including knowledge databases)

Additionally, a clear definition is required for surviving contractual clauses and continuing obligation of both the parties.

8.5.2   Contract changes

All outsourcing agreements should have a change management and control clause built into the contract that describes:

■   What constitutes legitimate causes for changes to the contract (e.g. environmental, economic, political, supply chain conditions, regulatory, scope, volume, technology, mergers and acquisitions or divestitures, strategic alliances or joint ventures, etc.)?

■ What is the change management process and templates? Who will document the changes? Track the changes? Execute the changes? Test the changes (if applicable)?

■ What impact will the change have on the customer's operation?

■ What can cause mandatory changes? Discretionary changes?

■ Who approves changes?

8.5.3   Contract risk areas

As in any business agreements, there are certain areas in contracts that present greater risk in terms of coming to an agreement and eventually enforcing them. The following are some of these risk areas:

■ Third party claims
  ● End-users
  ● Regulatory penalties
■ Customer paying for something it does not get (not being able to agree on scope, deliverables)
■ Service credits – exclusive remedies; incentives; buying at a point on the price: delivery curve
■ Wilful abandonment
■ Lost business revenue and profit (as a result of non-compliance to contract terms)
■ Reputational risk
■ Indirect / consequential liability
■ Suppliers assuming "new" areas of risk in outsourcing environment

8.5.4   Contract renegotiation

As the contract term gets closer to the end date, it is important to establish a schedule and framework for renegotiating the existing agreement. There are multiple points for consideration, depending on the desired outcome both parties wish. For example, if either party wishes to no longer be under a contract, a reasonable extension of contract term can be implemented to allow time for an orderly transition. On the other hand, if the current agreement is adequate, both parties can simply extend the termination date to a future one. In either case, it is important to set up a "lessons learned" session so that both parties can understand and evaluate what has worked and what has not worked in the current agreement and include those points for addressing in the new agreement.

Under certain circumstances, both parties can jointly agree to renegotiate an agreement *before* its normal term date. It can also be handled in a similar manner as described above, unless the reason for renegotiation is a dispute. In that case, the dispute resolution process must be exercised first before entering into renegotiation; since it can be a more effective and less expensive solution to the problem at hand.

8.6   List of key terms

Master Agreement, Services Agreement

See Appendix for a list of common commercial terms.

8.7   List of templates

8.1 Outsourcing Contract Structure

8.2 Common Outsourcing Contract Terms

8.3 Description of Interests for Outsourcing Contract Negotiations

8.4 Negotiation Checklist

8.8   Additional references

David Barrett, COP, "Outsourcing's New Global Deal Model" Keynote presentation at Outsourcing World Summit, 2007

Dr. Larry Ponemon, Sandra Hughes "Lose their data – lose their trust: Enabling secure vendor relationships," IAOP Data Security Chapter Webinar, 2007

Stephen Johnson, COP, Kirkland & Ellis LLP; Neil S. Hirshman, Kirkland & Ellis LLP; Min Wang, Kirkland & Ellis LLP, "Something Old, Something New: Contractual and Legal Issues Facing Top Industries for Outsourcing", Outsourcing World Summit Presentation, 2007

R. Etzkorn; Colliers International, M. Latshaw; H&R Block, "Scalability and Flexibility in Outsourcing Contracts" Outsourcing World Summit Presentation, 2008

John Beardwood, Fasken Martineau, Jeffrey Kastner, Air Canada, David Perez, Air Canada, "Risk Management in Outsourcing Transactions: Finding the Balance Between Certainty and Flexibility - An Air Canada Case Study", Outsourcing World Summit Presentation, 2009

Neil S. Hirshman, COP, Kirkland & Ellis, Stephen Johnson, Kirkland & Ellis, "Contracting in an uncertain world – aftermath of Satyam". Outsourcing World Summit Presentation, 2009

William P. Metz, COP, Procter & Gamble, "Key Components of an outsourcing agreement", Outsourcing World Summit Presentation, 2009

Danny Ertel, COP, Vantage Partners, "Help Me, Help you: Value creation takes two", Outsourcing World Summit Presentation, 2009

Ole Horsfeldt, Partner, LL.M., Gorrissen Federspiel, "Enforceable Outsourcing Contracts – New Approaches to Drafting Complex Outsourcing Contracts ", European Outsourcing Summit Presentation, 2009

Neil S. Hirshman, COP, Partner, Kirkland & Ellis, and Chair, IAOP's Chicago Chapter, Jagdish R. Dalal; COP, Managing Director of Thought Leadership, IAOP, "Hard and Soft side of managing talent in outsourcing" IAOP Global Human Resource Conference, 2009

Gregg I. Goldman, Executive Director, UBS, "Putting Power into Outsourcing Contracts: Understanding their Potential to Mitigate Risks", Outsourcing World Summit Presentation, 2010

Ken Adler, Partner, Loeb & Loeb LLP, Chris Malone, Director, Expense Management Solutions, "Cloud Computing: Contracting for the Silver Lining", Outsourcing World Summit Presentation, 2010

9 Managing the transition to an outsourced environment

9.1   Standards

9.0	**Managing the Transition to an Outsourced Environment**
9.1	**Ability to develop a comprehensive transition plan including:**
9.1.1	Transfer of assets, employees, processes and technology
9.1.2	Establishment of major mileposts and measurement for progress
9.1.3	Managing change through transition
9.1.4	Initial framework for governance
9.2	**Define and develop a comprehensive change management program for affected staff and understand various approaches and alternatives for implementing the program**
9.2.1	Understand human behavior and stages of human emotion during change and what types of programs enable staff to manage through the change
9.3	**Ability to oversee the transition plan to the outsourced environment, including considerations, such as:**
9.3.1	Detail definition of the operational interfaces between the customer and provider organization
9.3.2	Forecasting of volumes for ramp-up through production.
9.3.3	Risk assessment and contingency plan development.
9.3.4	Operationalizing the management structure, communications plans, and human resources plans.
9.3.5	Test, piloting, and conversion plans
9.4	**Ability to develop and coordinate the communication of an organizational agenda for change that demonstrates how customers, employees, and shareholders will benefit.**
9.5	**Ability to develop and coordinate an end-to-end process for managing the impact of outsourcing on the organization's personnel, including such considerations as:**
9.5.1	Identify applicable employment laws and precedents, in all applicable jurisdictions.
9.5.2	Leading the effort to identify the impact of an outsourcing decision on each and every affected individual, both those in-scope and those out-of-scope.
9.5.3	Overseeing the implementation and communication processes
9.5.4	Knowledge transfer where the work is transitioned but not the staff
9.6	**Ability to assess the potential community and media reactions and to develop and oversee action plans to minimize any negative aspects**
9.7	**Ability to develop a 'transition back' plan and model in event of termination and including the plan as a part of the contract model**
9.8	**Define knowledge management plan and implement it as a part of transition activities**

9.2.   Transition management

Transition is one of the most critical parts of outsourcing as it sets the stage for a successful engagement. There are many aspects to transition (and phases) as well as dimensions that need to be well defined, understood and implemented. In order to assure common terminology between the service provider and customer, the following definitions should be considered:

Transition

Transfer of responsibility from customer to the service provider. This occurs at a contractually agreed upon date (Start Date). Transition activities begin before the contract is executed and continues until all activities are completed - generally 60 to 90 days past the Start Date. There are four dimensions to the transition activities:

- Staff (employees as well as contractors)
- Work responsibility – continuation of activities and processes in place on the Start Date
- Assets and other tangible properties necessary to perform work responsibility by the service provider
- Fiduciary responsibility as agreed upon in the contract

Transfer

Activities to implement the solution that was the basis for the service provider's proposal to the customer. This includes knowledge acquisition and planning activities that will result in programs such as contractor replacement, off-on shore processing center establishment and implementation of the service provider's processes. Transfer activities are expected to be complete within the first 12-18 months of the contract, though a periodic review and re-planning will continue for the duration of the agreement.

Transformation

Activities that will transform the current customer's process (and/or systems) into a higher performing process. Transformation activities span the entire length of the agreement and are the basis for the savings to be accrued by the customer and profit levels achieved by the service provider.

9.2.1   Common problems with transition management

Experience has shown that the majority of failed outsourcing engagements begin with problematic transition management. Here are some of the reasons why transition management fails and why it creates a longer term problem for both the service provider and customer:

- Transition planning is not a key activity on the project plan for all outsourcing management teams (policy, idea, assessment, implementation and management)
- Transition planning is done in a vacuum and does not have "buy-in" by all parties involved – customer, service provider's sales and delivery teams

- The transition plan is not fully developed and documented and is a part of the contract
- The transition plan does not cover all aspects of the outsourcing engagement (people, processes, assets and financial) and all phases – from contracting through governance
- The transition plan implementation management team is not identified before the contract is signed so that the activities can begin as soon as the contract is signed
- The transition management team is either not involved in developing the original solution that was sold to the customer (and became the basis for the contract) or has a longer term accountability to create stability of operations
- Change management (as described in Chapter 3) is not considered a vital part of transition management

9.3 Developing and managing the outsourcing transition plan

The foundation for a successful transition to an outsourced environment is built in throughout the outsourcing process itself: in selecting the scope of the process to be outsourced; in developing the process diagram; in selecting the provider; in building the key performance indicators; and pricing, contracting, and negotiating the relationship.

The key aspects of the transition itself are defining the operational interfaces between the organization and provider in detail and, of course, testing, evaluating, and correcting any problems encountered. Volumes need to be forecasted for ramp-up to production. Risk assessments need to be performed and contingency plans developed. The management structure, communications plans, and human resources plans are all made operational.

There is simply no substitute for early identification and resolution of problems. Poor results during the transfer can create lasting perceptions that stay with the relationship for years to come.

The following provides a transition checklist to facilitate a transition for outsourcing functions and processes:

- Signed contract
- Transition customer and provider leads and teams
- Transition documentation
- Pilot test plan
- Transition training

- Transition schedule and timetable
- List of asset to be transferred (if applicable)
- List of people and other facilities to be transferred
- Transition communications plan
- Contingency and risk mitigation plan covering the transition
- Transition preparation meetings organized
- Integration plan

9.3.1 Test plan and pilot

In most outsourcing deals that are moderate to complex in scope, it is a good idea to plan a pilot and develop a test plan checklist consisting of the following:

- Finalize acceptance criteria
- Define test environment – functional, process, technical, integration, recovery, implementation/rollback testing, etc.
- Conduct pilot and test
- Document test results
- Fix discrepancies
- Approve test results to go live

9.3.2 Training

Often organizations are 'penny wise and pound foolish' by not allocating sufficient resources or time to training the customer's employees (who remain employed) in the new order of things and also making sure that the provider's employees are trained to assume their new roles and work assignments. Those employees who transfer to the outsourcing provider's payroll must also be trained in their new environment.

9.3.3 Cutover

Once all of the testing has been satisfactorily completed and the results approved, then - and only then - you are ready for the cutover. Once the cutover has occurred, update all documentation, databases and verify that any problems and discrepancies have been resolved. Part of the cutover must include operational and help desk support for the customer. Other cutover items that should be monitored include:

- Monitoring provider deliverables/process outcomes
- Mapping or describing the pre- and post implementation process impact of the outsourcing initiative
- Instituting a governance, relationship management and escalation process, metrics, controls and reports

9.4   Managing outsourcing's impact on the organization

9.4.1   Managing outsourcing's impact on employees

While most of the activities associated with managing the transition to an outsourced environment represent a classic exercise in project management, one aspect that is deserving of special focus is outsourcing's impact on employees – especially those working within the scope of what is being outsourced. Most of these employees will be offered a different job within their current company; offered a new job with the service provider; or told they no longer have a job. Even out-of-scope employees are affected as well. The company and the way they do their jobs are changing. And, most importantly, they can be expected to ask the question, "Am I next?"

Because of this impact on employees and on the communities within which the business operates, outsourcing professionals play an important role in helping to determine not only which employees are affected and how, but how employees and the communities are to be prepared for the changes taking place and supported throughout the process.

Outsourcing professionals are responsible for helping the organization demonstrate through words and actions that outsourcing can, and in very specific ways will, produce on balance positive outcomes for all of the organization's stakeholders. These communications must be clear, consistent, and in line with any and all employment laws and precedents, including such considerations as co-employment, protected groups, government-mandated programs, and the WARN Act – not to mention additional legislation that may be enacted in the future.

For employees, outsourcing opens up opportunities for taking on different jobs within their current company. Some of these will be in the management and integration of the outsourcing business relationship itself. New career opportunities are also created for employees going to work for the provider. Outsourcing can even result in the creation of brand new companies, through various forms of spin-outs, where employees have the ability to participate not just as employees, but as owners. Even for those who will not have a job in either company after outsourcing, the company has enormous resources at its disposal to assist these employees in ways that can lead to positive outcomes for these individuals, as well. Outsourcing professionals need to be well versed and experienced in all of these issues and approaches.

9.4.2   Managing change

Change management begins as soon as a decision is made to outsource. Hence, it is described in depth in Chapter 3. However, the impact of change management practice is actually felt when the transition of activities take place. If the change management process has not progressed through earlier phases, employees (affected as well as unaffected) may be still in a stage where the positive effect of change has not started. This may create difficult in assimilation of employees and can end up disrupting business during the period.

9.4.3   Employee communication to manage change

Figure 9.1 shows the key steps and timing in developing a robust plan for managing the communications and actions supporting outsourcing.

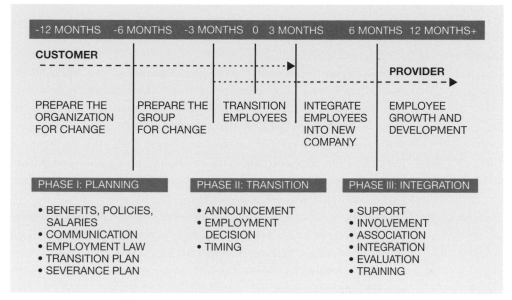

Figure 9.1: Creating Positive Employee Outcomes

Although specifics will need to be developed for every situation, common principles and generally accepted practices do apply.

For example:

- Even before evaluating its specific outsourcing plans, management should take stock of overall employee attitudes toward the organization and its management.
- The timeline for preparing employees for change and assisting them through the process should begin as early as 12 months before any actual deal is done and employee transition plans should extend 12 months past that date.
- Once the initial announcement is made, employees will quickly begin the process of comparing, very specifically and based on their individual criteria, the immediate and long-term implications at the personal, financial, and job level. Each and every one of these implications must be carefully thought through by management in advance.
- The organization's human resources professionals should play a major role throughout the process
- When employees have employment choices to make, the timelines for making these decisions should be clear.

9.4.4   Managing organization transition: pre- and post-outsourcing

One of the key elements of outsourcing transition management is managing the transition of the organization – pre- and post- outsourcing, Unfortunately, often the transition management activities do not receive enough emphasis and are not included in the plan, thereby creating potential problems in the outsourcing engagement.

Activities that are key to managing the organizational transition before outsourcing include:

- Establishing an organizational structure before outsourcing such that the outsourcing scope (and therefore people) would look natural to the rest of the organization. This is even more critical in European countries where the Acquired Rights Directive (and more specifically TUPE in the UK) requires that the organization that is outsourced represents a single work entity and not just an amalgam of resources working on disparate things (this is established to prevent companies from using outsourcing as a way to reduce staff off their payroll and adjust their compensation basis)
- Establishing a post outsourcing organization structure. This will ensure that the governance and management processes between the outsourcer and retained staff are well defined and responsibilities clearly understood.
- Identify skills (both the retained as well as outsourced) inventory to assure that the outsourced work does not adversely affect any longer term strategy dealing with skills acquisition and retention.

The table below clearly identifies the pre-outsourcing tasks.

Focus Area	Preparing to Transition the Organization	Preparing for the New (Retained) Organization
Employee alignment	Employee uncertainty	Unplanned attrition; correctly identified critical workforce
Communications	Negative PR (internal and external) and rumor mill	Alignment, change management
Knowledge	Critical knowledge flight	Knowledge transfer/transition management; managing distributed talent networks; getting more with less (talent shortages/premiums)
Culture	Career opportunities	Cultural integration
Skills/talent	Acquiring/retaining talent	Service provider resource skills; new and different skills (multidisciplinary/specialized)
Process management	Operational effectiveness and efficiency	Provider governance and SLA management
Compliance	HR and legal compliance	SAS 70, SARBOX, etc
Performance management	Compelling employment practices/performance indicators	Provider relationship management, escalations

Source: Deloitte Consulting LLP Outsourcing Advisory Services. Copyright © 2007 Deloitte Development LLC.

9.5   Outsourcing communications plans

There is a direct correlation between employee satisfaction and the way the company manages the outsourcing transition process. This means that in advance of any discussions about a specific outsourcing initiative or a specific contract, management should have already communicated a positive vision for the future of the organization – a vision that shows how customers, employees, and shareholders will benefit. Aspects of a communication plan and implementation are described in Chapter 3.

9.5.1   Creating a positive public perception for outsourcing

Since the media tends to sensationalize outsourcing's impact on employees and communities, it is important to assess the probability of media attention. The characteristics of the deal, the type of organization, the number and types of employees affected, and the impact on the community at large are the key factors.

In particular, in assessing the probability of media attention, consider the following:

- Does the company have a history of negative press coverage on outsourcing? Negative press on outsourcing has a cumulative effect with subsequent deals coming under increasing scrutiny following earlier negative public reactions.
- Will the deliberations be public? This is likely to be the case for public companies or organizations with unionized employees.
- How many people will be affected and what are their levels? Public reaction to outsourcing is decidedly more negative when large numbers of lower-wage, minority-group employees are affected or when it involves the offshoring of professional-level positions.
- Will employees be "kept whole" in terms of pay, benefits, and job security? This is a critical decision that management must make in formulating its strategy and should be done well in advance of announcing the deal. If employees will be kept whole, then there is often little story for the press to cover.
- Is outsourcing being driven by financial problems? Generally, outsourcing announcements by companies in financial difficulty receive more public scrutiny.
- What is the provider's reputation for dealing with transferred employees? Often, negative public reactions occur after the fact because of things the provider does or the provider's history of problems leading to greater media scrutiny.
- Will the executive team be visible and proactive in managing public perception? And does it have experience with outsourcing? Visibility when needed and experience are important in avoiding negative public reactions.

Once the probability of press coverage and a negative public reaction is assessed, an appropriate action plan is developed addressing both how the outsourcing deal itself should be structured as well as how it is communicated. Considerations here are:

- The public image is made in the media. It is clear that the amount and character of the media's coverage of an outsourcing engagement greatly determines the public's perception of the deal.
- The goal is not to have to manage public opinion. Outsourcing engagements do not require public opinion management when they do not attract media attention. Either create no public perception through little media coverage or create a positive perception by featuring innovative aspects of the deal.
- The deal and its perception unfold together. Many outsourcing deals are created with the public's perception in mind. Aspects of these deals are shaped to make the deal more acceptable to the public and the community.
- Like politics, all outsourcing is local. While there is currently a national debate on offshore outsourcing, outsourcing is still fundamentally a local issue. It is about local jobs and the impact on the local economy and community. Most negative public perceptions of outsourcing will center on this. It is important to treat outsourcing as a local issue in each affected community.
- Shape public opinion by shaping employee opinion. If the media is the connection to the public and the public's perception, then the employees are the key to the media. Layoffs and other features of the outsourcing deal attract the media, and disgruntled employees nourish negative press.

9.6   Knowledge management

A key success factor for outsourcing is the provider's ability to manage knowledge – acquire what is necessary from the customer, augment with experience and expertise and eventually share it with the customer. Experience has shown that a disciplined knowledge management process in place makes the relationship successful in the short and long term.

Knowledge management is defined as follows:
Knowledge management is the explicit and systematic management of vital knowledge – and its associated processes of creation, organization, diffusion, use and exploitation.

Thus, knowledge management (KM) comprises a range of strategies and practices used in an organization to identify, create, represent, distribute, and enable adoption of insights and experiences. Such insights and experiences comprise knowledge, either embodied in individuals or embedded in organizational processes or practice.

A typical life cycle of knowledge management is shown in Figure 9.2 and it also shows the phases of the outsourcing lifecycle where it is invoked and used.

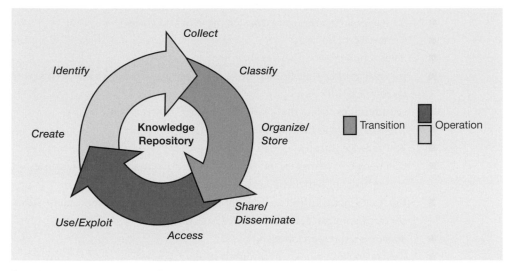

Figure 9.2: Knowledge Management Cycle

In order to establish an effective knowledge management process, the current state must be assessed and an action plan developed to reach the state where knowledge management can be effectively implemented. The assessment elements are organizational, process and technology.

Organizational
Champion for knowledge management
Detailed and effective communication throughout
Subject matter expert appointments and ownership of responsibility

Process
Definition of knowledge elements
Identification and documentation of collaborative process for identifying, capturing and maintaining knowledge
Established measurements for knowledge elements – may be more than SLAs

Technology
Repository for information
Knowledge capture tools
Knowledge utilization tools

There are several strategies that both the customer and service provider together can employ to assure that the knowledge management is effective and well implemented. These are:

- Rewards (as a means of motivating for knowledge sharing)
- Storytelling (as a means of transferring tacit knowledge)
- Cross-project learning
- After action reviews (Lessons Learned)
- Knowledge mapping (a map of knowledge repositories within a company accessible by all)
- Communities of practice ("birds of a feather" environment)
- Expert directories (subject matter experts)
- Best practice transfer
- Competence management (systematic evaluation and planning of competences of individual organization members)
- Proximity and architecture (the physical situation of employees can be either conducive or obstructive to knowledge sharing)
- Master-apprentice relationship
- Collaborative technologies (groupware etc)
- Knowledge repositories (databases, bookmarking engines etc)
- Measuring and reporting intellectual capital (a way of making explicit knowledge for companies)
- Knowledge brokers (some organizational members take on responsibility for a specific "field" and act as first reference on whom to talk about a specific subject)
- Social software (Lotus Notes, wikis, social bookmarking, blogs, etc)

A good knowledge management plan would identify "best fit" of these strategies and include them for implementation.

9.7   List of key terms

Knowledge Management
Migration
Transformation
Transition

9.8 List of templates

9.1 Outsourcing Transition Plan

9.2 Human Resources Planning

9.3 Knowledge Management Readiness Assessment

9.4 Knowledge Management Strategies

9.9 Additional references

Michael F. Corbett, "Managing the People Impact of Outsourcing," Michael F. Corbett & Associates, Ltd., August, 2002.

Phil Fersht and Derrick Sappenfield, "Preparing the new organization post outsourcing", IAOP Insight publication, 2007

Ron Kifer, COP,, Applied Materials, "Outsourcing and Change Impact - a view from Applied Materials", IAOP Insight publication, 2007

Till Lohman, PricewaterhouseCoopers "Managing the new. Getting the Change to Stick", Outsourcing World Summit Presentation, 2008

Thomas Tunstall, ACS "How Outsourcing is Impacting Management Styles and Organizational Structures", Outsourcing World Summit Presentation, 2008

Eulala Mills-Diment; Province of British Columbia, "Alternate Service Delivery: How to Conduct an Effective Transition", Outsourcing World Summit Presentation, 2008

Mark Peacock; Archstone Consulting, "Developing the retained organization", Outsourcing World Summit Presentation, 2008

Geetika Sinha; Genpact, "Achieving Predictable xcellence: Integrating Lean Six Sigma with Global Service Sourcing", Outsourcing World Summit Presentation, 2008

Vikas Bhalla, EXL service, "Setting up for success: getting things in place before you migrate processes", October, 2009

Roel Straetemans, Managing Director, Gitco BV, "Specifics of second generation transitions", European Outsourcing Summit Presentation, 2009

Sara Enlow; Principal, Vantage Partners, "Critical Skills for Outsourcing Professionals", IAOP Global Human Resources Conference, 2009

Danny Ertel, COP, Vantage Partners, "Danny Ertel; COP, Partner, Vantage Partners", Asia Outsourcing Summit Presentation, 2009

Dr. Phillip Hadcroft; General Manager - Strategy & International Development, Salmart BusinessForce, "Mapping the Boundaries:Cross-Cultural Knowledge Transfer: When East Meets West", Asia Outsourcing Summit Presentation, 2009

Kurt Kohorst, COP, Vice President, Liberty Mutual Insurance, "Practical Lessons on Onshore Transitions – Bringing Work Back In-House", Outsourcing World Summit Presentation, 2010

Garry Moore, Solutions Architect, Joe Farrell, IBM Program Executive, IBM Managed Business Process Services, "An IBM & ATT Case Study: HR Outsourcing as Innovation Driver – Creating Learning Ecosystems with Web 2.0 Innovations", Outsourcing World Summit Presentation, 2010

10 Outsourcing governance

Studies have found that more than half of all organizations spend two percent or less of an outsourcing contract's cost in managing the business relationship. However, more than sixty percent report losing ten percent or more of the contract's value because of poor working relationships between the customer and the provider. Fully twenty-one percent report losing more than twenty-five percent.

Given this, outsourcing professionals clearly have a leadership role to play in helping their organizations plan, invest in, and execute a cohesive set of business practices for managing outsourcing relationships.

10.1   Standards

10.0	Outsourcing governance
10.1	**Ability to define governance framework and its components such that the governance process is comprehensive and continuous.**
10.1.1	Define governance and "rules of engagement" as they apply to outsourcing and distinguishing their similarities and differences
10.1.2	Ability to discuss examples of good governance activities and process.
10.2	**Ability to design and oversee an organization's outsourcing governance model, including such considerations as:**
10.2.1	Establishing an Outsourcing Program Management Office (OPMO) and defining roles and responsibility for the OPMO as well as "rules of engagement"
10.2.2	Establishing a multi-level structure for linking the operational, management, and executive levels of all organizations involved in the outsourcing business relationship with defined roles, responsibilities, meeting frequencies, etc.
10.2.3	Identifying and promoting the use of technology to track, report, and facilitate communications
10.2.4	Ensuring a well-defined escalation process usable by all organizations
10.2.5	Implementing a change management process
10.3	**Ability to design and implement an interdependent project management office for managing across multiple organizations that addresses:**
10.3.1	*Project portfolio management* that ensures that the right projects are initiated with the appropriate priority
10.3.2	*Project execution* with a level of rigor reflective of the scope and effort that went into defining and crafting the outsourcing relationship initially and directs company resources to effect changing project objectives.
10.3.3	*Project tracking and reporting* using a well-defined and agreed-to system for measuring and reporting project information to the central repository, including standardized feeds based on information exchange architectures.
10.4	**Ability to define and implement an interdependent planning methodology that include such elements as:**
10.4.1	Regularly updated outsourcing business plan that puts in place a formal process for periodically reviewing and updating all aspects of the relationship between the companies, including strategies, operations, financial considerations, and business relationship management.
10.4.2	A joint risk assessment planning system that is a forward-looking tool that is an early warning system of potential future problems and opportunities.
10.5	**Ability to measure, assess, and achieve continual improvement in organizational outcomes through outsourcing relative to original goals and changing business needs**
10.5.1	Ability to use tools such as Value Health Check Survey (from IAOP) to assess the effectiveness of the relationship and delivery of service

10.6	Ability to evaluate and assess current providers relative to changing capabilities, competitiveness, and organizational needs, often referred to as vendor management
10.7	Ability to renegotiate or disengage and re-insource existing relationships relative to current performance, changing requirements and marketplace realities
10.8	Ability to define and manage a program of continuous improvement that integrates lessons from previous outsourcing implementations into future initiatives
10.9	Ability to govern knowledge management process and tools defined during the strategy phase

10.2 Outsourcing governance planning and set-up

According to Wikipedia, *"Governance makes decisions that define expectations, grant power, or verify performance. It consists either of a separate process or of a specific part of management or leadership processes. Sometimes people set up a government to administer these processes and systems. There are two fundamental requirements for establishing good governance practice for the outsourcing engagement:*

1. Outsourcing business performance
2. Corporate conformance to various regulations and legal requirements

Although corporate conformance is identified as a separate objective, the detailed requirements of compliance are aggregated as a part of the outsourcing business performance – for example, SOX compliance is identified as an audit governance process.

In the case of a business or of a non-profit organization, governance develops and manages consistent, cohesive policies, processes and decision-rights for a given area of responsibility. For example, managing at a corporate level might involve evolving policies on privacy, on internal investment, and on the use of data."

This is applicable to managing an outsourcing engagement. For outsourcing, in addition to providing for good governance, it is also important to provide for the rules of engagement. Figure 10.1 describes the difference between governance and rules of engagement. Governance is oversight of outsourced work conducted between the outsourcing program management office (see later for further discussion on this topic) while the rules of engagement is a set of policies and procedures that govern how the recipients of services deal with the service provider. The rules of engagement framework is completely defined and bound by the contract and provides no basis for any contractual dispute, unless it is escalated through the outsourcing program management office.

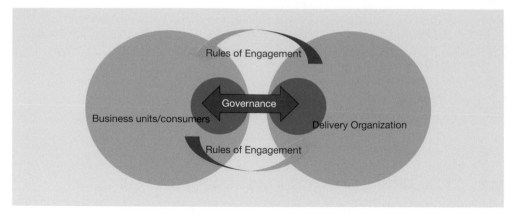

Figure 10.1: Governance framework

Rules of engagement are established by jointly by the outsourcing program management office and the service provider and uses contractual commitment as its basis. It provides for processes, procedures, forms and communication framework between the service provider and recipient. For example, it would define the form to use when requesting certain services or a procedure to follow for approving additional service.

The basic principles of outsourcing governance include:

- Start planning even before the deal is done
- Staff key roles with carefully selected individuals
- Develop a *Policies & Procedures Manual* that indicates how the customer and provider are going to live what the contract says
- Leverage governance models set up by companies that have gone before you
- Successful transition and cutover is the governance organization's first test

Common challenges are:

- No historic performance data, which makes setting KPI and SLA targets difficult
- The retained organization resists adoption of the rigor required to work in an outsourced environment
- Perception that things are slower and harder than before, value of outsourcing not recognized
- Actual value erodes due to lack of productivity measures
- Governance gets stuck in the middle vs. simply facilitating a direct relationship between customers and provider
- The provider is slow to react to changing needs (i.e. capacity issues)
- Coordinating work across multiple providers

- Lack of cross-organizational governance experience
- Maintaining enough competence to be a capable buyer

Critical processes include:

- Relationship Management
- Service Request Management
- Service Receipt Verification
- Performance Management
- Problem/Incident/Change Management
- Project Management
- Security, Business Continuity, Disaster Recovery
- Operations Management
- Financial Management
- Asset Management
- Contract Management

The following principles are commonly used by outsourcing professionals to shape outsourcing governance systems.

Strategic responsibility kept close to the top

Operational and management issues are dealt with at multiple levels within the organization (see below), but the strategic responsibility – the responsibility to ensure an ongoing alignment of the interests of both the customer organization and its providers – is a senior management responsibility. Some organizations even add a separate executive, reporting to the CEO, COO, or CFO, as the organization-wide coordinator for many of its major outsourcing business relationships.

Multilevel organizational links

Operating committees, made up of individuals directly involved in the day-to-day activities, ensure regular communications between organization and provider, resolve issues as they occur, and report upwards issues that cannot be resolved at this level.

A management committee, with overall responsibility for the contract and its deliverables, ensures that both customer and provider understand how current performance compares to expectations, is the focal point for approving changes in scope or deliverables, and is the arbitrator for unresolved operational issues.

Finally, an executive steering committee, led by the executive with overall strategic business relationship responsibility, is tasked with the ultimate responsibility of ensuring the ongoing health of the business relationship and with resolving issues that cannot be resolved at lower levels of their organizations.

Regular, goal-oriented meetings

Regular, goal-oriented meetings between the organizations are held with defined frequency, consistent attendance, and continuity from meeting to meeting through formal agendas, assigned action items, and follow-up. These meetings form the foundation of most outsourcing relationship management systems and are commonly seen as essential to overall success.

Use communications technologies

In addition to traditional face-to-face communications, technology is commonly used to support the outsourcing management structure. The internet, voice messaging, teleconferencing, e-mail, discussion groups, instant messaging, and online collaboration tools are all employed. Operational dashboards, fed by real time data systems, are often placed right online for all organizations to see.

Scorecard used to report results

The scorecard is an essential tool for gauging performance and is defined when the business relationship is created and is regularly updated. In so doing, the scorecard defines what is important, keeps all organizations focused, enables objective tracking, and is a motivator of achievement. Outsourcing professionals typically make sure that the ability to collect and report scorecard data is in place on 'day one,' maintained over time and used effectively.

Defined escalation process

A well-defined escalation process enables issues to be quickly brought to higher levels of management for review and resolution. This is critical to all parties involved in an outsourcing business relationship. Often simple, objective rating systems, such as "green – yellow – red," are used to rank problem severity and to systematize the steps that are to be taken and when. The process is often defined in advance for establishing working groups charged with investigating and making recommendations for issue resolution.

Implemented change management process

A final common element of most outsourcing governance models is change management. Each level of the management structure deals with change as part of its regular agenda, continually negotiating and implementing needed changes. A 360-degree review process is often used to encourage all parties to provide feedback on improvements that could be made to improve results for all parties involved.

10.2.1   Rules of engagement – industry best practices

A successful outsourcing relationship depends on not only having a strong governance process but also a well defined and implemented rules of engagement. These are some of the best practices from the industry examples:

- A "user's" version of the outsourcing contract, defining in business terms the requirements and obligations provided in the contract
- A training session for users of services on what has changed or will change under the outsourcing agreement (sometimes, this is referred to as "what's in, what's out")
- A book of policies, procedures and forms that define the normal interaction requirements between the using organization and the service provider
- A clear definition and communication path for escalation of issues that are not covered by the rules of engagement
- Periodic briefing on changes as a result of governance actions

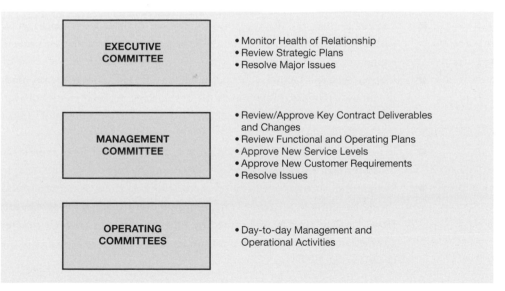

Figure 10.2: Multi-Layer Organizational Links

10.3 Outsourcing governance: performance management

The following factors will help to determine if your organization is effective in managing their outsourcing initiatives:

- Identify the critical success factors for the IT and outsourcing provider and identify the key performance indicators linked to factors
- Build key performance indicators into the contract performance evaluation system
- Make KPIs relevant, simple, comparable, easy to report and focused measurable outcomes
- Define and issue an outsourcing management control policy and related procedures, which identify all of the areas requiring management controls and integrate into contract
- Monitor, audit and assure that governance operates in accordance with the approved Management Controls
- Develop a risk management and mitigation plan, policy and process
- Balance stakeholder needs – companies that successfully outsource continuously "take the pulse" of all stakeholder groups to balance their needs over time
- Pursue stakeholder involvement – on governance boards and steering committees
- Remember that the customer is not always right – governance group participants must keep their minds open and reach across organizational boundaries to understand the motivations of all stakeholders
- Manage the expectations of all stakeholders well. Deliver what you promise; do not over-promise things you or the outsourcing provider cannot deliver. Credibility is a fleeting attribute that if lost, is extremely difficult or almost impossible to regain
- Experience matters – governance groups can rapidly fill their experience deficit through SME coaching or outside consulting support.
- SLAs are not enough – service level agreements are extremely important and should be continuously refined and improved over the life of the agreement. However, they must be augmented by other methods to ensure customer satisfaction (e.g. formal and/or informal surveys, listening to the Voice of the Customer, etc.)

In order to assure that there is a strong governance process is in place, a best practice is to conduct what would be the same as a due diligence exercise (as described earlier) and look at all aspects of the provider – from structure to performance to compliance with regulations and requirements.

Continuous monitoring is a key requirement for strong governance. This is also needed to assure that the disaster recover and/or business continuity programs are well maintained and can perform to expectations. In addition to continuous monitoring, "surprise" audits also help in discovering weaknesses in discipline and process deficiency. Generally, good governance requires a thorough audit at least annually, but preferably quarterly.

10.4   Outsourcing governance: management systems and tools

Outsourcing business relationships include not only pre-defined operational services that need to be managed, but, as described above, they also generate a constant stream of discrete projects in response to changing requirements and services. The challenge of project definition, estimation, and measurement grows in proportion to the increase in the number of organizations working together.

10.4.1   Outsourcing project management office

Without a project management office, project spending can spiral out of control, both in terms of the number of projects that get commissioned and the organization's ability to coordinate the work of its providers. The focus of the project management office is to ensure that the right projects get done the right way, and it is typically made up of four major components: project portfolio management, project execution, project tracking and reporting, and project management competency.

Project portfolio management

This means understanding the overall business objectives and ensuring that the right projects are initiated with the appropriate priority. It also means constantly check-pointing these projects back against the changing business needs to make sure that a project that might have been right a few months ago is still right today. It includes stopping projects when the business case no longer makes sense; looking for redundancies and overlaps in the project portfolio; and making project sponsors aware of opportunities to use or reuse work already being done and paid for elsewhere.

Project execution

This requires a level of rigor akin to the kind that went into defining and crafting the outsourcing relationship to begin with. Common internal methods typically prove inadequate for projects involving multiple internal organizations and multiple provider organizations. Greater attention to project definition and workflows is common, as is greater rigor in cost projections.

Project tracking and reporting

This requires a well-defined and agreed-to system for measuring and reporting project information to the central project tracking system. Project tracking and reporting also include the ability to compare project data against industry benchmarks. Project tracking systems are just as important for the project elements done internally as they are for the parts performed by the providers.

Figure 10.3 illustrates the functions typically performed by a project management office (PMO).

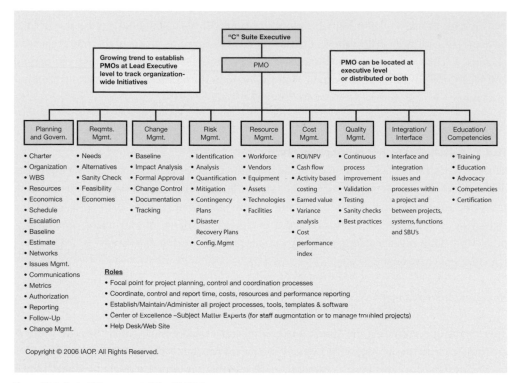

Figure 10.3: Project Management Office (PMO) Structure

Project management competency

This is the fourth element of a good project management office. Common activities here include: the ongoing development of project management standards and supporting tools; maintaining a center of excellence on the discipline of project management; promoting training and certification; and consulting with unit heads on project management.

10.4.2   Contract change management

The objective of contract change management is not to prevent change, but to permit change to occur in an orderly process. Guidelines and considerations include:

- Formal recognition, justification and approval are mandatory
- Mandatory versus discretionary changes
- For changes:
  - Why needed/necessary?
  - Cost/benefit?
  - Assessment of impact?
- For discretionary changes:
  - Who pays?
  - Negotiations
- Verify change requirement and obtain approvals through executive champion
- Define reserves (and contingencies) in time, cash, and resources
- Consider all the effects the change will have on the project baseline
- Evaluate alternatives
- Document the changes
- Track the changes and report on their progress

Figure 10.4 shows the common aspects of a robust change management process.

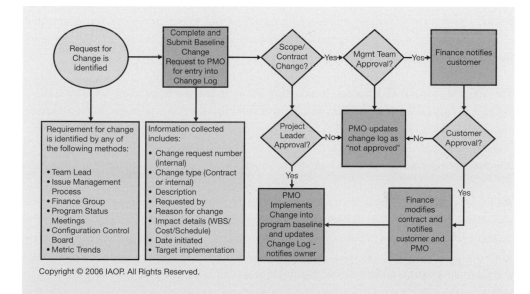

Figure 10.4: Change Management

10.4.3 The Outsourcing Business Plan (OBP) as a ongoing management tool

Outsourcing professionals also take the lead in implementing planning tools to help ensure alignment between the organizations involved in the outsourcing business relationship.

One example is a regularly updated outsourcing business plan putting a formal process in place for periodically reviewing and updating all aspects of the relationship between the companies. A shared commitment to its development as well as the process to be followed can be, and often is, written right into the outsourcing contract. Frequency can vary, but annually is the most common – aligned with the customer's annual planning cycle.

The business plan itself is made up of four key sections: strategy, operations, financial, and management. The strategy section of the business plan realigns the relationship and services to any changes in the organization's corporate direction and objectives, both operational and financial. In addition, it reviews the previous year's performance to identify any gaps that may have developed. It is also an opportunity to identify new initiatives and services that the provider will introduce to support the organization's changing needs. Changes in the business climate that may positively or negatively affect either the organization's business or the specific services and the way they are delivered are identified and assessed. Finally, the initiatives and targets in response to all of these considerations are described.

The next section of the business plan operationalizes the initiatives outlined in the strategic section. It describes the specific actions to be taken, along with the deliverables, dates, and responsibilities. The specific steps to be taken in achieving goals are stated, such as new service launches, process improvement, and cost reduction. New and revised scorecards are documented, as well as any required changes in the data collection and reporting. The required steps for any formal contract updates are laid out.

The financial section updates the outsourcing business case to reflect new investments and changes in costs, pricing, and pricing models. It ensures that the financial impacts of any changes are identified, justified, and agreed to by both parties.

The management section reviews the strengths and weaknesses of the current management process, along with any changes to be implemented during the upcoming period. This may include planned personnel changes, training programs, new management tools to be implemented, and so on. Communications is also an important part of the updated management plan. This includes communications in both the organization and provider, upward and downward, to the users of the services, and any other stakeholders who need to be updated on the current status and planned direction of the relationship and the services being provided.

Another type of interdependent planning tool is risk assessment. The purpose of joint risk assessment planning is twofold. First, it recognizes that as effective as scorecards are for managing performance, they are essentially trailing indicators – looking at what has happened and at best suggesting where things may be headed. Risk assessment, on the other hand, is a forward-looking tool that is an early warning system of problems to come. Second, it recognizes that, as organizations become increasingly interdependent through outsourcing, the risks any one company faces are risks that all of the companies in the delivery network face. As companies work with outsourcing providers worldwide in many areas that directly affect their ability to get products to market or support current customers, identifying the circumstances that could jeopardize a provider's ability to deliver is critical. When done jointly, it becomes a powerful planning tool for both organizations.

Outsourcing risk assessment uses a consistent, repeatable methodology to categorize and examine the business risks providers face. These risks are often grouped at the highest level into "risk families," such as infrastructure risks, business control risks, business value risks, and relationship risks. The specific risks within each category are then identified, ranked for potential impact, and evaluated for probability. By making this a joint review, looking at both the customer's and the provider's environment, the level of risk can be reduced.

10.4.4 Value health check survey

In any management system, there are three key fundamentals for making sure that the management system is sound and will deliver predictable results: **Effectiveness** (is the relationship yielding the results that were expected?), **Efficiency** (are the results being provided in line with the plans, expectations and productivity?) and finally, **Health of the relationship** (will the relationship consistently deliver results on an on going basis?). Most governance processes, tools and systems adequately provide support for the first two of these dimensions. However, without a thorough evaluation and continuous effort, the health of the relationship may not survive the test of time. Therefore, it is important that despite the ongoing governance success, the customer and providers periodically check the health of their relationship.

The Sourcing Relationship Value Framework (Figure 10.5) consists of the five key domains of business value delivered through global sourcing relationships: Financial Performance, Sourcing Capabilities, Service Quality, Risk/Compliance and Governance. Each domain is supported by a delineation of the value drivers (the standards) that are critical to outsourcing performance. By systematically and periodically reviewing customer/provider relationships through the lens of the five domains and key value drivers, customers and service providers are able to identify opportunities for value improvement and/or mitigate areas of potential value leakage. Our experience suggests that sustainable, high performing outsourcing and/or shared service center relationships typically strike a dynamic balance across these five key areas of business value. High performing relationships also consistently maintain alignment around the priority of the value drivers and the perception of value actually realized from the outsourcing or shared service center relationship.

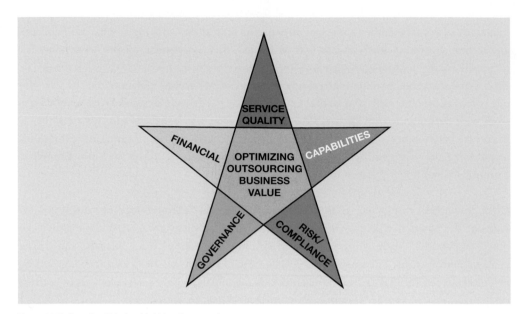

Figure 10.5: Sourcing Relationship Value Framework.

IAOP has developed a tool (available to members and non-members for a nominal fee) that assists the two parties in evaluating the health of their relationship. It is called "Value Health Check Survey". Figure 10.6 below shows the importance of this tool. More detailed information about the tool and its use is available from IAOP.

10.4.5 Knowledge management in governance

The cornerstone of a long term successful outsourcing engagement is managing the knowledge – throughout the entire life cycle of outsourcing. There are four key aspects of managing the knowledge:

1. Establishing the knowledge requirements (such as process diagrams, tools, metrics) and responsibility for creating, maintaining and communicating it
2. Creating a knowledge database where it is kept and maintained
3. Clearly defining the ownership and accountability for the knowledge database – done through the contract terms
4. Principles for using the database – especially when the database is being used by more than one function or companies.

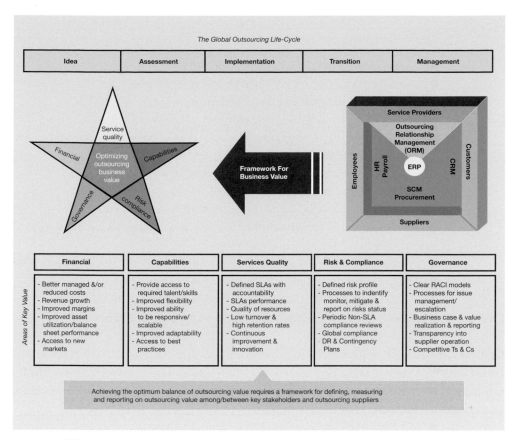

The Global Outsourcing Life-Cycle

Idea	Assessment	Implementation	Transition	Management

Financial	Capabilities	Services Quality	Risk & Compliance	Governance
- Better managed &/or reduced costs - Revenue growth - Improved margins - Improved asset utilization/balance sheet performance - Access to new markets	- Provide access to required talent/skills - Improved flexibility - Improved ability to be responsive/ scalable - Improved adaptability - Access to best practices	- Defined SLAs with accountability - SLAs performance - Quality of resources - Low turnover & high retention rates - Continuous improvement & innovation	- Defined risk profile - Processes to indentify monitor, mitigate & report on risks status - Periodic Non-SLA compliance reviews - Global compliance DR & Contingency Plans	- Clear RACI models - Processes for issue management/ escalation - Business case & value realization & reporting - Transparency into supplier operation - Competitive Ts & Cs

Achieving the optimum balance of outsourcing value requires a framework for defining, measuring and reporting on outsourcing value among/between key stakeholders and outsourcing suppliers

Figure 10.6: IAOP – Value Health Check Survey

10.5   Outsourcing governance: continuous improvement

- ■ Assessing goals and changing business needs
- ■ Assessing current providers
- ■ Renegotiating existing relationships
- ■ Integrating previous lessons into future initiatives

10.5.1   Provider management

How can you tell if your current provider is getting into trouble? Most important, how can you tell before their problem becomes yours?

There are two things to look for. The first is negative trends in the provider's current performance. The second is changes in the provider's overall business condition that may lead to performance problems down the road.

Current performance:

- Inconsistency in the level of service provided
- Increase in the 'noise level' about the provider's services
- Problems getting passed around and not solved
- More frequent need to escalate problems to get them fixed
- Increasingly rigid interpretation of scope of service, costs, and other contractual terms
- Unanticipated turnover at the management level
- Unanticipated turnover in the employee ranks
- Frequent requests for you to better prioritize your requirements
- Less interest in opportunities to provide new or expanded services to your company
- Increased visibility of problems with the provider's sub-contractors
- A perceived change in your importance as a customer
- Less frequent contact with the provider's senior management
- Inconsistent information from people on the provider's team

Overall business condition:

- Deteriorating financial condition at the balance sheet, P&L, cash flow, credit, or equity levels
- New marketplace, legal, or public relations issues
- Increase in executive turnover
- Increase in employee turnover
- Declining client retention rate
- Loss of one or more major current customers
- Negative change in financial condition of one or more major customers
- Win of a major new customer
- Entry to or exit from a new line of business, geography
- Problems in the parent company or other large business unit
- Problems with a major sub-contractor

10.5.2 Exiting

The key to getting the right exit provisions is asking the right key questions:

- Why will you want to terminate?
  - For cause
  - For convenience
  - Normal contract end

- What termination rights do each party have?
- What will you do when the contract terminates?
- What will you need from your service provider to make a smooth transition either to another service provider or to return to sourcing in-house?
- How and what incentives will you give the service provider to provide termination assistance?
- Can you build for exist? (e.g. have the service provider maintain some of your facilities on your premises, etc.)
- Could you use early termination assistance to reduce risk?

10.5.3 Transition back (or to third party) upon exiting

One of the key aspects of exiting is to understand the transition process that is necessary so that the work can be retrieved in-house or outsourced to another third party. There are some important issues that must be well defined during the strategy stage, negotiated during the implementation stage and then executed during the management stage. Although most of the issues and steps are similar to transitioning out to the outsourcer, there are some additional topics that must be addressed:

- Assistance required from the service provider to help in transition back. This may include use of SMEs, tools knowledge transfer and even transfer of "key" employees.
- Disposition of process related assets
- Access to and availability of systems, documentation etc during and after transition back
- Business continuity during the disruption stage

10.6 Assessing outsourcing process maturity

While the outsourcing process is a sequential five stages, it also needs to form a closed loop as the management of current relationships set the stage for what is strategically possible in the future.

This is not only true for each individual opportunity pursued, it is just as true for assessing the maturity of an organization's overall process.

An industry best practice framework (such as CMMI) can also be used to analyze current and target state maturity levels for outsourcing:

Initial Level: The outsourcing process is characterized as ad hoc and occasionally even chaotic. Few processes are defined and success depends on individual efforts.

Repeatable Level: Basic outsourcing processes are established. The necessary discipline is in place to repeat earlier successes.

Defined Level: The outsourcing processes are documented, standardized, and integrated into the management policies and procedures. All governance processes are implemented using approved, tailored versions of the IT governance policy.

Managed Level: The organization defines, collects and makes decisions based on outsourcing process measurements. Outsourcing processes and deliverables and metrics are quantitatively understood, reported and controlled.

Optimizing Level: Continuous process improvement is enabled by quantitative feedback from the process, from piloting innovative outsourcing ideas and from adopting external industry best practices and standards.

10.7 List of key terms

Governance
Outsourcing Project Management Office (OPMO)
Rules of Engagement
Value Health Check Survey

10.8 List of templates

10.1 Outsourcing Governance Plan

10.2 Assessing Results versus Expectations - Critical Success Factors (CSFs) and Key Performance Indicators (KPIs) for Outsourcing

10.3 Post-Operation Financial Review of an Outsourcing Decision

10.4 Outsourcing Process Maturity

10.9 Article on governance

Appendix H has a detailed article authored by Jagdish Dalal, Managing Director, Thought Leadership for IAOP on the topic of Governance. Professionals are encouraged to review it in the context of this module.

10.10 Additional references

William Metz, COP, "PMO as a Governance Tool," Outsourcing World Summit Presentation, February 24, 2004, Lake Buena Vista, FL.

David Jarman, "Welcome to the Workplace," Outsourcing World Summit Presentation, February 24, 2004, Lake Buena Vista, FL.

Jean-Francois Poisson, COP, "The Outsourcing Business Plan," The 2002 Outsourcing World Summit Presentation, February 20, 2002, Lake Buena Vista, FL.

James Brian Quinn, Frederick Julien, and Michael Negrin, "Outsourcing Strategy: Managing Strategic Risk," published April 4, 2001, http://www.outsourcingprofessional.org/firmbuilder

Zia Qureshi, COP, Business Catalyst, "Managing Outsourcing for Sustainable Value – Addressing the Missing Pieces of the Puzzle", Outsourcing World Summit Presentation, 2008

Marni Dicker & Jean Francois Poisson, COP; SNC Lavalin-Profac/Nexacor, "Re-Competing Outsourcing Agreements: A Third Generation of Outsourcing Contracts", Outsourcing World Summit Presentation, 2008

Unisys, "Beyond SLAs: Rethinking the Metrics of Outsourcing and Realizing True Bsuiness Value" published October 6, 2009

Matt Shocklee, COP, GSOS, "How to Optimize Outsourcing Value Through Advanced Tools and Technologies ", European Outsourcing Summit Presentation, 2009

Eus Pontenagel, COP International Business Development, Quint Wellington, "Supply-Demand Governance Framework & Outsourcing Globalization", Asia Outsourcing Summit Presentation, 2009

Danny Ertel, COP, Owner, Principal and Partner, Vantage Partners, LLC, "For Better or Worse: Maturing of Relationship Management in the Industry", Outsourcing World Summit Presentation, 2010

Kurt Kohorst, COP, Vice President, Liberty Mutual Insurance, "Practical Lessons on Onshore Transitions – Bringing Work Back In-House", Outsourcing World Summit Presentation, 2010

Appendix A
Glossary of outsourcing terms

A1.   Business terms

Activity-Based Costing: Activity-based costing looks at aspects of an organization's operations and attempts to answer the very simple, but sometimes hard to answer question, "How much does it cost to do *that*?" For example, how much does a company spend processing a receivable or taking a customer call? How much does it cost a city to fill a pothole? The term relates to outsourcing in that once an organization can answer the cost question at the activity level, it can more objectively compare the cost of internal versus external sourcing for performing it.

ARC: "Additional Resource Charge" is the pricing band for volume greater than baseline volume defined in the contract.

ASPs: Application Service Providers are companies that remotely host software applications and provide access to and use of the applications over the internet or a private network. Typically, the service fee is usage based, for example, per user per month. Although the term itself has somewhat fallen into disfavor because of the number of ASPs that were formed and then failed at the end of the dot-com bubble, today almost all outsourcing service providers rely on the ASP model for linking aspects of their services to the customer organizations.

Barriers to Outsourcing: Companies often see resistance, especially from inside the organization, to outsourcing. Commonly referred to as 'barriers to outsourcing' the most common ones are: fear of loss of control, viewing an activity as too critical to outsource, loss of flexibility, concern over potential customer issues, and concerns over potential employee issues. All of these barriers can not only be overcome but turned into positives through properly structured and managed outsourcing relationships.

Benchmark: An objective measure of performance that can be used to compare operations across organizations. Most commonly used to compare the cost for an activity, but can also be applied just as effectively to other aspects of an operation. For example, day's sales outstanding would be used to compare the performance of companies to each other in their collections activities. The comparison is often termed in quartiles, with the top quartile being the best 25 percent of companies and the bottom quartile being the poorest 25 percent.

Best-of-Breed Sourcing: When a business divides the outsourced work between different providers based on their capability matched against requirements, it is considered to be a "best of breed sourcing" model.

BPO: Business Process Outsourcing puts together two powerful business tools - business process management and outsourcing. Business process management uses technology to break down barriers between traditional functional silos, such as those found in finance, order processing, and call centers. Outsourcing uses skills and resources of specialized outside service providers to perform many of these critical, yet non-core activities. BPO means examining the processes that make up the business and its functional units, and then working with specialized service providers to both reengineer and outsource them at the same time.

Bundled Sourcing: When a company bundles multiple processes and sub-processes into a single transaction and outsources as a whole. Generally, this is done to achieve a greater level of process efficiency and take advantage of technology installation, such as ERP.

Captive Center: A company-owned offshore operation. The activities are performed offshore, but they are not outsourced to another company.

Case Study: A case study is a more collaborative approach to defining a customer's requirements styled after a Harvard Business Review case. It is used to engage a small number of pre-qualified providers in the conceptual design, development, and proposal of an outsourcing solution.

Change Management: Change management is recognizing and addressing the questions and fears expressed by various stakeholders who are affected by outsourcing. Communication is a key element within Change Management.

Commercialization: Outsourcing often provides an opportunity for an organization to 'commercialize,' that is, generate incremental revenue dollars or equity value, from its internal operations. This can be done in many ways, such as selling existing internal assets to the provider, licensing intellectual properties, and entering into a strategic alliance or joint venture with a provider.

Commoditization: Power is essentially shifting from the producers of goods and services to the consumers. As a result, a company's ability to command a higher price for the unique value it offers lasts only for a shorter and shorter period of time. Once commoditized, a product or service can no longer be differentiated in the marketplace and is selected by the customer based almost exclusively on price.

Consortium Sourcing: Several units and/or companies can jointly outsource an activity (by forming a formal or informal consortium) in order to gain economies of scale. Cloud computing is designed to provide a platform for such activity.

Core Competencies: The unique internal skills and knowledge sets that define an organization's competitive advantage – as seen by its customers. Core competencies are usually limited in number and are embodied in the organization's products and services rather than being the actual products or services themselves. For example, Microsoft's core competencies are software design, development, and marketing. Chrysler's are product design, process design, and marketing. These are the capabilities that enable these companies to produce and sell their uniquely competitive products for the customers they serve.

Critical versus Core: Many operations are critical to a business's operations but do not represent a differentiating competitive capability; that is, they are not core competencies. A classic example is payroll. Processing payroll accurately and timely is critical to the success of any organization, but is a core competency of very few organizations – mainly those that provide this service to other companies as their business.

Due Diligence: The due diligence – or provider evaluation - process begins before identifying the potential providers and continues through the acquisition process (RFI, RFP and contracting) and eventually becomes a part of the ongoing governance process.

EBITDA: "Earnings Before Income Tax, Depreciation and Amortization". This is a measure of net impact of savings on profit.

E-Sourcing: Internet-based outsourcing that takes advantage of the application service provider (ASP) delivery model. This approach enables the delivery of business process outsourcing over the Internet.

Functional Process Outsourcing: A company's business processes end at its true customers, the people paying the bills. There are, however, many internal processes that exist to support people within the company and are often performed within a single department. Human resources, finance and accounting, travel, and facilities services are examples. When these functional processes are outsourced, along with the supporting technologies and supply chains that feed into them, it is referred to as functional process outsourcing.

Gain-sharing: A contract structure where both the customer and provider share financially in the value created through the relationship. One example is when a service provider receives a share of the savings it generates for its client.

GBPOV: The Global BPO Value Equation is an expanded value model for outsourcing where: GBPOV = [(Business case) x (Acceleration + Flexibility)] ^ Innovation. That is, the full value of global business process outsourcing is the traditional business case multiplied by the improvement to the organization's acceleration and flexibility, all raised to the power of innovation.

Governance: The oversight and management of all aspects of an outsourcing relationship. Areas of focus include: change management, communications management, performance management, operational management, risk management, strategic management, and others.

Just-in-Time Sourcing: The organization adopts a continuous sourcing planning process that takes place on a project-by-project basis. Sourcing decisions are considered to last only as long as the projects that created the need for them. Shared services centers are often managed this way, with the organization's internal customers free to take their business on a project-by-project basis to the source they believe can best contribute to the outcomes they seek, whether that source is inside or outside the organization.

Knowledge Management: Knowledge management is the explicit and systematic management of vital knowledge – and its associated processes of creation, organization, diffusion, use and exploitation.

Knowledge Process Outsourcing (KPO): Knowledge process outsourcing is becoming prevalent to describe services where there is a greater content of using deeper level knowledge (domain, topic, data mining) as a part of the process.

Make versus Buy: Outsourcing is often referred to as a 'make versus buy' decision on the part of the customer. The question is, "Is it in the organization's best interests to continue to (or start to) perform the activity itself using its own people, process expertise, and technology or to 'buy' the activity from the service provider marketplace?"

Market-Driven Sourcing: A market-driven approach to sourcing means that the organization's sourcing decisions are in direct response to the capabilities of the marketplace of available providers. Where the organization's internal capabilities are superior to the marketplace of providers, the activity is performed internally; where they are not, the activity is performed externally.

Master Agreement: Agreement between customer and service provider containing terms that apply to all current and future services agreement. It also contains schedules that define overall conditions and requirements.

Nearshore Outsourcing: When companies select a destination country that is closer to the home country where work is performed (e.g. Canada, Costa Rica for US based companies or Ireland for English companies)

Net Present Value: Net present value (NPV) is a standard method for the financial appraisal of long-term projects. Used for capital budgeting, and widely throughout economics, it measures the excess or shortfall of cash flows, in present value terms, once financing charges are met.

Offshore Outsourcing: The outsourcing of any operation, whether information technology, a business process, or manufacturing, to a company whose principal base of operation is outside the country. Terms such as near-shore outsourcing or close-shore outsourcing are also used to indicate that while still outside the country, there is a closer proximity between the customer organization's primary operations and that of the provider. For example, for a US company Canada might be considered near-shore while India is offshore.

Offshore/Offshoring: Performing or sourcing any part of an organization's activities at or from a location outside the company's home country. Companies create captive centers offshore, where the employees work for them, or outsource offshore, where the employees work for the outsourcing provider.

Outsourcing: A long-term, results-oriented relationship with an external service provider for activities traditionally performed within the company. Outsourcing usually applies to a complete business process. It implies a degree of managerial control and risk on the part of the provider.

Outsourcing at the Customer Interface: Outsourcing where a provider assumes responsibility for direct interaction with an organization's customers. This interaction may be in person, over the telephone, via email, mail, or any other direct means.

Outsourcing Framework: The outsourcing framework is a structure for mapping all of the activities of an organization in a way that allows consistent evaluation, planning, implementation, and management of sourcing decisions.

Outsourcing Process: A repeatable, multistage, management process for identifying outsourcing opportunities and moving those opportunities from concept though implementation and ongoing management.

Outsourcing Process Maturity: Uses an industry best practice framework (such as CMMI) to analyze current and target state maturity levels for outsourcing

Outsourcing Teams: Multi-disciplinary working groups that form for specific purposes throughout the outsourcing process.

Out-tasking: The term out tasking implies that the business is responsible for the entire process except for a task that is done by a third party provider. It is often applied in the context of manufacturing processes where a business engages a third-party manufacturer to perform a manufacturing task (such as anodizing a formed part).

Performance-Based Pricing: Contractual pricing mechanisms that link compensation to meeting specific performance objectives or outcomes.

Process Enterprise: A process enterprise operates its business as a collection of end-to-end business processes where executive leadership, education, responsibilities, measurement, and reward systems are all oriented to this view of the business's operations. This process orientation is in direct contrast to the traditional hierarchical view of an organization.

Provider: See entry for *Service Provider*

Regulation Compliance: Outsourcing processes must comply to all regulations (state, country, industry, financial market) and the sourcing process must recognize the impact of these regulations on the strategy, implementation and governance of outsourcing

Risk: Risk refers to the chance for unexpected negative business outcomes resulting from internal or external factors. There are four major classes of risk associated with outsourcing: strategic risk, operational risk, result risk, and transactional risk.

RFI – Request for Information: A document requesting information from potential outsourcing service providers demonstrating their capabilities, resources, experiences, and overall approach to providing services.

RFP – Request for Proposal: A document detailing a customer's outsourcing requirements and the evaluation criteria that will be used for selecting the ultimate provider. RFP's are typically sent to a limited number of potential providers, around three to five, that have been previously qualified as capable of delivering the needed services.

RRC – "Reduced Resource Charges" The pricing band for volume lower than baseline volume defined in the contract.

Rural Sourcing: When a provider establishes a center in a rural area where the labor rates may be lower than an urban-metro area and companies take advantage of such an arrangement

Scope of Services: The services provided under an outsourcing agreement.

Scorecard (Balanced Scorecard): A scorecard, or balanced scorecard, is a way of measuring how much value has been delivered through the outsourcing relationship. Scorecards attempt to look at benefits beyond the mere level of service (see Service Level Agreement, below) and may include measures of overall economic value achieved, such as revenue, share price, market share changes, or measures of business-wide achievements, such as, speed to market and innovation.

Services Agreement: Agreement between customer and service provider containing terms for a specific process outsourcing and is supporting the terms laid out in the Master Agreement. However, a services agreement may overrule certain terms in the Master Agreement.

Service Level Agreement (SLA): Outsourcing is a service. The service level agreement, or SLA, defines the intended or expected level of service. For example, how quickly a service will be performed, what availability, quality and cost targets will be met, what level of customer satisfaction will be achieved. In essence, every outsourcing agreement is made up of three basic elements: a description of the services to be performed; a scorecard or SLA defining in objective, measurable terms the standards for the delivery of each service, and; a pricing formula for how the service provider will be compensated.

Service Provider: A company that provides outsourcing services. Terms such as provider, vendor, and partner are often used interchangeably each carrying a slightly different connotation intended by the user.

Shared Services (Shared Services Centers): Shared services are common activities that are used by more than one division or unit within the company. When these services are combined into a central operation they are often referred to as shared services centers.

Skills: Skills and disciplines required for the members of outsourcing teams through all phases. Some of the skills are common through all phases (such as communication) while some skills are specific – specialized for a particular phase (such as tax and treasury for implementation phase when contract terms are being defined)

Sourcing: Sourcing is generally the broadest term used in the field. It reflects the simple but essential point that everything the organization does has to be 'sourced' in some way – internally, externally, or a mix of the two.

Sourcing-as-Strategy: Sourcing-as-strategy is a powerful way to improve an organization's ability to serve customers, compete in its markets, and grow. It is a strategic approach to outsourcing that involves mapping the markets the organization plans to serve, the competitive advantages it seeks in each market, and then identifying the sources of those competitive advantages – whether they come from inside or outside the organization.

Stakeholders: Stakeholders represent all people whot have a vested interest in a business or organization (economically mostly). These include shareholders, affected employees, unaffected employees, shareholders, industry influencers (watchers as well as market makers), partners, customers, suppliers and even the civic community where the business is located.

Strategic Outsourcing: Outsourcing to achieve better return on investment and accelerated growth. Strategic outsourcing is approached as a redirection of the organization's resources toward its highest value-creating activities – its core competencies.

Supply Chain: The interlinked chain of contractors and subcontractors that provides components, subcomponents, and services that become part of the company's deliverable to its customers. Typically used to refer to the chain of suppliers in a manufacturing company's operation, but is also used more generally in regard to any product or service.

Tactical Outsourcing: Outsourcing to achieve operational efficiencies. Tactical outsourcing is approached as a competition between existing internal operations and outside service providers.

Transactions: Business process outsourcing often involves transaction-intensive processes. Transactions, by their very nature, are clearly defined sets of related actions making them easy to describe, measure, and monitor. They are information-intensive and repetitive. While they are certainly critical to the operation of any business, they seldom offer much opportunity for creating competitive advantage.

Transformation: Activities that will transform the current customer's process (and/or systems) into a higher performing process.

Transformational Outsourcing: Outsourcing to take advantage of innovation and new business models. Transformational outsourcing is approached as a way to fundamentally reposition the organization in its markets. The term *Business Transformational Outsourcing* is also used to combine this idea with that of *Business Process Outsourcing*.

Transition: Transfer of responsibility from customer to the service provider.

Value Proposition: What value is the organization looking to gain through outsourcing? Overall, about half of organizations state that reducing costs is their primary reason for outsourcing. This also means that something other than cost savings is the primary value sought in the other half of the cases. The other reasons most frequently cited are: focus on core competencies, a more variable cost structure, access to needed skills, grow revenue, improve quality, conserve capital dollars, and increase innovation.

X-sourcing: There is an extensive list of prefixes put on the word sourcing to suggest a specific approach to outsourcing. Co-sourcing, smart-sourcing, e-sourcing, in-sourcing, business process outsourcing, strategic sourcing, strategic outsourcing, and multi-sourcing are just a few. Each has a slightly different meaning intended by the person using it to indicate a slightly different approach to outsourcing.

Zero-Based Sourcing: Zero-based sourcing means that the sourcing decision for each and every aspect of a business's operation is re-justified every planning cycle from an assumed base of zero. This approach ensures that the organization is consistently and objectively re-testing its internal operations against the best available external solutions.

Appendix B
Templates

These templates are provided as reference only. Files containing template blanks are available from IAOP during the Master Class.

Template 1.1   Defining Outsourcing

Every organization needs to define outsourcing in clear, easy to communicate terms that individuals at all levels both inside and outside the organization can understand. Use the following template to develop that definition for your organization.

Key Outsourcing Criteria:	What Does This Mean to Your Organization?
Long-term: Organization 'divesting' itself of a capability or choosing not to create it.	
Results-oriented: Provider 'at risk' for delivery of operation or business outcomes, not simply providing resources/ doing the work.	
Specialized services provider: Provider chosen for expertise and focus, not just willing to take on the work and do it cheaper.	
Other	
Other	

Template 1.2   External Business Drivers

Understanding both external and internal business drivers upon the business is key to any decision to use outsourcing. For your organization, define and rate the criticality of each of the following external business drivers as an influencer to use outsourcing.

Define each external driver as it relates to your organization and then rate its priority as a influencer for or against outsourcing.

1	2	3	4	5
None	Low	Medium	High	Critical

External Business Driver	How Relates to Your Business	Priority 1 - 5
Shortened Product Life Cycle		
Changes in Customers, Customer Needs, Marketplace		
Competition		
Financials		
Technology		
Regulation, Deregulation, Laws		
Mergers, Acquisitions, Divestitures		
Others		

Template 1.3   Internal Business Drivers

Both external and internal business drivers are key to the increased use of outsourcing. For your organization define and rate the criticality of each of the following internal business drivers for outsourcing.

Define each internal driver as it relates to your organization and then rate its priority as a business driver for (or against) outsourcing.

1	2	3	4	5
None	Low	Medium	High	Critical

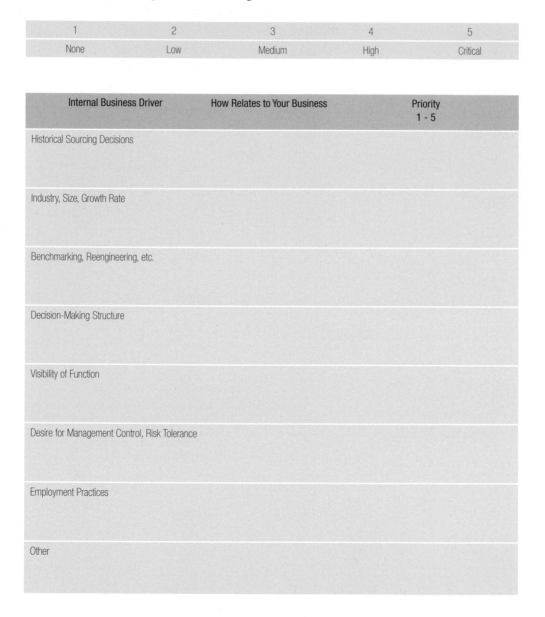

Internal Business Driver	How Relates to Your Business	Priority 1 - 5
Historical Sourcing Decisions		
Industry, Size, Growth Rate		
Benchmarking, Reengineering, etc.		
Decision-Making Structure		
Visibility of Function		
Desire for Management Control, Risk Tolerance		
Employment Practices		
Other		

Template 1.4 Organizational Evaluation Factors
(Shared Services and Outsourcing)

The following template provides for assessing the feasibility for the selection between establishing a shared services center or outsourcing the function. Importance to the business establishes the sensitivity of the factor. "Applies to us" determines whether that factor has a high, medium or low impact on the business. The last two columns may be used to indicate the appropriateness of the option based on the responses to the other columns. You can also assign weights to each factor, creating a numerical value.

Importance to business H/M/L	Consideration Factor	Applies to us H/M/L	Shared Services Y/N	Outsour-cing Y/N
	Political and functional maturity			
	Initial investment – start up capital/expense			
	On going capital investment availability			
	Subject matter expertise in the process			
	Systems platform (adequacy from functional and technical points of view)			
	Staffing availability			
	HR infrastructure to create new (or adopt) classes of employees and offer differing incentives for performance			
	Management availability for managing the center			
	Competitor's implementation			

Template 1.5   Anticipated Outsourcing Benefits

It is important to gain a common understanding of the anticipated benefits from outsourcing and their relative importance to the business. For each benefit, define it for your business (quantify the expected benefits if possible) and rate its relative priority.

Define each anticipated benefit from outsourcing as it relates to your organization and then rate its priority as a desired outcome.

1	2	3	4	5
None	Low	Medium	High	Critical

Anticipated Benefit	Define Benefit for Your Organization	Priority 1 - 5
Reduce, Contain, and/or Avoid Costs		
Improve Focus		
More Variable Cost Structure		
Access to Skills Not Available Internally		
More effective utilization of company resources – staff, money, etc		
Improved Quality		
Increased Speed		
Revenue and Margin Growth		
Reduce Capital Requirements		
Innovation		
Other		

Template 1.6 Gauging Organizational Outsourcing Maturity

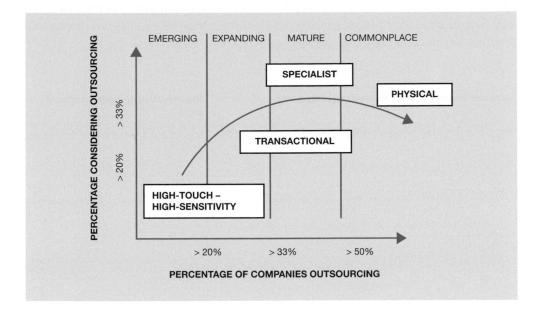

What areas does your organization currently outsource? List examples along the maturity curve as shown above and note the benefits sought and achieved for each.

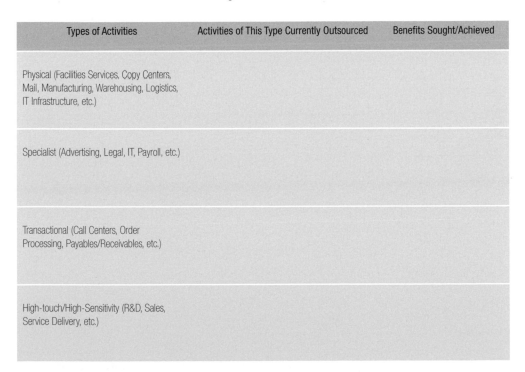

Types of Activities	Activities of This Type Currently Outsourced	Benefits Sought/Achieved
Physical (Facilities Services, Copy Centers, Mail, Manufacturing, Warehousing, Logistics, IT Infrastructure, etc.)		
Specialist (Advertising, Legal, IT, Payroll, etc.)		
Transactional (Call Centers, Order Processing, Payables/Receivables, etc.)		
High-touch/High-Sensitivity (R&D, Sales, Service Delivery, etc.)		

Template 1.7   Common Business Process Framework

The Common Business Process Framework (in the left-hand column below) provides a structure and terminology for identifying common business processes. Map your company's organizational structure and operational areas to the framework.

Common Business Process (Outsourcing) Framework	Company Structure and Operational Areas
1. Operational Services (Value Chain)	
1.1. Marketplace Research and Analysis	
1.1.1. Customer Needs Research and Analysis	
1.1.2. Customer Satisfaction Measurement	
1.1.3. External Business and Technology Research and Analysis	
1.2. Product Research, Development, Manufacture, and Delivery	
1.2.1. Product Research and Development	
1.2.2. Product Prototype and Test	
1.2.3. Capital Goods and Technology Acquisition	
1.2.4. Materials and Supplies Acquisition	
1.2.5. Inbound Logistics Management	
1.2.6. Component Manufacturing	
1.2.7. Product Assembly, Test, and Packaging	
1.2.8. Product Warehousing, Distribution, and Delivery	
1.2.9. Product Installation and Service	
1.3. Service Research, Development, Staffing, and Delivery	
1.3.1. Service Research and Development	
1.3.2. Service Prototype and Test	
1.3.3. Capital Goods and Technology Acquisition	
1.3.4. Materials and Supplies Acquisition	
1.3.5. Human Resources Acquisition and Development	
1.3.6. Service Delivery to Customer	

Common Business Process (Outsourcing) Framework	Company Structure and Operational Areas

1.4.	Marketing
1.4.1.	Marketing Plan Development
1.4.2.	Product and Service Advertising
1.4.3.	Product and Service Promotion
1.5.	Sales
1.5.1.	Sales Plan Development
1.5.2.	Field Sales
1.5.3.	Call Center Sales (Teleservices)
1.6.	Customer Relationship Management
1.6.1.	Customer Order-processing
1.6.2.	Customer Service, Inquiries, and Complaint-handling
1.6.3.	Customer Relationship Management (CRM) System Development and Management
2.	Management and Support Services
2.1.	Human Resource Management
2.1.1.	Human Resource Strategy Development
2.1.2.	Recruit, Select, and Hire Employees
2.1.3.	Develop and Train Employees
2.1.4.	Employee Relocation
2.1.5.	Outplacement Services
2.1.6.	Base and Variable Compensation Plan Development and Management
2.1.7.	Employee Satisfaction, Workplace Health, and Safety Management
2.1.8.	Employee Benefits Management and Administration
2.1.9.	Internal Communications and Labor Relations Management
2.1.10.	Human Resource Information Systems (HRIS) Development and Management
2.2.	Information and Communications Technology Management
2.2.1.	Information and Communications Technology Strategy Development
2.2.2.	Data Center Design and Management

Common Business Process (Outsourcing) Framework	Company Structure and Operational Areas
2.2.3. Distributed System Design and Management	
2.2.4. Desktop/Mobile System Design and Management	
2.2.5. Data Network Design and Management	
2.2.6. Communications Systems and Network Design and Management	
2.2.7. Internet Services (including Web hosting)	
2.2.8. Application Development and Maintenance	
2.2.9. Enterprise Resource Planning (ERP) System Development and Maintenance	
2.2.10. Data and Database Management and Maintenance	
2.2.11. Help Desk Services	
2.2.12. Systems Security and Controls Management	

Common Business Process (Outsourcing) Framework	Company Structure & Operational Areas

2.3.	Document Management
2.3.1.	Document Layout and Design
2.3.2.	Document Imaging, Storage, and Distribution
2.3.3.	Printing and Publishing
2.3.4.	Centralized and Convenience Copy Services

2.4.	Financial Management
2.4.1.	Budget, Cash Flow, and Risk Management
2.4.2.	Accounts Payable Processing
2.4.3.	Payroll Processing
2.4.4.	Invoicing, Accounts Receivables, Credits, and Collections Processing
2.4.5.	Travel and Entertainment Expense Management and Processing
2.4.6.	Internal and External Financial Accounting and Reporting
2.4.7.	Internal Auditing
2.4.8.	Tax Management and Processing
2.4.9.	Financial Information Systems (FIS) Development and Maintenance

2.5.	Real Estate and Capital Asset Management
2.5.1.	Real Estate and Capital Asset Plan Development and Project Management
2.5.2.	Real Estate and Capital Asset Transaction Management
2.5.3.	Real Estate and Capital Asset Engineering and Maintenance
2.5.4.	Energy Management

2.6.	Facility Services
2.6.1.	Food and Cafeteria Services
2.6.2.	Mailroom Services
2.6.3.	Shipping and Receiving
2.6.4.	Security
2.6.5.	Parking

2.7.	Administrative Services
2.7.1.	Secretarial/Clerical Services
2.7.2.	Data Entry/Transcription Services
2.7.3.	Records Management

Common Business Process (Outsourcing) Framework	Company Structure & Operational Areas
2.7.4. Travel Services	
2.7.5. Workplace Supplies Management	
2.8. Corporate Services	
2.8.1. Purchasing	
2.8.2. External Communications and Public Relations Management	
2.8.3. Legal Services	

Template 1.8   Outsourcing and Offshoring Considerations

Use this template to weight (1-5) and score (1-5) each location being considered for offshore outsourcing. Later templates will examine these factors again relative to specific outsourcing projects.

Factors	Weigh (1-5)	Score (1-5)	Total Score (Weigh x Score)	Notes
Exogenous Factors				
Government Support				
Educational System				
Geopolitical Environment				
Infrastructure				
Catalyst Factors				
Physical and time zone displacement				
Cultural compatibility				
Labor pool				
Language proficiency				
Business Environment				
Cost advantage – direct labor and indirect process				
Process maturity/competitiveness of suppliers				
Supportive people factors				
Security, IP protection				
TOTAL				

Template 2.1   Organizational Capability

Assessing organizational capability (and maturity) is important in establishing and managing the sourcing process. Each of the factors below must be evaluated and, in instances where the capability is deemed to be low, an alternative considered as a part of the decision making process.

Factor	H/M/L	Alternatives / Corrective Actions to be Considered
Outsourcing Competency		
Strategic Coalition		
Customer Impact		
Sourcing Capability		
Process Expertise		
Governance Style		
Relationship Management		

Template 2.2   Outsourcing End-to-End Process

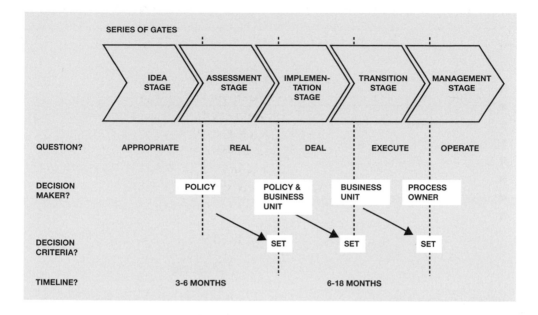

Organization:

Use this template to develop an organization-specific end-to-end process for outsourcing. Refer to each of the five stages of the Outsourcing Process and the Outsourcing Process Checklist on the left column. Considering the existing processes already present in your organization, develop and describe your organization's outsourcing process on the right column.

Outsourcing Process Checklist	How Will This Be Done in Your Organization?
1.0 Idea Stage	
Key Business Question: Which outsourcing opportunities are appropriate for this organization?	
Who are the decision makers for this stage?	
What is the process to be followed in determining the decision criteria?	

Outsourcing Process Checklist	How Will This Be Done in Your Organization?
When will this be done/what is the timeframe for this stage?	
How will the following key activities be performed?	

- Develop concept.
- Perform high level strategic review of operations.
- Identify corporate direction.
- Develop "high insight" reports on outsourcing competitive intelligence.
- Perform business comparative or situation analysis.
- Identify outsourcing potential.
- Get executive concurrence and sponsorship.
- Assign steering committee.

Outsourcing Process Checklist	How Will This Be Done in Your Organization?
2.0 Assessment and Planning Stage	
Key Business Question. With development of the business case and analysis of the provider marketplace, are the anticipated benefits real?	
Who are the decision makers for this Stage?	
What is the process to be followed in determining the decision criteria?	
When will this be done/what is the timeframe for this stage?	
How will the following key activities be performed?	

- Identify current processes.
- Understand user needs.
- Identify internal baseline costs and organization.
- Develop process requirements.
- Perform risk assessment analysis.
- Explore supplier alternatives.
- Develop preliminary outsourcing business case.
- Present to business prime.

Outsourcing Process Checklist	How Will This Be Done in Your Organization?
3.0 Implementation Stage	
Key Business Question: Can we reach agreement on a deal with one of the qualified providers?	
Who are the decision makers for this stage?	
What is the process to be followed in determining the decision criteria?	
When will this be done/what is the timeframe for this stage?	
How will the following key activities be performed? ■ Select appropriate requirements model (collaborative, RFP, etc.) ■ Develop outsourcing contract terms ■ Finalize human resources plan ■ Finalize deal structure ■ Negotiate contract. ■ Ratify contract. ■ Execute contract.	

Outsourcing Process Checklist	How Will This Be Done in Your Organization?
4.0 Transition Stage	
Key Business Question. Can we execute successfully?	
Who are the decision makers for this stage?	
What is the process to be followed in determining the decision criteria?	

Outsourcing Process Checklist	How Will This Be Done in Your Organization?
When will this be done/what is the timeframe for this stage?	
How will the following key activities be performed?	

- ■ Communicate project, team, and leadership.
- ■ Develop detailed transition plan.
- ■ Finalize communication plan.
- ■ Implement new organization structure.
- ■ Transition activities.
- ■ Monitor transition and implementation.

Outsourcing Process Checklist	How Will This Be Done in Your Organization?
5.0 Management Stage	
Key Business Question: With the transition complete, are we ready to operate under the new agreement? Are the benefits being realized?	
Who are the decision makers for this stage?	
What is the process to be followed in determining the decision criteria?	
When will this be done/what is the timeframe for this stage?	
How will the following key activities be performed?	

- ■ Perform daily management activities.
- ■ Monitor performance.
- ■ Implement relationship management processes.
- ■ Complete outsourcing business plan.
- ■ Change management process.
- ■ Assess strategic review.
- ■ Reconfirm business case.
- ■ Review outsourcing performance assessment model.

Template 2.3 Outsourcing Business Plan

| Outsourcing Project: |
| Project #: |

The Outsourcing Business Plan will be built throughout the decision-making process followed by your organization, updated regularly, and refined at each stage of the process. The three main purposes of the Outsourcing Business Plan are:

- Document in a comprehensive manner the strategic analysis leading to the outsourcing decision.
- Document rigorously how outsourcing upon the contemplated terms is an attractive opportunity for the organization.
- Clearly define the future mode of operations by providing a "blueprint" of how it will be achieved.

Subsequent templates (Sections 3 through 10) will guide a more detailed analysis of many of these sections.

Executive Summary	
Strategy:	Risk Mitigation:
Operation:	Human Resources:
Financial:	Communication:
Schedule:	

Strategy

The Strategic section/plan outlines the assessment of the client seeking outsourcing solutions. It describes the client's current situation, highlights industry trends and benchmarks, and shows process comparisons between the client and the industry. The following analysis supports the rationale for selecting the proposed alternate service delivery model or outsourcing.

Overall Strategy:

A clear articulation of the business definition, a description of the key factors driving change within the client's organization as well as the market within which they operate, the client's strategy to respond to these changes and the impact this will have on its operation, customers, and labor force.

Business Requirements:

A clear articulation of what the client's organization is seeking to do and what it will gain from outsourcing the activity (i.e. cost competitiveness, improve quality, access to technology, increase control, variable cost structure, flexibility, etc…)

Strategic Choice:

An assessment of the outsourcing options and the competitive options and the competitive advantages over the status quo.

Strategic Objectives:

A description of what the client is seeking from the outsourcing transaction and relationship. This would include future opportunities between the client and the provider and the importance of the relationship to the client.

Structural Model:

A review of potential outsourcing structural models such as: Divestiture, Sale of business, Subsidiary, Joint Venture, etc. and the recommendation of the most desirable financial structure.

Contractual Model:

An evaluation of potential business models (General/Sub Contractor, Consignment, Principal/Agent, etc.) with a recommendation of a contractual model that will meet the outsourcing objectives.

Provider Selection:

A recap of the potential providers and a brief review as to why these providers could be selected (i.e. financial stability, management, ownership, market growth, expertise, past experience, business fit, etc.)

Risk Mitigation

A risk mitigation matrix highlighting the major risks in proceeding with the outsourcing as well as the mitigation tactics to address these risks.

Strategic Risks:

Operational Risks:

Result Risks:

Transactional Risks:

Unique Project Specific Risks:

Operation

The operational section/plan outlines how the outsourced activities will be transitioned, and how the relationship will be structured and managed. The operation plan sets out the mechanisms through which the client's organization will implement its strategic plan. This section usually includes the following key elements:

Division of Function, Roles and Responsibilities:

A description of the outsourcer functions, roles and responsibilities. From the client's perspective, a description of the 'stay back team' retained in the client. Such a team is usually required to take over the management of the business relationship and to act as the point of contact between the client and the provider.

Transition Activities:

A description of the transition phases and their respective timelines.

Division of Assets and Systems:

A description of which assets and systems will need to be shared with the provider and how the risks of giving such access to a third party will be controlled and safeguarded. (Gateways, Restricted Access, Logical Access Control, etc).

Management of Day to Day Operations:

A day to day interface and escalation protocol.

Management of Overall Relationships:

A description of how the overall relationship would be managed. This must include identification of the key people involved and the protocol for periodic senior executive interfaces.

Management of the Outsourcing Contract Performance:

A description of how performance under the contract would be measured and managed, including the description of the key performance measures and incentive formula if any.

Exit Strategy:

A description of the alternatives available if the relationship proves unsatisfactory and/or re-entry strategies if the client decides to return the function in-house in the future.

Human Resources

The Human Resource section/plan outlines in some detail how the client Human Resource members are affected by the outsourcing and what the potential outcomes are. This section would usually include the following clarifications;

Division of Human Resources:

Diagnostic of the Client Organization Human Resources Needs:

An identification and diagnostic of the human resources required
within the client organization to implement the plan set out above
(transition team, ongoing management team, 'on site manager',
etc.). An emphasis on the competencies or expertise required
to excel in the new mode of operation. If required, the skills and
knowledge gaps with a plan for filling such gaps.

Diagnostic of the Provider's Human Resources Needs:

An identification of human resource (management and non-
management) required by the provider to implement the
outsourcing set out above.

Financial

The financial section/plan outlines the financial rationale for outsourcing this business activity and the financial impact that the transaction
will have on the client's bottom line.

Financial Baseline:

A set of financial pro forma reflecting the impact on the business
after proceeding with the outsourcing as proposed for the duration
of the outsourcing term.

Incremental Impact of Transaction on the Provider:

If relevant, a set of financial statements reflecting the impact on
the provider of the transaction as proposed.

Provider's Valuation:

A valuation of the provider's business as a standalone business
operating as a going concern.

Management of the Financial Process:

A description of how the financial relationship would be managed.
This will include elements such as: the mechanism for billing and
payments, etc.

Communication

The communication section/plan outlines the communication components of the outsourcing project; moreover, how it will be implemented. The communication plan ensures that the current partner relationship is well known to all stakeholders in a timely manner.

Client Organization Employee Communication Plan:

This plan should have two components: first, a general communication strategy designed to keep employees affected by the outsourcing and their union (if any) informed of the status of the transaction; and second, an individual communication strategy designed to keep each employee informed of the impact of the outsourcing on him or her.

Customer Communication Plan:

This plan should have two components: first, a general communication strategy designed to keep employees affected by the outsourcing and their union (if any) informed of the status of the transaction; and second, an individual communication strategy designed to keep each employee informed of the impact of the outsourcing on him or her.

Provider Communication Plan:

This plan should address communications with the provider organization, at all levels, pertaining the client, goals, objectives, etc.

Regulatory, Government and Community Communication Plan:

If required, a communication strategy to demonstrate to any regulatory organization the resulting impact of the outsourcing decision on the constituents.

Union Communication:

A communication strategy that complies with the current union and any legal board requirements.

Schedule Summary and Milestones

Project Initiation:	3.0 Implementation Stage:
Idea Stage:	4.0 Transition Stage:
2.0 Assessment and Planning Stage:	5.0 Management Stage:

Scope of Work

Project Quality Statement

Key Project Stakeholders

Review and Authorization
Reviewed by:
Authorized by:

Special thanks to Certified Outsourcing Professional (COP) Jean-Francois Poisson for his ideas upon which the template was developed.

Template 3.1   Top-Down Strategic Planning

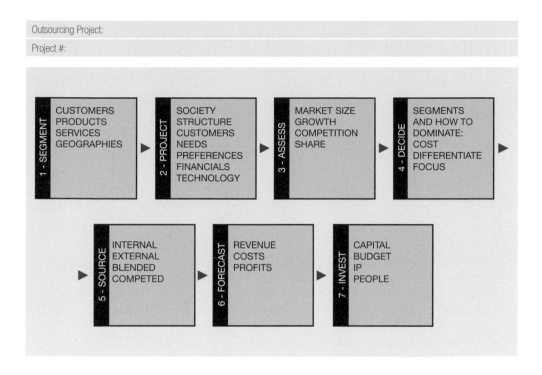

Refer to the figure above. The Top-Down Approach to integrating outsourcing into a business strategy focuses on identifying where the organization's competitive advantage will come from and then ensuring that its investments and execution plans are aligned with that strategy. Review your organization's business strategy; map it to the seven steps below showing how this project helps achieve the organization's business strategy.

Steps	Project-Specific Mapping
Step 1 – Segment the Marketplace	
Customers	
Products	
Services	
Geographies	

Steps	Project-Specific Mapping
Step 2 – Project Changes in Each Segment	
Society	
Structure	
Customer Needs and Preferences	
Financials	
Technology	
Step 3 – Assess Size and Growth	
Market Size	
Market Growth	
Competition	
Market Share	
Step 4 – Segment Selection and How to Dominate	
Cost	
Differentiate	
Focus	
Step 5 – Sourcing	
Internal	
External	
Blended	
Completed	

Steps	Project-Specific Mapping
Step 6 – Forecast Business Outcomes	
Revenue	
Costs	
Profits	
Step 7 – Invest in Execution	
Capital	
Budget	
IP (Intellectual Property)	
People	

Template 3.2   Bottom-Up Strategic Planning

| Outsourcing Project: |
| Project #: |

The Bottom-Up Approach to integrating outsourcing into the business strategy focuses on identifying on a continuous basis activities that do not contribute to a unique competitive advantage of the organization and then competing these activities against the marketplace of service providers. Using Template 1.8 Common Business Process Framework as a guide, assess your organization's business processes reviewing the Key Questions below and identifying business processes that do not meet the criteria.

Key Question	Assessment
1. If we started from scratch today, would the business build the capability internally?	
2. Is the business so good at the activity that others would hire it to do it for them?	
3. Is this an activity of the business where its future leaders will come from?	

Template 3.3 Outsourcing Decision Matrix

| Outsourcing Project: |
| Project #: |

The Outsourcing Decision Matrix provides a tool to perform a weighted rating of an area being considered for outsourcing. The criteria for both "Performance Relative to Market" and "Importance as a Differentiator" are considered and the resulting score is located on the chart at the end of this template. Complete the evaluation below by entering an Importance Weighting and Effectiveness Rating for each criteria.

Performance Relative to Market – Criteria	Importance	Effectiveness	Score
	(1-5)	(1-5)	
Financial:			
Is expense/revenue ratio favorable compared to best-in-class (BIC)?			
Have ratios been moving in a positive direction over the past two years?			
What is the volume compared to the largest provider?			
Process:			
Is performance in key quality measures favorable compared to BIC?			
Is cycle-time competitive?			
Is the process positively/negatively affecting time to market?			
Technology:			
Has technology investment kept pace with the marketplace? How strong is the organization's bench strength?			
Employees:			
Employee attrition/satisfaction compared to BIC?			
Is an adequate labor pool available geographically?			
Organizational Strength:			
Does change management/sponsorship exist?			
		Total Performance Score	

Importance as a Differentiator - Criteria	Importance	Effectiveness	Score
	(1-5)	(1-5)	
Core versus Non-core:			
Is there a highly valued unique asset involved in the activity?			
Do we have institutional capabilities/experiences that are hard for our competitors to replicate?			
Is this a unique source of leverage?			
Brand:			
Is the activity done to raise brand awareness?			
Can the activity strengthen/weaken the brand?			
Impact of Customers:			
Does the activity involve direct interaction with customers or prospects?			
Is the activity important to our customers in the long term?			
Is the activity directly related to the delivery of product versus a support function? Would loss or disruption of this service harm the organization?			
	Total Differentiator Score		

Example — For a business are with a score for "Performance Relative to Market" of 150 and a score for "Importance as a Differentiator" of 85, the result indicates that it would be outsourced for scale advantage and Inceased focus on differentiators. Enter the score for the area under consideration for outsourcing in the lower chart.

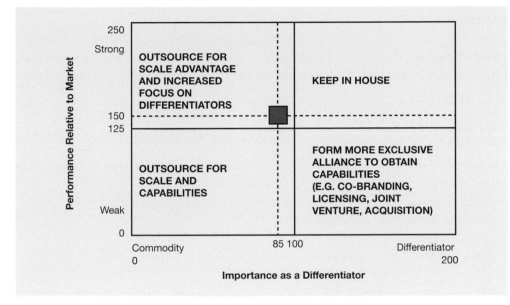

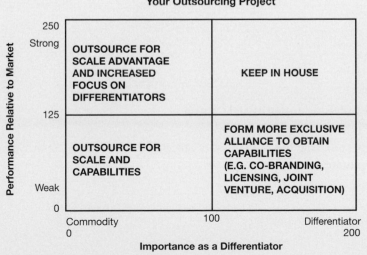

Template 3.4   Stakeholder Analysis

| Outsourcing Project: |
| Project #: |

Objective

To ensure the success of an outsourcing business initiative by identifying, gaining and keeping the appropriate levels of support and involvement of all individuals and groups having a stake in the outcome.

Stakeholder Definition

An individual or group of individuals with an interest (stake), something to be gained or something to be lost in the outcome of the outsourcing initiative.

Stakeholder Involvement and Commitment

Oppose	Will attempt to block an action.
Allow	Will allow the project to proceed but may not directly support it.
Assist	Will help in some way to ensure the success of the project.
Perform	Will take responsibility for a significant portion of the project.
Sponsor	Will provide the resources and leadership necessary for the success of the project.

Stakeholder Influence, Authority and Control

The ability to affect the behavior of others through the control of information, expertise, resources, or authority.

Influence and Involvement Matrix

Objective

To identify the influence and involvement of key stakeholders and identify actions that will:

- Fill influence and involvement gaps
- Move high influence/low involvement stakeholders to high influence/high involvement or low influence/low involvement
- Move low influence/high involvement stakeholders to high influence/high involvement or low influence/low involvement

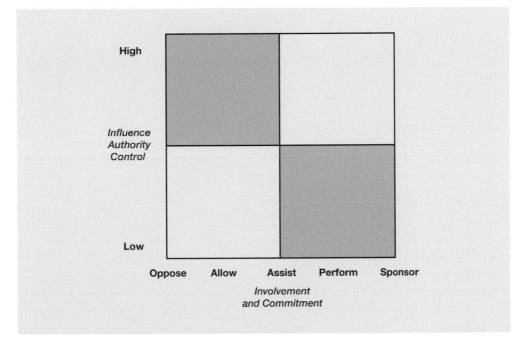

Stakeholder Assessment

Stakeholder Individual or Group	Influence Assessment Low • Medium • High	Involvement Assessment Oppose • Allow • Assist • Perform • Sponsor	Identify Stakeholder Issues and List Actions Needed to Change Influence and/or Involvement

Assessment Process

1. Identify individuals or groups that will be most affected by the outcome of the outsourcing project and list them on the chart above.

2   Determine their current level of influence, authority and control.

3. Determine their current level of involvement and commitment.

4. Locate each stakeholder's current position on the Influence and Involvement Matrix above.

5. Identify the outstanding issues associated with each stakeholder. Identify the desired location for each stakeholder and draw an arrow from their current location to the desired location.

6. Create an action plan to resolve these issues and reposition stakeholders by changing their influence and/or involvement.

Template 3.5   Stakeholder Communication Plan - Messages

Outsourcing Project:

Project #:

Use this template to develop the Project Communication Plan. For each of the five stages of the Outsourcing Process, identify the key stakeholders and main messages about the project that should be communicated to these stakeholders. Review Template 3.4: Stakeholder Analysis to ensure all stakeholders are identified. Write the communication strategy for each stakeholder at each stage of the process, identifying the main messages to be communicated, as well as the communications plan (timing (when), format (written, verbal), context (how it fits in), and frequency).

1.0 Idea Stage		
Key Stakeholder	Main Messages	Communications Plan

2.0 Assessment and Planning Stage		
Key Stakeholder	Main Message	Communications Plan

3.0 Implementation Stage		
Key Stakeholders	Main Message	Communications Plan

4.0 Transition Stage		
Key Stakeholders	Main Message	Communications Plan

5.0 Management Stage		
Key Stakeholders	Main Message	Communications Plan

Template 3.6 Stakeholder Communication Plan Framework

| Outsourcing Project: |
| Project #: |

Developing a comprehensive communication plan framework is important and it must be established during the strategy phase and implemented throughout the entire lifecycle of outsourcing. In the template, the first row is shown as an example.

Stakeholder	Objectives	Communication Tools
Directly affected employees	1. Reduce their fear 2. Communicate the facts about outsourcing 3. Solicit their input in the process	1. One-on-one meetings 2. Status Reports 3. Website 4. "Town Hall" Meeting
Other affected employees (e.g. users)		
Customers		
Suppliers		
Shareholders		
Community		

Template 3.7   Scoping an Outsourcing Opportunity

| Outsourcing Project: |
| Project #: |

Identify a potential business process or service area candidate for outsourcing. Describe the discrete activities that make up the business process. Identify activity inputs and outputs and the resources used in the activity. After entering this information, review the full list of activities and place a check in the left column to identify activities that are likely to be included in the outsourcing arrangement

√- to be included in outsourcing projects	Describe the discrete activities making up the business process	Process Inputs	Process Outputs	Resources Used
❑				
❑				
❑				
❑				
❑				
❑				
❑				

Template 3.8 Offshore Outsourcing: Country Specific Risk Assessment

Outsourcing Project:	
Project #:	
Country:	

There are strategic and operational benefits offered by various offshore locations. The Offshoring Decision Matrix provides a tool to perform a country specific assessment of the various offshoring risk factors. Identify both the business process and country/location under consideration. Assess the risk factors and rate each risk from Low to High.

Source: The OffShore Nation, Atul Vashistha and Avinash Vashistha

Offshoring Risk Factor	Country Specific Research & Assessment	Rating (1-3)
Government Support		
Labor Pool		
Infrastructure		
Educational System		
Cost Advantage - Direct/Indirect		
Quality		
Cultural Compatibility		
Time/Distance Advantage		
Language Proficiency		
Geopolitical Environment		
Process Maturity/ Competitiveness		
Supportive People Factors		
Supportive Economic Scenario		
TOTAL		0

	Low	Medium	High
	1	2	3

Template 3.9   Impact of Business Regulations and Statutes

Outsourcing Project:

Project #:

Identify the governing agencies in each country and the applicable regulations and statues administered by each agency for both the client and service provider. In the lower table, list the regulations and statutes and describe the impact each has on the outsourcing project. Then rate the impact of each regulation and statute.

Client, Provider, or Both	Governing Agency	List Applicable Regulations and Statutes

Applicable Regulations and Statues	Describe Project Impact	Rate L-M-H
		☐ L ☐ M ☐ H
		☐ L ☐ M ☐ H
		☐ L ☐ M ☐ H
		☐ L ☐ M ☐ H
		☐ L ☐ M ☐ H

Template 3.10   Scoping an Outsourcing Opportunity

Outsourcing Project:

Project #:

Identify a potential business process or service area candidate for outsourcing. Describe the discrete activities that make up the business process. Identify activity inputs and outputs and the resources used in the activity. After entering this information, review the full list of activities and place a check in the left column to identify activities that are likely to be included in the outsourcing arrangement.

√- to be included in outsourcing projects	Describe the discrete activities making up the business process	Process Inputs	Process Outputs	Resources Used
❑				
❑				
❑				
❑				
❑				
❑				
❑				
❑				

Template 3.11   Prioritizing Outsourcing Opportunities

| Outsourcing Project: |
| Project #: |

Once the outsourcing candidate areas have been listed and scoped in process terms, they need to be prioritized. The goal is to ensure that the opportunities that offer the organization the greatest return at the lowest risk are pursued first. Use this template to evaluate and prioritize candidates being considered for outsourcing.

Factors in Gauging the Opportunity	Document in Objective and Comparable Terms
Financial - budgets affected; size of budget opportunity (amount and percent); other.	
Providers - size and expertise; unique advantages of each provider; other.	
Benefits - cost savings; freed-up resources; flexibility to ramp up and down quickly; gap between current interval quality levels and marketplace of service providers; capital spend avoided; other.	
Ease of Execution - process understood, defined and measured; ease of transfer to new environment; level stakeholders understand and support the change; other.	
To prioritize each opportunity, rate how effectively the outsourcing candidate addresses the specific factor.	

1	2	3	4	5
Not Effectively	Somewhat Effectively	Effectively	Very Effectively	Extremely Effectively

Factors in Gauging the Opportunity	Rate 1- 5
Financial - the size of the financial opportunity affects a large enough portion of the business's operations to be worth pursuing the opportunity.	
Providers - there are providers of sufficient size and expertise to pursue this opportunity.	
Benefits - the preliminary assessment of potential benefits to be realized affects a large enough portion of the business's strategy to be worth pursuing the opportunity.	
Ease of Execution - the business process is understood, defined, and measured well enough to support transfer to the new environment.	
Total	

Template 3.12   Public Affairs Risk Analysis

| Outsourcing Project: |
| Project #: |

Use the Public Affairs Risk Analysis to determine whether the risk level is low, medium or high for a negative public reaction to an outsourcing announcement. Review each risk factor and check the appropriate response. Count the total responses in each column and multiply the column sub-total by a weight of 1 (low), 3 (medium) or 5 (high). The higher the total score, the higher the overall risk. (For example, a total score of 10-15 could be considered low, 16-30, medium, and 31-plus high. This process also helps identify actions that can be taken to lower the risk level of specific factors by changing the organization's response to a specific risk factor.

Risk Factors	Rating		
	High	Medium	Low
Does the company have a corporate communications or public relations group?	☐ No	☐ No but will be Mgmt Led	☐ Yes
Does the company have a strict policy limiting only the public relations people to speak to the press?	☐ No	☐ Yes but employees have not been trained frequently	☐ Yes and quarterly reminders
Does the company have a continuous relationship with local press?	☐ No	☐ Infrequent - one or two times per year	☐ Regularly - at least quarterly
Has the company made other announcements related to jobs?	☐ No	☐ Yes, but more than a year ago	☐ Within the last 12 months
Has the company produced strong positive economic impacts for the change at hand?	☐ No	☐ Wage only	☐ Full economics with provider and growth opportunities
Is the company's local industry releasing similar job affecting notices?	☐ No	☐ Yes, but only fractionally	☐ Yes, many have released similar strategies
Does the community have other high growth areas creating jobs?	☐ No	☐ Yes, but area is net negative	☐ Yes, and many have moved to new roles

Risk Factors	Rating		
	High	**Medium**	**Low**
Is the initiative labeled a downsizing?	☐ Yes	☐ No, but staff labels it this way	☐ No
Are the affected employees long term?	☐ Yes; turnover is less than 5%	☐ Maybe; turnover is 6-10%	☐ No; the turnover is high and above 10% on average
What is the level of the affected employees?	☐ Trade and front line	☐ Mid Management	☐ Professionals and Executives
Column Total			
Column Weight	5	3	1
Weighed Column Total			
Total Risk Score			

Template 4.1 Outsourcing Professional Roles

| Outsourcing Project: |
| Project #: |

For each of the following roles, identify the resource(s) and their role in executing the outsourcing end-to-end process. What role do you as an outsourcing professional have and how will it contribute to the success of the outsourcing decision?

	Lead Role	Support Role	None
Design & Manage End-to-End Process			
Strategy and Policy			
Identify Opportunities			
Set up Project Team(s)			
Manage Project Team(s)			
Perform Preliminary Assessment			
Financial Analysis			
RFP			
Provider Selection			
Deal Structure			
Negotiate			
Contract			
Go/No Go Decision			
Implementation			
Change Management			
Relationship Governance			
Operational Management			
Performance Management			
Renegotiate, Renew, Terminate			
Other			
Other			

Template 4.2   Creating and Leading Outsourcing Teams

Outsourcing Project:
Project #:

Identify the business areas required to provide needed support to the project during each stage. Identify and recruit team members from these business areas, indicating the contributing strengths and key reasons for adding this person to the Project Team. Also identify subject matter experts and other contributors who may be called upon periodically to provide support to the project.

Policy Team
Responsible for setting the organization's overall policy on outsourcing and determining the appropriateness of outsourcing in specific areas under consideration.

Business Area	Team Member	Contributing Strengths and Reason for Joining the Team

Subject Matter Experts and Other Contributors

Stage 1 – Idea Team
Responsible for generating outsourcing project ideas for review by the Policy Team.

Business Area	Team Member	Contributing Strengths and Reason for Joining the Team

Subject Matter Experts and Other Contributors

Stage 2 – Assessment and Planning Team
Responsible for performing detailed evaluation and plan development for selected outsourcing initiatives.

Business Area	Team Member	Contributing Strengths and Reason for Joining the Team

Subject Matter Experts and Other Contributors

Stages 3 & 4 – Implementation and Transition Team(s)		
Responsible for reaching agreement on a deal with one of the qualified providers and ensuring an effect transition to the new arrangement.		

Business Area	Team Member	Contributing Strengths and Reason for Joining the Team

Subject Matter Experts and Other Contributors

Stage 5 – Management Team
Responsible for ongoing oversight and effectiveness of the outsourcing relationship.

Business Area	Team Member	Contributing Strengths and Reason for Joining the Team

Subject Matter Experts and Other Contributors

Template 5.1 Checklist for Objectives and Boundary
                  Conditions

Outsourcing Project:
Project #:

Before initiating the outsourcing provider selection process it is important that objectives and boundary conditions are well identified, documented and an organizational buy-in obtained. This template provides a framework for capturing them. An example of how to use the template is shown.

Business Factors	Objectives ST – Short Term LT – Long Term	Boundary Conditions N – Non-negotiable C – Can be approved by steering committee
Cost Savings	15% (LT) 5% or better first year	There must be year-on-year cost decrease against baseline (N)
Variable cost structure	At least 70% of cost baseline must be variable (S/LT)	No penalty for fixed cost baseline beyond 3rd year (C)
People	80%+ employees must be offered a position (ST) and retained for at least 1 year (LT) Critical employees must have a retention program (LT)	All labor laws must be met (N) Employees must have parity in their compensation once transitioned (C)
Other		Service provider must meet certification requirements before engagement (N)

Template 5.2   Checklist for Developing Outsourcing
Requirements

| Outsourcing Project: |
| Project #: |

Developing and communicating outsourcing requirements effectively to potential providers is key to receiving high quality responses. Review the requirements below to ensure each is addressed appropriately in your communication and supporting management processes. Describe in the "Notes" column how and where each requirement has been addressed.

√ complete	Developing and Communicating Requirements	Notes
☐	Does the team developing the requirements document have representation from functional management, process experts, customers/users, procurement, finance, human resources, and legal?	
☐	Has the current process been diagramed, including clear distinction and rationale for in-scope and out-of-scope activities?	
☐	Have current costs been captured for each activity, including people, supplies, equipment, overheads, and capital costs?	
☐	Have the critical success factors and key performance indicators for the current process's quality, customer satisfaction, timeliness, financial performance, conformance to requirements, speed, flexibility, and innovation been measured and documented?	
☐	Have future process requirements, based on reasonable potential scenarios, been identified and documented?	
☐	Objectives and desired results, while allowing providers to propose specific resources and methodologies to be employed?	
☐	Current and future volumes in sufficient detail for providers to forecast workload levels?	
☐	The number and location of recipients of the services?	
☐	The desired relationship between the companies, including such considerations as transfer of assets, people, exclusivity, sharing of risks and rewards, and pricing?	

√ complete	Developing and Communicating Requirements	Notes
☐	How the relationship should be managed over time?	
☐	Current problems and costs; projects currently underway, status and expectations for provider to assume and complete?	
☐	Key contract considerations, such as intellectual properties, length, termination options, liabilities and warranties?	
☐	Why the company will be a good customer for the provider?	

√ complete	Does the requirements process include:	Notes
☐	A defined process for identifying the companies to receive the document?	
☐	Compilation of the appropriate contact information for the individuals at the companies to receive the document?	
☐	Definition of the key activities and dates for the distribution, response, review and selection process?	
☐	Sufficient guidance on response structure; the evaluation criteria described; what constitutes a valid response?	
☐	A definition of the internal review process, including roles, responsibilities, and timelines?	
☐	A weighted evaluation criteria; a standardized format for documenting reviewer notes and positions?	
☐	Completion of all required internal reviews and approvals before any providers are contacted?	
☐	When and by whom responders are advised; the next steps to be followed with the selected provider(s)?	

Template 5.3   Critical Success Factors (CSFs) and Key
Performance Indicators (KPIs) for Outsourcing

Outsourcing Project:

Project #:

Identify your organization's critical success factors, key performance indicators, and applicable attributes for the scope of services being evaluated for outsourcing. Different types of services may require different performance metrics even if they are to be evaluated as a single opportunity.

For each category of Critical Success Factor (CSF) indicate the relative key performance indicators (KPIs), the specific attribute of the KPI to be tracked and how it will be measured and rated. To be meaningful, no more than six to twelve KPIs should be selected for any single service.

For example:

For the CSF of 'Financial' a Key Performance Indicator is likely to be cost. But what attribute of cost is most important? Total cost, cost variance against plan, cost per unit? Finally, if cost variance is selected as the best attribute, how will it be measured and rated? What will be used as the baseline costs and for the actual costs? What is and is not an acceptable variance?

Critical Success Factors (CSF)	Key Performance Indicator (KPI)	Specific Attribute	How Measured and Rated
Financial			
Customer			

Critical Success Factors (CSF)	Key Performance Indicator (KPI)	Specific Attribute	How Measured and Rated
Employee			
Process and Product Innovation			
Service Level Innovation			
Other			

Template 5.4   RFP (Request for Proposal) Document
Development

| Outsourcing Project: |
| Project #: |

Use this template to outline the sections, content, and responsible individuals/organizations and dates for developing the sections of the RFP.

Sections	Sub-sections	Content	Who/When
Objectives, Scope and Key Dates			
Background			
Provider Relationship Model			
Services Requested			

Sections	Sub-sections	Content	Who/When
Transition/Migration Services			
Performance Requirements			
Requirements for Proposal			
General Terms and Conditions			
Proposal Evaluation			
Pricing			

Sections	Sub-sections	Content	Who/When
Attachments			

Template 5.5   Collaborative Approach to Document
Development

Outsourcing Project:

Project #:

This collaborative approach to engaging providers uses a Harvard Business Case-style document as a tool to explore solutions and test alignment of interests of all parties. First develop your organization's response to each of these areas in the form of an Organization Statement. Provide these responses to each provider of interest and obtain the provider's response. Compare responses and assess for alignment.

Describe what the organization believes is likely to occur in the industry and business over the next few years.

Organization Statement	Provider's Response Statement

Describe the challenges and opportunities these changes will create.

Organization Statement	Provider's Response Statement

Describe the issues, constraints facing the organization in meeting these challenges and opportunities.

Organization Statement	Provider's Response Statement

Describe the types of approaches to addressing and leveraging those changes that are currently under consideration

Organization Statement	Provider's Response Statement

Template 6.1   Identifying Potential Outsourcing Service Providers

Outsourcing Project:
Project #:

Use this template to develop the list of business resources available to you for identifying potential service providers. List the individuals and organizations to contact and the provider name, contact information, and key characteristics identified.

Business Resources	Organizations/ Individuals	Provider Names, Contact Information	Key Insights
Professional Associations			
Current service provider relationships			
Board members and company executives			

Business Resources	Organizations/ Individuals	Provider Names, Contact Information	Key Insights
Accounting Firms			
Law Firms			
Consultants			
Direct Research (Industry articles and publications, Internet, conferences, etc.)			
Other			

Template 6.2   Evaluating Potential Service Providers

| Outsourcing Project: |
| Project #: |

Use this template to develop the list of activities to be performed in evaluating potential service providers. For each, indicate the organizations and individuals to be involved, where, when and how they will be conducted, and the information to be collected and reported (documents, checklists, meeting reports, etc.)

Business Resources	Organizations/ Individuals	Where, When How	Information to be Collected/ Reported
Bidders Conference			
Provider Presentations			
Reference Checks			

Business Resources	Organizations/ Individuals	Where, When How	Information to be Collected/ Reported
Due Diligence			
Site Visits			
Debriefing Sessions			
RFP, other Document Responses			
Scoring and Selecting (see Template 6.3)			
Other			

Template 6.3   Scoring and Selecting Service Providers

Outsourcing Project:

Project #:

Identify the factors most relevant to your organization's evaluation of provider responses; some suggested criteria factors are given. Then assign a relative weight of from 1 to 5 to each factor (this is the same for all service providers) and a rank of from 1 to 5 reflecting how well the provider meets your organization's expectations in comparison to the other providers under consideration. The provider's total score is the sum of its weighted rankings for each factor considered.

Outsourcing Service Provider:			
Factors to Consider	Weight 1 - 5	Rank 1 - 5	Score
Demonstrated Competencies			
People	0	0	0
Process	0	0	0
Technologies	0	0	0
Experience	0	0	0
Proven Performance	0	0	0
Track Record of Innovation	0	0	0
Other	0	0	0
Total Capabilities			
Financial Strength	0	0	0
Infrastructure and Resources	0	0	0
Management Systems	0	0	0
Complete Suite of Services	0	0	0
Other	0	0	0
Relationship Dynamics			
Culture	0	0	0
Mission and Strategy	0	0	0
Relationship Management	0	0	0
Relative Importance	0	0	0
Other	0	0	0

Competitiveness of Solution			
Solution Itself	0	0	0
Service Delivery	0	0	0
Risk and Risk Sharing	0	0	0
Financial Proposal	0	0	0
Terms and Conditions	0	0	0
Human Resources Requirements	0	0	0
Other	0	0	0
Achievement (especially Existing Relationship)			
Evaluate Performance	0	0	0
Assess Value Achieved	0	0	0
Continuous Improvement	0	0	0
Other	0	0	0
Total Score			0

Template 7.1   Cost Elements for Creating Baseline Costs

Outsourcing Project:

Project #:

The following checklist of cost elements should be looked at while constructing the cost baseline. Such a checklist is important in making sure that the cost elements that may not be a part of the department budget are properly identified and accounted for. These cost factors are then aggregated for the appropriate sections of Template 7.2.

Cost Elements	Applicable Y/N	Source (for data)
Staff Expense		
■ Salaries and wages		
■ Benefits (employee benefits plan and legislated benefits)		
■ Bonus		
■ Temps		
■ Contractors		
■ Travel and Entertainment		
■ Overtime		
■ Recruiting		
■ Training/tuition		
■ Severance		
■ Relocation		
■ Other		
Facilities/Office Costs		
■ Rent		
■ Utilities		
■ Depreciation (building, leasehold		
■ improvements, furniture, equipment)		
■ Work orders/space reconfiguration		
■ Property taxes		
■ Maintenance and repairs		
■ Property manager administration		
■ Mail services/postage		
■ Security		
■ Janitorial		
■ Copiers, faxes, other office equipment		
■ Shared operators, word processors		

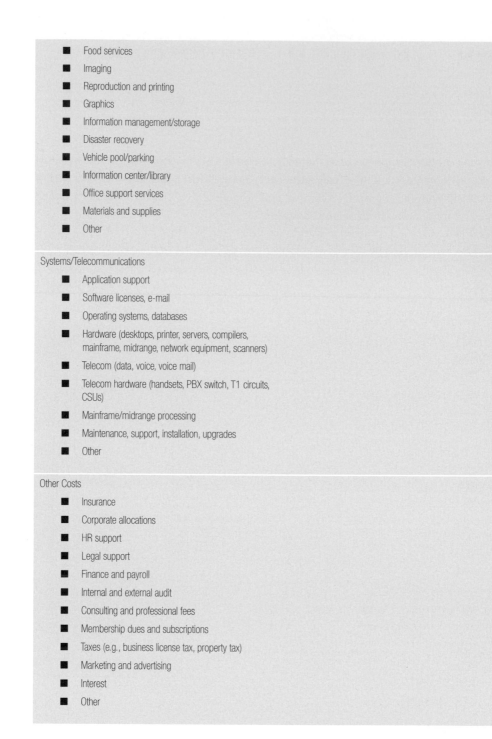

- Food services
- Imaging
- Reproduction and printing
- Graphics
- Information management/storage
- Disaster recovery
- Vehicle pool/parking
- Information center/library
- Office support services
- Materials and supplies
- Other

Systems/Telecommunications

- Application support
- Software licenses, e-mail
- Operating systems, databases
- Hardware (desktops, printer, servers, compilers, mainframe, midrange, network equipment, scanners)
- Telecom (data, voice, voice mail)
- Telecom hardware (handsets, PBX switch, T1 circuits, CSUs)
- Mainframe/midrange processing
- Maintenance, support, installation, upgrades
- Other

Other Costs

- Insurance
- Corporate allocations
- HR support
- Legal support
- Finance and payroll
- Internal and external audit
- Consulting and professional fees
- Membership dues and subscriptions
- Taxes (e.g., business license tax, property tax)
- Marketing and advertising
- Interest
- Other

Template 7.2   Financial Analysis of an Outsourcing Decision

| Outsourcing Project: |
| Project #: |

Use this template to develop the financial analysis of an outsourcing decision. Create additional sheets in this workbook for individual elements as needed and then link those calculations to this sheet as appropriate.

Discount Rate for NPV:	8%				
Category	Year 1 ($000)	Year 2 ($000)	Year 3 ($000)	Year 4 ($000)	Year 5 ($000)
Net Financial Benefit (Loss)	0	0	0	0	0
Net Present Value	0				
Base Case	0	0	0	0	0
Salary					
Equipment					
Outside Services					
Supplies					
Direct Overheads (Occupancy, Training, Benefits, etc.)					
Indirect Overheads (Management, HR, Finance, Admin, etc.)					
Capital Costs (Depreciation, Cost of Capital)					
Other					

Outsource Case	0	0	0	0	0
Vendor Proposal	0	0	0	0	0
Price					
Start-Up Costs					
Other					
Additional Costs	0	0	0	0	0
Planning Costs (Staff, Travel, Professional Services)					
Transition Costs (Staff, Travel, Professional Services, Fees, Penalties, Bonuses, Taxes, etc.)					
Oversight Costs (Staff, Travel, Systems, Professional Services)					
Other Costs					
Risks and Risk Mitigation					
Additional Benefits	0	0	0	0	0
Quality (Reduced defects, increased yield, improved services, etc.)					
Capacity (Increased throughput, additional services, market growth, etc.)					

Focus (Reduced competition for capital, cash infusion, reduced cost of capital, resource redeployment, management focus, etc.)					
Revenue (New markets, new customers, additional revenue current customers, etc.)					
Other (Speed, flexibility, innovation, organizational change, employee morale, unexpected synergies, etc.)					
Retained Costs	0	0	0	0	0
Salary					
Equipment					
Outside Services					
Supplies					
Direct Overheads (Occupancy, Training, Benefits, etc.)					
Indirect Overheads (Management, HR, Finance, Admin, etc.)					
Capital Costs (Depreciation, Cost of Capital)					
Other					

Template 7.3   Selecting the Optimum Pricing Model

| Outsourcing Project: |
| Project #: |

Review each of the pricing models below and assess the advantages, disadvantages, and resulting financial implications of each model relative to the outsourcing service(s) being evaluated. Rank each to determine the preferable pricing model(s).

Pricing Models	Project	Potential Financial Implications	Rank
Cost Plus – provider is paid for actual costs plus a pre-determined fixed amount or percentage for profit margin.	Advantages: _____ Disadvantages:		
Unit Pricing – customer pays based on the amount of service, number of service units used.	Advantages: _____ Disadvantages:		
Fixed Price – provider's fee is the same regardless of the volume of services provided.	Advantages: _____ Disadvantages:		
Incentive-Based Pricing – payments are connected to achieving specified service levels or other specific aspects of delivery or performance.	Advantages: _____ Disadvantages:		
Gain-sharing – provider receives a portion of additional benefits, typically savings, it can generate for its customer.	Advantages: _____ Disadvantages:		

Pricing Models	Assessment	Potential Financial Implications	Rank
Achievement Bonuses – one-time payments for achieving certain milestones.	Advantages: _____ Disadvantages:		
Risk/Reward Sharing – both customer and provider have money at risk, and each gain a percentage of additional value created by their collaborative efforts.	Advantages: _____ Disadvantages:		
Combining two or more options	Advantages: _____ Disadvantages:		
Other	Advantages: _____ Disadvantages:		

Template 7.4   Value Proposition

Outsourcing Project:

Project #:

This template helps establish the importance of the value proposition and how it is expected to impact the outsourcing decision (as defined in the Outsourcing Business Plan). First establish 1-5 scoring priority for the five categories – (1 being the most important, 5 least important) then for each subcategory, identify the priority as High, Medium or Low. In the Expected Impact column identify how achieving the value proposition will affect the Outsourcing Business Plan (High, Medium or Low impact).

Value Factors	Priority	Expected Impact
Financial		
Reduce operating costs		
Reduce capital costs		
Improve asset utilization		
Reduce liabilities		
Improve "free cash flow"		
Improve revenue potential – new markets, greater penetration		
Create a more variable cost structure		
Capabilities		
Access to unavailable skills		
Provide flexible skill acquisition and utilization		
Access to and utilization of best practices and proven operational performance		
Access to unavailable technology platform		
Quality		
Predictable SLA commitment		
Repeatable process and performance		
Lower defect rates and rework opportunities		
Improved customer service? reaction / satisfaction		
Access to and use of Quality Tools (e.g., Kaizen, 6 Sigma) and process knowledge		
Risk and Compliance		
Lower company' risk profile and exposure		
Provide risk management alternative and evidence of compliance		

Value Factors	Priority	Expected Impact
Governance		
Transparency into providers' operation		
Other		
Provides the opportunity for access to new markets and relationships for the business		
Enhances alignment of the business to its strategy and mission		

Template 8.1   Outsourcing Contract Structure

Outsourcing Project:
Project #:

Review the main sections of the outsourcing contract structure below; ensure each item is specifically addressed in the outsourcing agreement.

Section 1: Contract Terms		
Check	Item	How Addressed
☐	Define the intent of the relationship.	
☐	Define outsourcing business drivers and anticipated benefits.	
☐	Define outsourcing goals and objectives.	
☐	Define the plan for converting the customer's operation to the provider's including cost allocations, timelines, and operational certification.	
☐	Define availability of customer equipment and facilities for use by the provider.	
☐	Define transfer of third party services, equipment and facilities to provider.	
☐	Define the transfer of personnel from the customer to the provider organization.	
☐	Define how the outsourcing relationship will be managed and compliance assured	
☐	Define roles and responsibilities of customer and provider.	

Section 2: Scope of Services (one for each type of service)

Check	Item	How Addressed
☐	Define the scope, type and nature of all the services including detailed description of services and the responsibilities and duties associated with it.	
☐	Where and when services will be provided	
☐	Criteria by which acceptance for cutover to the provider for provisioning of services is agreed	
☐	Standards of performance defined by the key performance indicators (KPIs) and Service Level Agreements (SLAs)	

Section 3: Pricing (one for each type of service)

Check	Item	How Addressed
☐	Pricing model	
☐	Price points	
☐	Payment terms	

Template 8.2   Common Outsourcing Contract Terms

Outsourcing Project:
Project #:

Review the common contract terms below to ensure they are addressed in the outsourcing contract.

Check	Definition	Where and How Addressed
☐	*Assignment* is the ability of a company to subcontract or assign its obligations to a third party with or without consent. The contract should specify when, where, and under what circumstances and with what pre-approvals subcontractors can be used.	
☐	*Audit* is the ability of a company to review the financial records and performance information as they relate to an agreement.	
☐	*Change of character* clauses give one or both of the parties the right to change other aspects of the contract, including services and prices, if there are significant changes in where or how the services are delivered.	
☐	*Compliance with laws* states that both parties will be compliant with all federal, state, and local laws and regulations. If there is a law or regulation that governs the particular relationship, it can be specifically stated.	
☐	*Confidentiality* describes what information is confidential and the party's rights and restrictions in the use of any confidential information.	
☐	A great deal of customer data may be used and generated in the delivery of the services. Issues such as the provider's rights to access that data, its security, backup, and accessibility should be addressed.	
☐	*Definition of the relationship* describes the parties, their business interests, and their goals and objectives in entering into the relationship.	
☐	The contract should specify how *disputes* are to be resolved, including under what conditions and in what manner they are escalated within and between the organizations. For issues that cannot be resolved between the two parties, alternative dispute resolution methods may be agreed to.	
☐	Outsourcing providers will frequently seek to be the *exclusive* provider of services within the agreement's scope. If granted, the organization typically seeks protections, which recognize its loss of control.	
☐	*Force majeure* limits performance and delivery in the case of uncontrollable events, such as acts of God or government actions. Responsibilities for maintaining adequate backup, recovery, and business continuity plans should be described, including how any costs are allocated.	
☐	The contract typically restricts the parties from *hiring each other's employees* for specified periods of time. Alternatively, it may establish a payment structure for compensating the current employer if its employees are hired by the other party.	

Check	Definition	Where and How Addressed
☐	*Indemnity* is a promise by one party to hold the other party harmless from loss or damage of some kind, irrespective of the liability of any third party. The liability for a loss is shifted from one party held legally responsible to another party.	
☐	The agreement should state that the provider is an *independent contractor* excluding any rights or privileges associated with being an employee of the organization not specifically granted in the agreement.	
☐	*Insurance* requirements vary depending on the type of activity and risk involved. It is important to understand which party's insurance covers what risks and to specify the requirements of each party to maintain appropriate coverage as well as how these costs are allocated.	
☐	When organizations outsource, they are combining their existing *intellectual properties,* the intellectual properties of other outside organizations, those of the service provider, and new intellectual properties that may be generated. Questions around the use and ownership rights of these assets should be addressed.	
☐	*Limitation of liability* clauses are standard in most contracts. Typically, certain types of consequential or special damages (punitive, indirect, and incidental) are excluded.	
☐	*Liquidated damages* is the sum that a party to a contract agrees to pay if it breaches the contract. It determined by a good faith effort to estimate the amount of actual damage that would result.	
☐	*Most favored customer* clauses are used to assure the customer that the level of service and prices they are receiving now and in the future are the provider's best for customers of similar services and volumes.	
☐	*Multi-providerr considerations* apply when more than one provider will need to work together to deliver the desired services. The responsibilities to coordinate these activities and how any costs will be allocated across the parties are specified.	
☐	*Personnel requirements,* such as skills, experience and training of personnel, where the work is performed, the provider's right to change personnel, the organization's right to review and approve personnel changes, and any specific obligations of the provider about screening, security, confidentiality, non-compete clauses, and succession planning should be specified.	
☐	*Safe harbors* protect certain payment and business practices that are implicated by the anti-kickback statute from criminal and civil prosecution.	
☐	In some cases, the service provider may seek to serve other clients from the organization's premises or from an offsite location that is primarily serving this customer. Any rights, restrictions, liabilities and indemnifications for *sharing resources* by either the provider or the customer should be addressed.	

Check	Definition	Where and How Addressed
☐	Outsourcing relationships are entered into with the general intent of being long-term, strategic relationships that will continue into the foreseeable future. For practical purposes, however, most contracts have a specified *term,* or period of time, for which they are in force.	
☐	Outsourcing contracts specify *termination* for cause, for convenience, as a result of other qualifying events, and at the end of the planned term. There are two key considerations: the definition of the types of termination and their trigger events, and the specification of the responsibilities of the parties and the allocation of costs in each situation.	
☐	*Venue* or governing law designates which state (and possibly which county) will govern and interpret the contract.	
☐	A *warranty* is essentially a guarantee that a product will perform as promised for a specified limited amount of time.	

Template 8.3 Description of Interests for Outsourcing Contract Negotiations

Outsourcing Project:
Project #:

Successful contract negotiations are based on a clear understanding of your organization's interests and the interests of the other party. First, clearly identify your interests and describe each interest in the appropriate customer or provider section. Then, based on what you already know about the other party, describe what you expect are their interests. Also list their interest areas that you need to understand in greater detail. Compare your organization's interest with that of the other party and look for common interests to build upon. Identify potentially divergent interest areas and look for ways that both sets of interests can be met.

Contract Negotiations - Customer Interests		
Ref.	Description of Interest	Divergent or In Common with Provider Interest Ref.

Contract Negotiations - Provider Interests		
Ref.	Description of Interest	Divergent or In Common with Customer Interest Ref.

Template 8.4   Negotiation Checklist

Outsourcing Project:

Project #:

With an understanding of the interests of both parties, review the checklist of negotiation principles below. Make notes and list action items in response to each principle.

√ Reviewed	Negotiation Principles	Project Notes and Actions
☐	Define negotiating team members and roles.	
☐	Include individuals with all relevant discipline knowledge including legal, HR, procurement and functional management.	
☐	Define the organization's key interests. (See Template 8.3)	
☐	Define the other party's key interests. (See Template 8.3)	
☐	Include individuals from both parties with sufficient decision-making authority on the negotiating team.	
☐	For negotiations with multiple providers, establish dates for "best and final" offers	
☐	Identify sources of objective information for evaluating proposed terms.	

Template 9.1   Outsourcing Transition Plan

| Outsourcing Project: |
| Project #: |

Develop the Transition Plan for the new outsourcing arrangement. Review the transition activities below along with the relevant templates that have been created up to this stage and add any other activities and sub-activities necessary to achieving a successful transition. Describe each activity, the responsible party, and its projected start and end date.

Operational Transition Plan (See OPBOK for Additional Details)	Description	Who	Start	End
Forecasting volumes				
Assessing risk and developing contingencies				
Establishing the transition governance process				
Establishing the communications plan				
Establishing the HR plan				
Establishing the change-over date				
Establishing the Technology plan				
Establishing the Knowledge Management plan (see Templates 9.3 and 9.4)				
Other				
Other				

Employee Transition Plan (See Template 9.2 for Additional Details)	Description	Who	Start	End
Developing and communicating the end-to-end process for managing the impact on employees.				
Identifying applicable employment laws.				
Identifying the changes and impact on all employees.				
Establishing an employee issue identification and resolution process.				
Other				
Other				
Other				
Other				
Other				

Communication Plan (See Templates 3.13 and 3.14 for Additional Details)	Description	Who	Start	End
Communicating with employees				
Communicating with suppliers				
Communicating with external customers				
Communicating with shareholders				
Communicating with media				
Other				
Other				
Other				
Other				
Other				

Template 9.2 Human Resources Planning

Outsourcing Project:

Project #:

- 12 MONTHS - 6 MONTHS - 3 MONTHS 0 3 MONTH 6 MONTHS 12 MONTHS+	

CUSTOMER

PROVIDER

PREPARE THE ORGANIZATION FOR CHANGE	PREPARE THE GROUP FOR CHANGE	TRANSITION EMPLOYEES	INTEGRATE EMPLOYEES INTO NEW COMPANY	EMPLOYEE GROWTH AND DEVELOPMENT

PHASE I: PLANNING

- BENEFITS, POLICIES, SALARIES
- COMMUNICATION
- EMPLOYMENT LAW
- TRANSITION PLAN
- SEVERANCE PLAN

PHASE II: TRANSITION

- ANNOUNCEMENT
- EMPLOYMENT DECISION
- TIMING

PHASE III: INTEGRATION

- SUPPORT
- INVOLVEMENT
- ASSOCIATION
- INTEGRATIONE
- VALUATION
- TRAINING

Creating positive employee outcomes requires careful Human Resources Planning. For each affected group of employees determine the responsible party, key considerations, and action plan.

Phase I: Planning	Responsibility		Key Considerations	Action Plan
	Client (Who)	Provider (Who)		
Benefits, Policies, Salary				
Communication				
Employment Law				
Transition Plan				
Severance Plan				
Other				

Phase II: Integration	Responsibility		Key Considerations	Action Plan
	Client (Who)	Provider (Who)		
Announcements				
Employment Decisions				
Timing				
Conversion				
Other				
Transition				

Phase III: Integration	Responsibility		Key Considerations	Action Plan
	Client (Who)	Provider (Who)		
Support				
Involvement				
Association				
Integration				
Evaluation				
Training				
Other				

Template 9.3   Knowledge Management Readiness
Assessment

Outsourcing Project:
Project #:

This template helps assess the organizational readiness for establishing a knowledge management process for the outsourcing engagement. It is to be developed jointly between the customer and service provider and an action plan for improving the readiness becomes a part of the transition plan. Identify the current state (CS) of readiness (0 - non-existent to 5 - completely ready) in the first column; show the impact of lack of readiness on the outsourcing engagement in the second column (Low, Medium, High). The last column may be used to prioritize actions.

Readiness Factor	C.S.	Impact	Priority
Organizational			
The champion for knowledge management is appointed and accepted			
Importance is communicated and understood by everyone			
SMEs are identified and own responsibility			
Process			
Knowledge elements are well defined and understood			
There is a collaborative process for identifying, capturing and maintaining knowledge			
Measurements are identified (for knowledge elements – may be more than SLAs)			
Technology			
A repository for information is defined and established			
Knowledge capture tools are identified and established			
Knowledge utilization tools are identified and established			

Template 9.4   Knowledge Management Implementation Strategies

Outsourcing Project:
Project #:

This template helps assess the organizational strategies that are needed to assure success of a knowledge management process/program. Identify whether it exists in the current environment or not, importance of the strategy (high, medium, low) and the priority for implementation to improve it from its current state.

Strategies	Exist?	Import.	Priority
Rewards			
Story telling			
Cross project learning			
After action reviews (lessons learned)			
Knowledge mapping			
Community of practice ("Birds of a feather")			
Expert (SME) directories			
Best practice transfer			
Competence management			
Proximity and architecture			
Master-apprentice relationship			
Collaborative technology (groupware)			
Knowledge repositories			
Intellectual capital measurement and reporting (e.g. copyrights, patents)			
Knowledge brokers			
Social software to promote interaction and story telling			

Template 10.1 Outsourcing Governance Plan

| Outsourcing Project: |
| Project #: |

Use this template to identify and outline the implementation plan for the major aspects of the outsourcing governance program.

Management Processes	Implementation Outline
Relationship Management	
Service Request Management	
Service Receipt Verification	
Performance Management	
Problem/Incident/Change Management	
Project Management	
Security, Business Continuity, Disaster Recovery	
Operations Management	
Financial Management	
Asset Management	
Contract Management	
Other	

Management Systems & Tools	Implementation Outline
Service Catalog / Request Tool	
Service Performance Dashboard	
Joint Business Planning Tool (The Outsourcing Business Plan)	
Project Portfolio Management Tool	
Project Execution Dashboard	
Issue Management System	
Contract Management System	
Other	

Identify where and how each of the following management principles are reflected in the implementation outlines provided above.

Management Principles	Applies to which systems and tools? How is it reflected?
Keep strategic responsibilities kept close to the top	
Create multilevel organizational links	
Conduct regular, goal-oriented meetings	
Use advanced communications technologies	
Use objective techniques to report and manage results	

Template 10.2 Assessing Results versus Expectations

| Outsourcing Project: |
| Project #: |

In Template 5.3 you identified the critical success factors, key performance indicators, and applicable attributes for the scope of services being outsourced.

Key to performance management is tracking results against these expected outcomes. Use the added column in this template to do this.

Critical Success Factors (CSF)	Key Performance Indicator (KPI)	Specific Attribute	How Measured and Rated	Results Achieved
Financial				
Customer				
Employee				
Process and Product Innovation				

Critical Success Factors (CSF)	Key Performance Indicator (KPI)	Specific Attribute	How Measured and Rated	Results Achieved
Service Level Innovation				
Other				

Template 10.3 Post-Operation Financial Review of an
Outsourcing Decision

Outsourcing Project:
Project #:

Use this template to develop the actual financial performance of an outsourcing business relationship. Perform a gap analysis with the projected financial performance as recorded on Template 7.1 Create additional sheets in this workbook for individual elements as needed and then link those calculations to this sheet as appropriate.

Discount Rate for NPV:	8%				
Category	Year 1 ($000)	Year 2 ($000)	Year 3 ($000)	Year 4 ($000)	Year 5 ($000)
Net Financial Benefit (Loss)	0	0	0	0	0
Net Present Value	0				
Base Case	0	0	0	0	0
Salary					
Equipment					
Outside Services					
Supplies					
Direct Overheads (Occupancy, Training, Benefits, etc.)					
Indirect Overheads (Management, HR, Finance, Admin, etc.)					

Discount Rate for NPV:	8%				
Category	Year 1 ($000)	Year 2 ($000)	Year 3 ($000)	Year 4 ($000)	Year 5 ($000)
Net Financial Benefit (Loss)	0	0	0	0	0
Capital Costs (Depreciation, Cost of Capital)					
Other					
Outsource Case - Actual	0	0	0	0	0
Provider Costs - Actual	0	0	0	0	0
Fees Paid					
Start-Up Costs					
Other					
Additional Costs - Actual	0	0	0	0	0
Planning Costs (Staff, Travel, Professional Services)					
Transition Costs (Staff, Travel, Professional Services, Fees, Penalties, Bonuses, Taxes, etc.					
Oversight Costs (Staff, Travel, Systems, Professional Services)					
Other Costs					
Risks and Risk Mitigation					

Discount Rate for NPV:	8%				
Category	Year 1 ($000)	Year 2 ($000)	Year 3 ($000)	Year 4 ($000)	Year 5 ($000)
Net Financial Benefit (Loss)	0	0	0	0	0
Additional Benefits - Actual	0	0	0	0	0
Quality (Reduced defects, increased yield, improved services, etc.)					
Capacity (Increased throughput, additional services, market growth, etc.)					
Focus (Reduced competition for capital, cash infusion, reduced cost of capital, resource redeployment, management focus, etc.)					
Revenue (New markets, new customers, additional revenue current customers, etc.)					
Other (Speed, flexibility, innovation, organizational change, employee morale, unexpected synergies, etc.)					
Retained Costs - Actual	0	0	0	0	0
Salary					
Equipment					

Discount Rate for NPV:	8%				
Category	Year 1 ($000)	Year 2 ($000)	Year 3 ($000)	Year 4 ($000)	Year 5 ($000)
Net Financial Benefit (Loss)	0	0	0	0	0
Outside Services					
Supplies					
Direct Overheads (Occupancy, Training, Benefits, etc.)					
Indirect Overheads (Management, HR, Finance, Admin, etc.)					
Capital Costs (Depreciation, Cost of Capital)					
Other					

Template 10.4 Outsourcing Process Maturity Assessment

| Outsourcing Project: |
| Project #: |

Use this template to assess the current and target maturity level for the organization's outsourcing process, both for each stage and at the overall level. The following definitions apply for each maturity level:

1. Initial Level: The outsourcing process is characterized as ad hoc and occasionally even chaotic. Few processes are defined and success depends on individual efforts.

2. Repeatable Level: Basic outsourcing processes are established. The necessary disciplines are in place to repeat earlier successes.

3. Defined Level: The outsourcing processes are documented, standardized, and integrated into the management policies and procedures. All governance processes are implemented using approved, tailored versions of the IT governance policy.

4. Managed Level: Define, collect and make decisions based on outsourcing process measurements. Outsourcing processes and deliverables and metrics are quantitatively understood, reported and controlled.

5. Optimizing Level: Continuous process improvement is enabled by quantitative feedback from the outsourcing process, from piloting innovative outsourcing ideas and from adopting external industry best practices and standards.

Outsourcing Stage	Current Maturity Level	Why?	Target Maturity Level	How?
Idea Stage				

Outsourcing Stage	Current Maturity Level	Why?	Target Maturity Level	How?
Assessment and Planning Stage				
Implementation Stage				
Transition Stage				
Management Stage				
Overall Assessment				

Appendix C
The common business process framework

The outsourcing framework is a common list of the activities that take place in most organizations. It provides a common structure for developing a mapping of any organization's opportunities for outsourcing as well as a common language for comparing and contrasting across organizations.

C1.   Operational services (value chain)

1.1. Marketplace Research and Analysis
     1.1.1.   Customer Needs Research and Analysis
     1.1.2.   Customer Satisfaction Measurement
     1.1.3.   External Business and Technology Research and Analysis

1.2. Product Research, Development, Manufacture, and Delivery
     1.2.1.   Product Research and Develop
     1.2.2.   Product Prototype and Test
     1.2.3.   Capital Goods and Technology Acquisition
     1.2.4.   Materials and Supplies Acquisition
     1.2.5.   Inbound Logistics Management
     1.2.6.   Component Manufacturing
     1.2.7.   Product Assembly, Test, and Packaging
     1.2.8.   Product Warehousing, Distribution, and Delivery
     1.2.9.   Product Installation and Service

1.3. Service Research, Development, Staffing, and Delivery
     1.3.1.   Service Research and Development
     1.3.2.   Service Prototype and Test
     1.3.3.   Capital Goods and Technology Acquisition
     1.3.4.   Materials and Supplies Acquisition
     1.3.5.   Human Resources Acquisition and Development
     1.3.6.   Service Delivery to Customer

1.4. Marketing
     1.4.1.   Marketing Plan Development
     1.4.2.   Product and Service Advertising
     1.4.3.   Product and Service Promotion

1.5. Sales
     1.5.1.   Sales Plan Development
     1.5.2.   Field Sales
     1.5.3.   Call Center Sales (Teleservices)

1.6. Customer Relationship Management
    1.6.1. Customer Order-processing
    1.6.2. Customer Service, Inquiries, and Complaint-handling
    1.6.3. Customer Relationship Management (CRM) System Development and Management

C2.   Management and support services

2.1. Human Resource Management
    2.1.1.   Human Resource Strategy Development
    2.1.2.   Recruit, Select, and Hire Employees
    2.1.3.   Develop and Train Employees
    2.1.4.   Employee Relocation
    2.1.5.   Outplacement Services
    2.1.6.   Base and Variable Compensation Plan Development and Management
    2.1.7.   Employee Satisfaction, Workplace Health, and Safety Management
    2.1.8.   Employee Benefits Management and Administration
    2.1.9.   Internal Communications and Labor Relations Management
    2.1.10. Human Resource Information Systems (HRIS) Development and Management

2.2. Information and Communications Technology Management
    2.2.1.   Information and Communications Technology Strategy Development
    2.2.2.   Data Center Design and Management
    2.2.3.   Distributed System Design and Management
    2.2.4.   Desktop/Mobile System Design and Management
    2.2.5.   Data Network Design and Management
    2.2.6.   Communications Systems and Network Design and Management
    2.2.7.   Internet Services (including Web hosting)
    2.2.8.   Application Development and Maintenance
    2.2.9.   Enterprise Resource Planning (ERP) System Development and Maintenance
    2.2.10. Data and Database Management and Maintenance
    2.2.11. Help Desk Services
    2.2.12. Systems Security and Controls Management

2.3. Document Management
    2.3.1.   Document Layout and Design
    2.3.2.   Document Imaging, Storage, and Distribution
    2.3.3.   Printing and Publishing
    2.3.4.   Centralized and Convenience Copy Services

2.4. Financial Management

    2.4.1.   Budget, Cash Flow, and Risk Management

    2.4.2.   Accounts Payable Processing

    2.4.3.   Payroll Processing

    2.4.4.   Invoicing, Accounts Receivables, Credits, and Collections Processing

    2.4.5.   Travel and Entertainment Expense Management and Processing

    2.4.6.   Internal and External Financial Accounting and Reporting

    2.4.7.   Internal Auditing

    2.4.8.   Tax Management and Processing

    2.4.9.   Financial Information Systems (FIS) Development and Maintenance

2.5. Real Estate and Capital Asset Management

    2.5.1.   Real Estate and Capital Asset Plan Development and Project Management

    2.5.2.   Real Estate and Capital Asset Transaction Management

    2.5.3.   Real Estate and Capital Asset Engineering and Maintenance

    2.5.4.   Energy Management

2.6. Facility Services

    2.6.1.   Food and Cafeteria Services

    2.6.2.   Mailroom Services

    2.6.3.   Shipping and Receiving

    2.6.4.   Security

    2.6.5.   Parking

2.7. Administrative Services

    2.7.1.   Secretarial/Clerical Services

    2.7.2.   Data Entry/Transcription Services

    2.7.3.   Records Management

    2.7.4.   Travel Services

    2.7.5.   Workplace Supplies Management

2.8. Corporate Services

    2.8.1.   Purchasing

    2.8.2.   External Communications and Public Relations Management

    2.8.3.   Legal Services

Appendix D
Outsourcing professional skills

The following is a list of the skills required of outsourcing professionals. The skills are organized by the three phases of the outsourcing lifecycle – strategy, implementation, and management; by professional skills; by additional skills unique to provider and advisory roles; and by emerging areas of specialty, such as, offshoring, and the use of technology to streamline the outsourcing process and enhance outsourcing results.

This skill profile provides complements the Outsourcing Professional Standards contained with the OPBOK.

Each skill is weighted, where:

- Primary skills are skills required by outsourcing professionals
- Secondary skills are skills outsourcing professionals must either possess themselves or have sufficient knowledge of to direct and integrate through others

As shown in Figure D1, the skills of outsourcing professionals are in direct response to the requirements for ensuring continuous improvement in the results organizations receive.

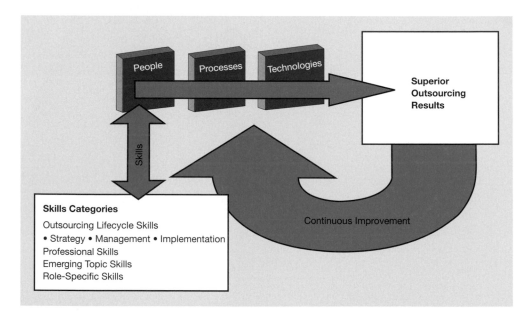

Figure D1: Outsourcing Professional Skills

Outsourcing Lifecycle Skills	Weight
Strategy	
Develop Outsourcing Value Model for the Organization	Primary
Integrate Outsourcing Value Model into Organization's Strategic Planning Process	Primary
Develop End-to-End Outsourcing Project Management Process	Primary
Develop Opportunity Identification and Assessment Criteria and Process	Primary
Determine Scope of Potential Outsourcing Opportunities	Secondary
Benchmark Current Operations	Secondary
Assess Potential Outsourcing Opportunities	Primary
Accept, Reject, and Prioritize Potential Outsourcing Opportunities	Primary
Implementation	
Structure and Manage Project Teams, Including Internal and External Resources	Primary
Establish Required Outcomes (Balanced Scorecard)	Primary
Determine Optimal Structure for Relationship(s), Including Pricing Models	Primary
Design Governance Model	Primary
Establish Provider Selection Criteria	Primary
Develop Pool of Potential Providers	Secondary
Determine Optimal Approach(s) for Engaging the Marketplace of Providers	Primary
Manage Provider Evaluation and Selection Process	Primary
Develop Supporting Materials, such as RFIs, RFPs, Case Studies, etc.	Secondary
Functional and Financial Analysis of Proposal(s)	Secondary
Negotiate Final Deal Structuring	Primary
Negotiate Final Contract	Secondary
Finalize Implementation Plan	Secondary
Manage Transition to New Environment, Including Governance	Primary

Management	
Manage Governance System	Primary
Evaluate and Manage Performance	Secondary
Evaluate and Manage Change	Secondary
Identify and Resolve Conflicts	Primary
Reassess Value and Renegotiate	Primary

Professional Skills	Weight
Project Management	Primary
Change Management	Primary
Communications	Primary
Contracting	Primary
Interpersonal/Trust Building	Primary
Marketing	Primary
Negotiating	Primary
Team Leadership	Primary
Balanced Scorecards	Primary
Strategic Analysis	Secondary
Process Analysis	Secondary
Benchmarking	Secondary
Financial Analysis	Secondary
Human Resources Analysis	Secondary

Emerging Topic Skills	Weight
Offshoring	
Strategic Global Sourcing Model Development	Primary
Global Source Evaluation	Primary
Engagement Model Evaluation (Outsourced, Captive, Build-Operate-Transfer, etc.)	Primary
Cross-Cultural Collaboration	Primary
Technology	
Outsourcing Process Analysis for Continuous Improvement	Primary
Communications and Management Technology Assessment	Secondary
Outsourcing Management Technology Assessment	Primary
Technology ROI Development	Secondary
Technology Implementation	Secondary

Additional Role Specific Skills	Weight
Providers	
Strategy Development and Management	Varies
Brand Management	Varies
Marketing	Varies
Sales	Varies
Opportunity Qualification	Primary
Engagement Process Management	Primary
Deal Structuring and Negotiation	Primary
Operations	Varies
Governance	Primary
Advisors	
Third Party Relationship Facilitation	Primary

Appendix E
Code of ethical and business practice standards for outsourcing professionals

E1.   Professional responsibility

Core principle

To adhere to the highest standards of ethical business practices in all business dealings, especially those that involve business decisions on entering, maintaining, or discontinuing outsourcing relationships. To conduct oneself in a way that contributes to a positive image for the individuals and organizations that work in the field of outsourcing.

Intent

- Ensure that outsourcing relationships developed, implemented and managed by outsourcing professionals are based on well recognized and sustainable ethical and business practice standards
- To build respect, credibility, and ongoing value for the individuals and organizations that work in the field of outsourcing
- To directly contribute to the success of the organizations we work in and influence, and through them to the success of communities at large
- To encourage, through example, the highest professional standards among all those with whom we work

Guidelines

1. Understand and comply with all ethical and business practice standards of all of the organizations with which one works
2. Identify and resolve standards conflicts, discrepancies, and omissions between the organizations with which one works, using generally-recognized international principles, such as the United Nation's Global Compact (www.unglobalcompact.org), as a guide
3. Understand and comply with all laws in all countries involved in one's work
4. Promote decisions that support the best long-term interests of businesses, their customers, shareholders, and the communities in which they operate
5. Freely share and encourage discussion of this Code of Ethical and Business Practice Standards with others, both within and outside the field of outsourcing
6. Bring attention to and encourage corrective action when there is observed non-compliance by others
7. Work with fellow professionals to identify and promote changes to this code intended to enhance the field's professionalism

E2.   Professional representation

Core principle

To represent one's skills, knowledge, and experiences with honesty and integrity enabling customers, employers, and other business partners to make fully informed hiring and contracting decisions.

Intent

- To make certain that outsourcing professionals and the organizations they work for and advise accurately represent their skills, knowledge, capabilities, and experiences
- To help ensure fully-informed decisions that lead to better outsourcing outcomes
- To enable professionals and organizations to effectively differentiate themselves based on the skills, knowledge, capabilities, and experiences they have invested in and developed

Guidelines

1. In all written and verbal communications to accurately represent one's skills, experiences, and capabilities in a format that facilitates effective comparisons
2. Engage only in activities for which the individual and the organization they represent have the requisite education and experience; freely sharing those qualifications whenever appropriate
3. When acting as an outsourcing customer, provider, or advisor to accurately represent information regarding current and future business operations and strategies, costs, pricing, resources, methods, requirements, risks, and assumptions
4. When acting as an outsourcing customer, provider, or advisor to accurately represent the extent of executive support for an outsourcing relationship and the intended decision-making and management process
5. To disclose all existing and potential business relationships that may, or may be perceived to, influence or affect an individual or organizational business decision or commitment
6. When providing references to make every possible effort to ensure that they accurately reflect all of one's relevant experiences and accomplishments
7. To not knowingly misrepresent or mislead when sharing information about other professionals or organizations
8. Disclose all material facts known to them that, if not disclosed, may distort the decision making of their clients, prospects, employers, employees, or others.
9. To properly cite and credit the source of all information and ideas used, presented, and shared with others

E3. Accountability for outcomes

Core principle

To measure and share accomplishments in terms of the business outcomes actually achieved over time, using industry defined terms and thresholds where available, and in a way that can be objectively evaluated by others.

Intent

- To ensure that outsourcing and outsourcing professionals are focused on and evaluated based on actual outcomes achieved
- To enable the field and industry to better demonstrate its economic value in objective, standardized, and measurable terms

Guidelines

1. Establish objective and standardized measures of success for all outsourcing relationships that reflect the full range of business outcomes sought
2. Establish objective and standardized measures of risks for outsourcing relationships
3. Collect and report actual outcomes achieved over time in objective measurable terms
4. Whenever possible, use outcomes-based data as the basis for business recommendations to clients, employers, employees, and businesses and communities at large
5. Build and continuously seek to employ and enhance effective communications, change management, and dispute resolution processes for outsourcing relationships
6. Build and continuously seek to employ and enhance effective risk management and risk-reward sharing mechanisms for outsourcing relationships

E4. Professional development

Core principle

To continuously increase the economic value derived through outsourcing by building one's professional skills and knowledge through ongoing education, expanded experience, and a focus on innovation.

Intent

- To promote the fact that it is the skills of the professionals that design, implement and manage outsourcing relationships that ultimately produces economic value for organizations

- To ensure continuous improvement in outsourcing outcomes by developing the skills and knowledge of the field's professionals
- To continuously understand and mitigate current and emerging risks associated with outsourcing
- To minimize total outsourcing costs through a focus on learning and the promotion of best practices on an industry-wide basis

Guidelines

1. Invest on a regular basis in training and professional development activities to improve one's skill and knowledge in the outsourcing field
2. Freely share, within recognized guidelines for the protection of proprietary intellectual properties, learning and experiences with fellow professionals
3. Contribute directly, through training and knowledge sharing activities, to the education and professional development of professionals in the field
4. Proactively seek new ways of doing business that expand the economic value derived through outsourcing
5. Proactively seek relevant professional certifications

E5.   Outsourcing advocacy

Core principle

To be an effective, proactive advocate for outsourcing as a management practice and as a profession.

Intent

- To ensure an ever-better educated business and public community on what outsourcing is, why organizations outsource, and its impact on businesses and communities
- To continually improve the overall business and public perception of outsourcing as a management practice, industry, and profession
- To ensure open discussion and debate of the impact of outsourcing on businesses and communities
- To attract top talent and resources to the field and industry of outsourcing

Guidelines

1. Proactively invest professional time and organizational resources in outreach and advocacy for outsourcing as a management practice, industry, and profession

2. Opening engage in dialogue and discussion with those outside the field to both promote outsourcing and better understand and shape business and public opinion

3. Strive to stay on top of the latest trends in outsourcing, which may include new industry, academic or government initiatives, in order to influence the outcome

E6.   Issue resolution

Core principle

For these standards to fully benefit the field and profession, customers, employees, and others need a reliable method for reporting and resolving issues with the standards and how they are being applied.

Intent

- To ensure that these ethical and business practice standards are put into practice
- To provide a way for those both inside and outside the profession to resolve any concerns with the adherence of outsourcing professionals to these standards
- To create a forum for ongoing dialogue and understanding of the evolving nature of outsourcing in the global business community

Guidelines

1. Outsourcing professionals should provide a copy of these ethical and business practice standard to customers, employers, employees, and other business associates early in the development of their relationships

2. Complaints of violations of these standards should be reported to member services at the International Association of Outsourcing Professionals (IAOP) at 845.452.0600 or email **memberservices@iaop.org**

3. Complaints should state the specific issue, when and how it occurred, all supporting material, along with a statement of the alternative practice that would have been expected under these standards

4. Complaints are forwarded to the Outsourcing Standards Board for assignment of an ombudsman responsible for their review and resolution, during which time there is a full sharing of information among all involved parties

5. In the case of multiple complaints that reflect a failure to adhere to these standards, sanctions, up to and including permanent loss of membership in organizations that have adopted these standards and any all privileges that represents, may be imposed at the sole discretion of the board working with the association that has licensed the use of these standards

Appendix F
Common contract terms and general guidelines for application

F1. Products and services to be provided

Thorough, detailed descriptions should include whether each product/service is to be provided on the customer's, provider's or third party's site/facilities.

F2. Business-related terms

Effective Date	
Initial Term	
Renewal Term	
Termination – without cause	X days prior written notice by either party
Termination – with cause	■ Material breach X days prior written notice of breach Breaching party fails to cure within X-day period. ■ Insolvency, etc. – 60 days from date of filing
Fee Increases	■ X days prior written notice ■ Limited to X% increase from the fees of immediately preceding term.
Payments	■ Due within X days of receipt of invoice ■ Schedule for milestone payments (Exhibit X)
Late fee	1-1/2% interest for overdue payments
Related Contracts - Pre-existing	■ This contract amends "Original Agreement," dated 1/1/99 ■ Other agreements terminated: "Other Pre-Existing Agreement," dated 1/1/93 "Amendment No. 1," dated 1/1/94
Related Contracts - New	■ Service Level Agreement (Exhibit X) ■ Software escrow agreement (Exhibit X) ■ Third party software license agreement (Exhibit X) ■ Any other third party contracts

F3. Provider's obligations during and after the term

Services	■ Statement of Work ("SOW" - Exhibit X) ■ Schedule of due dates for Deliverables (Exhibit X) ■ Specifications (Exhibit X) ■ Any applicable Change Orders
Additional Services	■ Use Change Order form ■ Submit fully executed copy to Legal.

Acceptance Procedure	■ Exhibit X on acceptance criteria, procedure, notice of acceptance or rejection, testing, etc.
	■ Failed Acceptance Testing Limit of X business days for testing, acceptance/rejection and corrections unless otherwise agreed to in writing. If exceed limit, then the provider refunds to the customer fees paid for Services or Deliverables related to such testing. Applicable SOW is then terminated.
Security of Confidential Information	■ Exhibit X on safety and physical security procedures.
	■ Includes personally identifiable information.
	■ The provider must immediately notify the customer of any breaches of security or unauthorized access to the provider's system if related to the Services.
Protection of Personally Identifiable Information	Exhibit X on compliance and inspection requirements.
Key Personnel	Provide list and inform customer of any updates.
Customer's clients	■ No solicitation during Term and thereafter (indefinitely).
Records	■ Keep records related to fees.
	■ Maintain for three years after termination.
	■ Customer inspection once per calendar year, during business hours, upon 30 days prior written notice.

F4.   Customer's obligations during the term

Related to provider's Services	■ Provide information in accordance with the schedule for submittal of Deliverables. (Exhibit X)
Records	■ Keep records related to use of the Service.
	■ Provider inspection twice per calendar year, during business hours, upon 10 business days prior written notice.
Equipment	■ Procure and maintain certain equipment, at customer's expense, necessary to use Services.
Software configuration	Exhibit X
Provider's trademarks and name	■ Use in accordance with provider's policies and maintain all attribution on provider's Deliverables and Services.
Key Personnel	Provide list and inform provider of any updates.

F5.   Provider's rights during the term

Suspension of Services	■ Customer's negligent or intentional misuse of Services or any content provided through Services.
	■ Provider may terminate for material breach (after 30 day cure period) or suspend upon two days prior written notice.
	■ Provider may resume Services if customer cures misuse within 30 days.

F6.   Customer's obligations upon termination

| Provider's IP | ■ Destroy provider's intellectual property ("IP") on customer's system and, upon provider's written request, certify this was done. |

F7.   Other key contract provisions

Order of Precedence	■ SOWs, Specifications, Change Orders, Amendments, and then Agreement.
Assignment to Competitors	■ Neither party can assign or delegate without other party's prior written consent.
	■ No assignment to either party's competitors (as defined in Section X).
	■ Violation is material breach.
Non-Solicitation	■ No active solicitation of employees who performed material work under this agreement.
	■ During the Term and for one year thereafter.
	■ Sole remedy for breach: 25% of employee's first year base salary.
Intellectual Property	■ Customer owns certain intellectual property, documentation, and technology provided and created by customer.
	■ Provider owns technology, documentation, etc. used to provide the Services and Deliverables.
	■ Third parties retain ownership of third party data.
	■ Ownership of derivative works.
Publicity	Prior written consent required
Confidentiality	Period and application
Indemnification	For various events and violations
Limitation of liability	■ Cap on damages: X times total fees or $X dollars (whichever greater).
	■ Exceptions to cap: indemnity, breach of IP obligations, confidentiality, willful misconduct, misappropriation of IP.
Warranties	Definitions and voidance
Governing law and jurisdiction	

Appendix G
The Global Outsourcing 100® and the World's Best Outsourcing Advisors

IAOP annually conducts an independent assessment of the capabilities of outsourcing service providers and advisors and, based on this assessment, publishes The Global Outsourcing 100® and The World's Best Outsourcing Advisors.

The Global Outsourcing 100 and its sub-lists are essential references for companies seeking new and expanded relationships with the best companies in the industry. The lists include service provider and advisory companiesfrom around the world that provide the full spectrum of outsourcing services. They include not only today's leaders, but also tomorrow's rising stars.

Companies apply for inclusion on the list by completing an online application. Applications are then judged by an independent panel of experienced outsourcing buyers on four critical characteristics: size and growth; customer references; organizational competencies; and management capabilities.

Each company selected for The Global Outsourcing 100 is recognized by IAOP on its website and at various events and programs throughout the year and in a special advertising feature in FORTUNE® magazine reaching the magazine's worldwide circulation of over one million and readership in excess of five million. The annual lists are made a permanent part of the knowledge center in FirmBuilder.com®. Please go to www.outsourcingprofessional.org/content/23/152/1793 page of IAOP's website to view the current lists.

Appendix H
Reference article on governance

By: Jagdish R. Dalal, President,JDalal Associates, LLC
Managing Director, Thought Leadership, IAOP

Although the best time to plan governance is during the strategy formulation stage, most companies wait until after implementation, when a problem arises, to address governance. This is true whether the function is a part of a newly established shared services organization or is being outsourced. Governance is not just setting up formal reviews and periodic status report; it requires creating processes that create success in the new relationship. This is even more important when considering the challenges associated with off shore outsourcing.

As Churchill once said: "…. this is not the end, it is not even the beginning of the end. It is only the end of the beginning". So it is when an outsourcing agreement is signed - it is only the beginning of the relationship. Unfortunately, many miss this nuance, sigh a deep breath of relief and let the outsourcing go forward without being managed.

H1. Defining governance

Governance is the act of managing the outsourcing engagement, and it is this discipline, instituted by governance processes, that guarantees results meet outsourcing objectives. At the same time, there is a need to establish relationships between the end users of services and the service provider. The protocol for this relationship is what we refer to as the "rules of engagement". Experience has shown that many businesses fail to distinguish between "governance" and "rules of engagement".

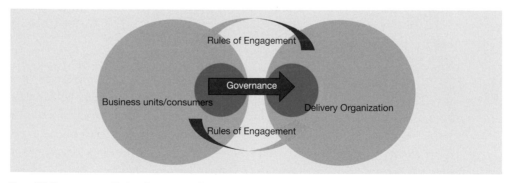

Figure H1 Governance and 'rules of engagement'

Governance is defined as a set of pre-defined contractual and implied commitments between the outsourcer and the business to assure successful delivery of services. The governance principles are directly managed by a group or a designated individual, generally known as the Outsourcing Manager (or group). Non-compliance of governance principles generally results in either or both parties not meeting a contractual term.

Rules of Engagement are the rules, framed by contractual agreement, which govern the relationship between the outsourcing service provider and the end users of services in the business. Unlike governance, non-compliance to the rules of engagement may not directly result in violation of any contractual term. The rules of engagement are used by the Outsourcing Management Organization to socialize the contractual terms within the using organization.

One of the best practices we have seen was the creation of a documented set of Rules of Engagement, distributed throughout the organization, along with classes held for users outlining them.

H2.   Lessons learned – what can prevent good governance?

Although outsourcing has been around for well over two decades, the governance of these agreements has remained more an after-thought than a pre-planned activity. There are many lessons learned from these past engagements, so let's outline some of the problems that have prevented the establishment of good governance programs.

The need for a strong governance program is not recognized until after the outsourcing agreement is signed, and usually not until after a problem arises and the lack of a clear communication and problem-solving process becomes evident.

The existing governance program only addresses the issue of contract management between the outsourcing management organization and the service provider. Confusion between governance and rules of engagement creates many points of conflict for the service provider, the sourcing manager and the service users.

Governance principles, meaning the objectives and anticipated outcomes of the governance process, are not established before entering into an outsourcing agreement. In addition, contractual requirements and governance principles are often not well integrated and therefore create difficulty in managing the contractual compliance. Governance problems are further exacerbated by a lack of well defined reporting processes. Lack of governance tools makes it difficult to create a holistic view of performance on a continuous basis.

The cost of governance is not included in the overall business case, and as a result, many are surprised at the "overhead" costs once the outsourcing deal is consummated. Often, the budget for governance is limited to what can be "afforded" rather than what is necessary to oversee a contract.

The principles of governance are determined only by legislative requirements or worse, fail to comply with US or foreign laws. This is a crucial issue when considering offshoring, since it will involve at least two countries' laws.

Both businesses and outsourcers believe that the responsibility for governance rests with the "other" party. Offshore providers especially believe that a detailed reporting of measurements on a regular basis is sufficient and constitutes fulfilling the governance requirements. On the opposite side of the table, client businesses often view governance as a way to address "non-performance" after the fact, rather than preventing it in the first place.

H3. Stages in the growth and maturity of governance

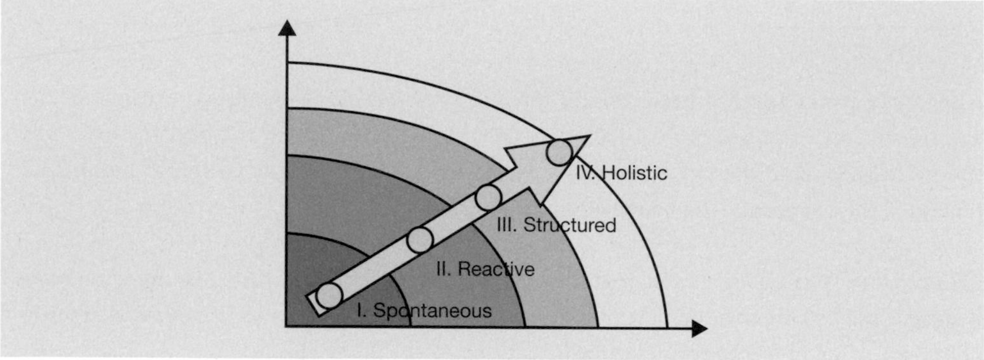

Figure H2 Stages of growth in governance

Before we look at the governance model, let's examine the stages of growth in the governance program. Companies that have outsourced have gone through these stages in their evolution of the discipline. There are only a few examples of successful programs that have been designed and implemented at the higher end of the maturity growth curve.

Stage I – Spontaneous
This is the stage where governance is an afterthought and is implemented only when needed. Once the issue that raised the governance discussion ceases to exist, both companies revert to their non-existing governance stage. Outsourcing engagements, in this stage, usually lead to an acrimonious relationship, and the cost of governance becomes a surprise to both parties. The outsourcing provider, who normally operates in this stage, usually finds that the customer relationship is weak and the governance program results in a competitive disadvantage. Many offshore service providers are in this stage of growth. Unless the service providers make a commitment, this will become a major obstacle to their success in outsourcing.

Stage II – Reactive

This second stage is where most companies are in their growth of governance. The discipline required results when some event triggers a closer management of the outsourcing arrangement. The customer generally drives the process through this reactive stage, and since it results from an unanticipated event, it leads to dissatisfaction with the provider's service. It also leads to a higher level of cost in implementation, especially if the event requires investment in a process that was not initially planned as a part of the governance.

Stage III – Structured

This begins the stages where governance is included as a part of the initial outsourcing engagement. Although both parties are actively engaged in the governance process, it is driven by customers' demands and providers reluctantly agreeing to implement process. In this stage, costs are identified before the contract is signed and are appropriately included in the outsourcing benefit analysis. Benefits gained in this stage include avoidance of conflicts or events that may result in surprises or higher cost of delivery. This is the final stage that many engagements reach and our experience has shown that most offshore engagements do not go beyond this stage.

Stage IV - Holistic

This may be the ultimate stage of maturity in the governance of an outsourcing contract. Both the customer and the provider play an active role in defining responsibilities, processes and actions well in advance. Both view the cost of governance as an investment in assuring short and long-term success in meeting outsourcing objectives. A strong relationship will be evident and lead to a high degree of customer satisfaction. Sometimes, the two parties begin to refer to their contract as "true partnership" and see competitive advantages for both of them.

H4.   Governance model

J Dalal Associates, LLC has developed a comprehensive model establishing an effective governance program. It is based on two foundation blocks and four pillars of success in governance.

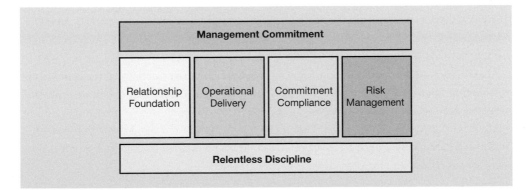

Figure H3 Governance model

The two foundation blocks are required before a strong governance program can be designed and implemented. They are *management commitment* and *relentless discipline*.

Management commitment

It is essential to have a strong management commitment to the outsourcing engagement and the governance program. This management commitment must be in place, by both the customer and the provider, before the contract is signed. Appropriate funding for the governance program, periodic management review of the results, actions and a willingness to engage fully in making the governance successful are hallmarks of a strong management commitment.

Relentless discipline

No governance program, no matter how well designed and implemented, can be successful without a commitment by both parties to manage it with relentless discipline throughout the life of the agreement. We have often observed that it is the lack of discipline that begins to erode the efficacy of a well-designed governance program. This discipline requires that the governance activities are identified and included as a part of the overall outsourcing engagement project plan.

Let's review the four frameworks of a good governance program: *operational delivery*, *relationship foundation*, *commitment compliance* and *risk management*.

Operational delivery

A large financial services institution wanted to make sure that the global delivery of the services was standardized and that there was a focus on "continuous improvement" of service. They also believed that establishing many metrics and associate penalties with missed service levels would not address the root cause of the problem and therefore not provide appropriate incentives for improving the results systematically. The company established improved services as an objective before completing the outsourcing agreement and contractually bound the service provider to perform "root cause" analysis – using quality tools – and providing them with a 30-60-90 day corrective action plan to address the problem. Over a period of three years, the service delivery performance was one of the best in the industry- benefiting both company and service provider alike.

First and foremost, the governance process must oversee the basic operational functions of the outsourcing relationship. The process should, for example, validate that operational delivery processes are well defined and performed in a controlled fashion.

This control should be gauged by measurements that have a defined basis for collection and are reported consistent with the requirements of the agreement.

Reporting should include current performance and trend analysis, and offer recommendations for improvement in metrics gathering and reporting. In addition, specific penalties associated with missed metrics outlined in the service level agreement would be the responsibility of the governance team to discuss and trigger when appropriate.

Ideally, this aspect of the process would also conduct "lessons learned" and "root cause analysis" exercises for service delivery metrics out of control. The team responsible for governance should also produce a management presentation of delivery metrics and communicate with all stakeholders in the process about delivery levels and control. This can be accomplished, for example, through a service delivery dashboard, that incorporates key metrics for the stakeholder in question.

The governance team should also review processes that interface between the provider(s) and customer in managing the work effort between them. Work change requests and project status reporting are examples of such processes. Where these are not defined, develop and implement them. Finally, the team should be responsible for reviewing and monitoring a security, disaster recovery and business continuity program.

Relationship foundation

A well-recognized technology firm wanted to make sure that the outsourcer would be well integrated into their operations when they outsourced their Information Technology function. The company and the outsourcer created a team (not a staff function but consisting of the line management) and tasked them with creating a two-year "integration" process. The teams, consisting of four sub-teams; addressed specific topics: culture, processes, structure and people.

The objective of the team was to establish a process by which the outsourcer would become an integral part of the company's Information Technology function and not just be a supplier of services. Much of the early success of the outsourcing agreement was credited to this "innovative" approach of establishing a relationship between the outsourcer and the company with a view towards long-term success.

Another critical task for the governance team is to create and validate the effectiveness of the relationship framework. Because the governance team is the point where the two organizations – customer and service provider – come together, it needs to make sure that the two organizations can work together effectively, and can do so from a relationship point of view. Cultural congruence, organization clarity and ease of communication are factors that assure a good relationship foundation. On an ongoing basis, it is important to review the organizational framework and communication process to assure that the two organizations remain in synchronization. Satisfaction surveys, organizational charts, newsletters and bulletin boards are some of the tools that are used in creating and maintaining the relationship.

Cultural assimilation is one of the key success factors for offshore outsourcing. Any outsourcing brings the cultures of two companies together, and if one is offshore, it introduces the social culture as yet another dimension. Experience has shown that a professionally managed cultural introduction and assimilation program, before and during the term of the agreement, is important. A cultural assimilation program would introduce the nuances – differences and similarities – of the two cultures. For example, it is important to understand that the typical Asian culture promotes the notion that it is not good to be the bearer of bad news. Hence, it is important that a process is put in place that would allow an Asian offshore service worker to identify problems without facing criticism. A good governance program will make sure that the other dimensions of governance take this into account when dealing with an Asian service provider.

Another example of a cultural difference is the use of measurements in managing work. Indian service providers value the importance of measurements and hence they measure many things, even some seemingly unimportant to American clients. They believe that decision making is based on measurements alone, while American businesses use measurements as one of many inputs for decision making. If this difference in approach is not well discussed throughout the governance program, it has the potential of creating differences of opinions in managing the work effort.

Commitment compliance

A multi-industry giant had entered into a long term Information Technology agreement with a leading service provider. The agreement between the two companies was "solidified" with the use of measurements, critical metrics and penalties associated with non-performance. There was an ironclad agreement between the two companies based on over a hundred critical measurements. As time passed, numbers of measurements became too numerous to manage and without the support of any automated information system, it became almost impossible to view the monthly metrics and determine if there were any "missed" commitments and if so, how much penalty was due the company from the outsourcer. After two years of trying to get "control" of the situation, both the company and the outsourcer came to the conclusion that the contractual commitment compliance, as structured, was impossible to manage. Clearly, having so many metrics did not improve the governance for either company. In fact, voluminous reporting, lack of follow-up and constant negotiating penalties for missed service levels became a "joke", defeating the purpose of a strong governance process.

The governance process should also be used to assure both sides of an ongoing contractual commitment and, if required, to amend the contract to reflect changes in the operational environment. Many contractual terms require ongoing responsibilities and obligations for both parties. These range from setting and reviewing pricing to assuring that disaster recovery plans are tested on a regular basis. There are also terms that govern how the outsourcing engagement is managed. It is in both the parties' interests to review these terms periodically and evaluate their efficacy against the original objectives and, if necessary, initiate the contract change request process to modify the terms.

Review and processing of billing and payments is one of the key aspects of commitment compliance. Since most contracts include credit for services that did not meet a minimum level, billing is not as consistent as one would imagine and hence, reconciliation of billing against payments and service credits is a time-consuming activity. Usually, there are terms that govern how the pricing is to be adjusted as a result of other factors – such as inflation, foreign exchange variation, and volume of work. Periodically, the service provider and customer should review these factors and initiate discussion to adjust the pricing to reflect the changed conditions

Flexibility on the part of both parties can be important to making a business relationship more workable, as overly specific contracts can prove to be a burden.

Risk management

When a noted US bank outsourced a part of its application development and maintenance function to India, it had done a thorough job of identifying risks and developed a detailed plan for mitigating them. In fact, the US governing body for banks – Office of Currency and Comptrollership -- had commended the bank for its diligence in developing a robust risk management program. But a key aspect of the risk management program depended on the bank knowing when to institute the mitigation plan, and they were dependent on the provider notifying them of the occurrence of any extraordinary event. It was only during one of these "mini-events" that it became clear that the provider did not have an effective notification process in place. A solution (involving morning email) was developed and implemented to cover for the omission from the earlier risk management program.

Finally, the governance team needs to review and analyze the on-going risk profile of the engagement and take the steps necessary to improve controls, compliance and risk mitigation.

The entire issue of managing risks in outsourcing has become an important issue in recent times. In fact, we believe that more and more outsourcing decisions – selection of providers or destination country – are driven by the risk profile rather than just the direct benefits of outsourcing. Significant issues, such as data security, privacy of information, and a vigilant monitoring of the outsourced activities are driving risk management. Any governance process that does not include stringent risk management monitoring cannot be judged as adequate in today's environment.

Risk management in an offshore engagement has additional challenges brought about by the distance, different socio-economic environment and changing political landscape.

There are many risks faced by clients in outsourcing relationships, particularly in offshore engagements:

- Reputation risk
- Transaction risk
- Operational risk
- Security risk.

The governance process should include a periodic review of ongoing risk management activities (e.g. information and physical security, disaster recovery, and business continuity plans, compliance, and provider reputation) and recommend changes and improvements, if required.

Finally, the governance team should determine and issue a risk profile for the engagement. The risk profile will pinpoint weaknesses in the delivery of services and will ensure that those weaknesses are examined on a periodic basis. If the risk level exceeds the risk profile, corrective actions are initiated between the two parties.

The review process can be invaluable in catching omissions in the original design of a risk mitigation plan. We have seen that most governance processes do not include Risk Management as an ongoing activity, and most consultants and service providers underplay its importance.

H5.   Governance and legal requirements

Until recently, legal requirements had little impact on governance and if they were taken into account, it was only for obvious legal issues – such as bribery or egregiously unlawful acts. With the enactment of recent regulations such as Sarbanes-Oxley Act, Privacy Act of 1974, USA Patriot Act (HR3162) as well as more industry specific regulations imposed for banking (Graham-Leach-Blicly Act, OCC notices, HIPAA requirements, Telecommunication Act of 1996) the importance of assuring legal compliance has become critical to businesses and service providers alike. There are additional requirements imposed under the European Union Data Privacy Act (or "safe harbor act" as it is known) that require diligent monitoring.

Businesses not only have to certify their results but also compliance to processes that produce the results. Contractual compliance, as a part of governance, is now more critical than it was in the past. Outsourcing agreements must clearly identify applicable legal regulations, violations reported, corrective actions taken and compliance monitored.

These legal requirements are further complicated when the service provider is located offshore and is operating under foreign jurisdiction and laws. Also, depending on the country, there are other US government regulations that may apply to the outsourcing agreement such as Foreign Corrupt Practices Act, labor laws governing employees, the Export Administration Regulations (EAR), the International Traffic in Arms Regulations (ITAR). Compliance to these and similar

Acts requires that a strong governance process is in place that can demonstrate to an examining agency its efficacy in assuring compliance.

H6.   Implementing governance

Experience with offshore outsourcing deals has shown that implementing a governance program after a contract has been signed is not effective and does not provide both parties with an adequate level of assurance for the outsourcing engagement. The governance program needs to be defined during the early stages of the outsourcing process. For an ideal implementation of a governance program, a variety of activities are expected to be performed over the lifecycle of the outsourcing process at specific junctures.

Pre-contract – definition
During the pre-contract stage, the framework for the ongoing audit of the relationship is identified, with processes established for the audit and audit evaluation/corrective action. It is also in this stage that the contractual terms are identified and negotiated between the two parties. A diligent preparation in this phase will assure that there are no surprises in the future and the processes and the outcomes are planned and anticipated.

During transition – implementation
As soon as the contract is signed the transition period begins, when the service provider begins to establish the processes for the engagement – ranging from knowledge acquisition to the establishment of the governance program. It is at this stage that the governance program is completely detailed. Processes required for governance are defined, documented and implemented by both parties. Typically, baselines for measurements are established and agreed upon. The transition process efficacy is measured to assure that the foundation for measurements are defined and can yield the anticipated results.

Post implementation - audit
The majority of the governance activities take place once the transition is completed and a steady-state achieved in the outsourcing engagement. A quarterly or at least an annual audit of the entire engagement, using the model given above, will provide an assessment of the program, establish variances and form the basis for an improvement program. From this work, a corrective action program can be established and reviewed with the customer and service provider management teams. Implementing this corrective action will strengthen the outsourcing engagement and help provide the results sought by both parties. Some of the best practices we have come across include:

- Service providers doing a self-audit and making the results available to the customer before a formal audit. A self-audit can also give the outsourcer the opportunity to address the weaknesses in their process or other issues before they become impediments to contractual obligations.

- Engaging a third party to perform the audit, assuring both parties of an objective review. Consultants and public auditors are good options for such audits. As consultants, we have worked with service providers in performing such audits before a customer audit and helped address weaknesses beforehand.

- Performing surprise audits and thereby testing the governance framework of "relentless discipline". We have come across a few service providers who claimed to have sound processes and practices in place, but could only demonstrate them during a pre-announced audit.

Monitoring governance metrics

Most outsourcing contracts provide for many metrics and are generally adequate to cover much of the requirement for monitoring the delivery of service. However, as we have seen in the framework described above, that is not adequate to properly govern an outsourcing engagement. In order to assure coverage for all dimensions of governance, it is important that a monitoring tool is developed – or acquired – and used. Key characteristics for such a tool are:

It must be a "common" system for use by both the customers and the service providers, thereby assuring congruence of information. It should be a "web" based system, which would assure access from anywhere – on or offshore - and provide for a sound security framework. Ideally, it should easily integrate (or at least enable email interface) with the email systems for both the customer and service provider, so that it would make it easy to communicate results, causes and corrective actions.

It should integrate effortlessly with the service provider's information source (ideally, directly but at the least, through an automated feed mechanism) and must be able to support standard reporting required by the contract.

It should provide for a complete drill down capability – including across multiple service provider sources, so that there can be an opportunity to examine the "root cause" of a problem.

It should provide a complete view of all metrics, not just for the current reporting period but also the trend. Trend data is extremely useful in ascertaining that the measurement process itself is under control and can highlight systemic problems versus less serious ones.

It should enable easy access to all supporting documents (for example, organization charts to reflect the relationship foundation) and keep them maintained.

A common repository of information – current and historical - will form a sound basis for some of the legal requirements imposed by Sarbanes-Oxley Act.

H7.   Summary

There are a number of examples where a successful governance program was implemented and helped to deliver the success expected from outsourcing. Many of these success factors have been addressed in the framework discussion above. However, experience has shown that management commitment – from senior management on down – is essential in all cases. We have also seen that there is a need for defining the governance rules and framework in the early stages of the negotiations process, and that the contract must contain definitive language regarding this, rather than general intent. This precision in the contract will prevent any misunderstanding or misinterpretation at a later date and will allow the customer and the service provider to establish a governance program in a timely manner. In recent times, we have seen that as more lawyers become knowledgeable about outsourcing (and especially offshore outsourcing), they are including some standard requirements and processes of governance in the contract. However, we have also seen a disturbing trend where customers and service providers alike do not clearly understand governance requirements and fail to take the necessary steps to implement and monitor them on an ongoing basis. This is why the "relentless discipline" step of the model above is so important for success.

We believe that as the industry learns more about the principles of governance, we will have a stronger set of governance requirements identified and followed in every engagement. This will lead to a stronger relationship between the customer and the service provider, and create the outsourcing success that will deliver long-term value to both.